Measuring Globalisat...

OECD Handbook on Economic Globalisation Indicators

OECD

ORGANISATION FOR ECONOMIC CO-OPERATION AND DEVELOPMENT

ORGANISATION FOR ECONOMIC CO-OPERATION AND DEVELOPMENT

The OECD is a unique forum where the governments of 30 democracies work together to address the economic, social and environmental challenges of globalisation. The OECD is also at the forefront of efforts to understand and to help governments respond to new developments and concerns, such as corporate governance, the information economy and the challenges of an ageing population. The Organisation provides a setting where governments can compare policy experiences, seek answers to common problems, identify good practice and work to co-ordinate domestic and international policies.

The OECD member countries are: Australia, Austria, Belgium, Canada, the Czech Republic, Denmark, Finland, France, Germany, Greece, Hungary, Iceland, Ireland, Italy, Japan, Korea, Luxembourg, Mexico, the Netherlands, New Zealand, Norway, Poland, Portugal, the Slovak Republic, Spain, Sweden, Switzerland, Turkey, the United Kingdom and the United States. The Commission of the European Communities takes part in the work of the OECD.

OECD Publishing disseminates widely the results of the Organisation's statistics gathering and research on economic, social and environmental issues, as well as the conventions, guidelines and standards agreed by its members.

Also available in French under the title:

Manuel de l'OCDE sur les indicateurs de la mondialisation économique

Foreword and Acknowledgements

In response to increasing demand for better measures to analyse the trends of globalisation, the OECD took the initiative to draw up a conceptual and methodological framework for gathering quantitative information and constructing indicators. This work has led to the present "Handbook on Economic Globalisation Indicators". It is the outcome of co-operation among experts from member countries and with international organisations. The work was carried out primarily in the Directorate for Science, Technology and Industry under the aegis of the experts of the Special Session on Globalisation of the Working Party on Statistics of the Committee on Industry and Business Environment (CIBE).

Recognising the multidimensional nature of globalisation, the Secretary-General of the OECD, Donald J. Johnston, recommended that the work be undertaken collaboratively with other OECD groups with expertise in foreign direct investment, international trade and technology. These include the Investment Committee and its Workshop on International Investment Statistics (WSII) serviced by the Directorate for Financial and Enterprise Affairs; the International Trade Statistics Expert Group and the OECD-Eurostat Experts in Trade in Services Statistics served by the Statistics Directorate; and the Working Party of the Trade Committee serviced by the Trade Directorate. Among groups serviced by the Directorate for Science, Technology and Industry, the Committee for Scientific and Technological Policy (CSTP) and its working parties, the Working Party of National Experts on Science and Technology Indicators (NESTI) and the Working Party on Technology and Innovation Policy (TIP), also participated in the preparation of the Handbook. The Handbook was approved and declassified by the CIBE. In addition, Chapter 2 was approved and declassified separately by the Investment Committee.

While the Handbook is the work of many individuals, the principal contributor has been Thomas Hatzichronoglou of the Directorate for Science, Technology and Industry who organised the subject matter and prepared drafts of all of the chapters except Chapter 2. This chapter was prepared by Ayse Bertrand of the Directorate for Financial and Enterprise Affairs. Other members of the Secretariat who also made significant contributions include Paul Atkinson, Andrew Wyckoff, Daniel Malkin, Candice Stevens, Pierre Poret, Dominique Guellec, John Neighbour, Bernard Damsma, William Cave, Nadim Ahmad, Andreas Lindner, Anthony Kleitz and Peter Walkenhorst.

The OECD Secretariat wishes to thank all of the experts who participated in the preparation of the Handbook and, in particular, Dr. Hartmut Fest of the German Ministry of Economics and Labour, who played a particularly important role throughout the preparation of the Handbook as Chair of the Special Session on Globalisation. Roger De Boeck, Chair of the Workshop on International Investment Statistics of the Investment Committee also played a key role. The Secretariat also wishes to mention the experts from international organisations who participated in the meetings and offered their comments, in particular Margaret Fitzgibbon (IMF), Maria Montanjees (IMF), Neil Patterson (IMF), Guy Karsenty (WTO), Katja Weigl (UNCTAD), Torbjörn Fredriksson (UNCTAD), Masataka Fujita (UNCTAD), David Cieslikowsky (World Bank), Brian Sloan (European Commission), Bettina Knauth (Eurostat), Arto Luhtio (Eurostat), Michaela Grell (Eurostat) and Paolo Passerini (Eurostat).

The Secretariat also wishes to thank David Belli (former head, International Investment Division, Bureau of Economic Analysis, United States) and Yvan Gervais (Statistics Canada) who served as consultants in 2003 and brought their expertise to bear on the final revision of the Handbook. Other important contributions were made by Obie Whichard (United States), William Zeile (United States), John Jankowski (United States), Edouard Mathieu (France), Fabrice Hatem (France), Claire Plateau (France), Giovanni Balcet (Italy), Lelio Iapadre (Italy), Anne-Christine Strandell (Sweden), Enrica Morganti (Italy), Frédéric Boccara (France), Vincent Thollon Pommerol (France), Lionel Fontagné (France), Martyn Vaughan (United Kingdom), Angelo Zanetta (Switzerland) and Raoul Depoutot (France).

Nobuo TANAKA
Director
Directorate for Science, Technology
and Industry

Enrico GIOVANNINI
Chief Statistician and Director
Statistics Directorate

William WITHERELL
Director
Directorate for Financial
and Enterprise Affairs

Jean-Marie METZGER
Director
Trade Directorate

Table of Contents

• • •

Boxes

Figures

Tables

ISBN 92-64-10808-4
OECD Handbook on Economic Globalisation Indicators

Introduction

1. The term "globalisation" has been widely used to describe the increasing internationalisation of financial markets and of markets for goods and services. Globalisation refers above all to a dynamic and multidimensional process of economic integration whereby national resources become more and more internationally mobile while national economies become increasingly interdependent.

Why a *Handbook?*

2. In a globalising economy, distances and national boundaries have substantially diminished as most of the obstacles to market access have been removed. In this global market, multinational enterprises (MNEs) are perceived to be a key vector through which globalisation has occurred and continues to evolve. Thanks to information and communication technologies, firms continue to organise themselves into transnational networks in response to intense international competition and the need for strategic interactions. Despite the fact that economic integration is a dominant feature of globalisation, other dimensions are also of significance, including the social, cultural, political and institutional realms.

3. The globalisation process has accelerated in the second half of the 20th century and has gone through significant developments over the past 20 years. Understanding globalisation based on facts and findings is indispensable for policy making, strategic decisions, as well as many other economic, social and other types of analysis.

4. In this context, the crucial question is whether or not adequate tools are available to measure and assess the globalisation process, and to analyse its economic impact. This leads to the following considerations:

i) Traditional statistics no longer suffice to analyse fully the magnitude and consequences of globalisation, and they need to be supplemented by, and combined with, other indicators.

ii) New concepts resulting from a global economy have to be identified, defined and explained, and they have to be integrated with existing tools into a common analytical framework.

iii) Comparable statistics, based on international standards, must be developed. These standards must be adjusted to take new developments into account.

5. These considerations have led the OECD to reflect on the ways and means of developing a framework in order to analyse the process of globalisation in economic, technological, commercial and financial dimensions, and to construct internationally comparable indicators. This task does not necessarily entail the organisation of new surveys. Most of the existing national data could be adjusted to accommodate the new concepts and definitions needed to analyse economic globalisation and ensure that

indicators are comparable from one country to another. To this end, the development of this *Handbook* has been undertaken with two primary objectives:

- Identify a set of relevant globalisation indicators to gauge the magnitude and intensity of the globalisation process, and to enable policymakers and other analysts to track how it evolves over time.
- Provide national data compilers with the methodological and statistical guidelines needed to construct the chosen indicators and make them compatible with international standards.

6. These objectives entailed that the scope of this *Manual* be built, whenever possible, on the methodological work already established in other manuals. Thus, the recommended definitions and concepts concerning the collection of data on foreign direct investment were taken from the *IMF Manual of Balance of Payments* (MBP5) and its accompanying documents, as well as the *OECD Benchmark Definition of FDI* (3rd edition, 1996). The basic definitions concerning research and development and technology balance of payments are based on those described in the *Frascati Manual* (OECD, 2002) and in the *Technological Balance of Payments Manual* (OECD, 1990), respectively. In addition, some of the concepts and recommendations linked to the activity of foreign affiliates in the service sector which are also presented in this *Manual* come from the *Manual on Statistics of International Trade in Services* (2002).

7. The present *Handbook* recalls the main concepts and definitions already adopted by the aforementioned manuals, putting them within the framework of globalisation and showing the existing links between these manuals. Beyond these reminders and appropriate references, however, the *Handbook* goes further by developing in more detail the concepts linked to the activity of multinational firms and proposing recommendations that can be used to develop harmonised statistics. Given the practices observed in the majority of OECD countries, it is in this area that most of the new recommendations are made. The proposed priorities take these practices into account, along with the need for better analysis of the process of economic globalisation.

Areas covered by the *Handbook*

8. Improving the understanding of the impacts of globalisation requires quantitative work in at least three areas: measurement of its magnitude and intensity, its economic impact, and lastly its links with structural adjustment policies. The *Handbook* covers only the first area, for which a set of indicators is proposed, essentially in the form of ratios derived from basic statistics measuring the magnitude and intensity of the process of globalisation in its different dimentions. The last two areas are not dealt with as they are too complex and cannot therefore be described using simple indicators. Consequently, they most often require models and extensive analytical work inappropriate for a manual. However, they do require data relating to the first area.

9. However, even though the scope of the *Handbook* is limited to measuring the magnitude of the globalisation process, the task encompasses a potentially large number of areas. Priority is given to those that are considered the mainsprings of globalisation: *international trade, foreign direct investment*, the *activity of multinational firms* and the *production and international diffusion of technology*. Most of these areas are dealt with in other, more specialised manuals as indicated above, but the intention with this *Handbook* is not to present all the relevant indicators but to select those which are linked directly to

globalisation and for which the OECD countries are directly involved in data collection. Other driving forces of globalisation, including financial portfolio movements, international migration of persons, and government action, are not addressed in the current version of the *Handbook*. The five chapters contained in this *Handbook* are followed by a brief description of the sources of data for the proposed indicators, a list of acronyms and a glossary which recalls the definitions of the principal terms used.

10. Chapter 1 sets out to define the concept of globalisation and identify its main driving forces. It will also propose a limited list of reference indicators based on the current availability of the underlying data and some of the policy issues confronting policymakers and analysts of globalisation.

11. Chapter 2 covers foreign direct investment. It reviews the basic concepts and definitions that apply to the FDI statistics in the *IMF Balance of Payments Manual* (5th edition) and the *OECD Benchmark Definition of Foreign Direct Investment* (3rd edition). In respect of application of the standards recommended by the member countries, the chapter refers to the joint OECD/IMF *Survey of Implementation of Methodological Standards for Direct Investment* (SIMSDI). The survey also provides a brief description of future methodological work that could lay the groundwork for an extension of FDI statistics.

12. Chapter 3 deals with the economic activity of multinational firms. It develops the main concepts and definitions regarding activity data for multinational firms, notably the concept of control of an enterprise and the identification of the country of the investor which has the ultimate control over its activities. Building on national statistical agencies' best practices, pragmatic and operational recommendations are made in order to enhance international comparability of indicators and basic data. The definitions proposed are consistent with those contained in the fourth chapter of the *Manual on Statistics of International Trade in Services*.

13. Chapter 4 is devoted to the internationalisation of technology. Several forms of internationalisation are analysed: the internationalisation of R&D, technology balance of payments and trade in high-technology products. The chapter benefits from the guidelines set out for the measurement of research and development developed in the *Frascati Manual* and the *Technology Balance of Payments Manual*.

14. Chapter 5 deals with certain aspects of the globalisation of trade. The purpose is not to repeat what readers can easily find in other manuals, books and articles on the subject, but to focus on several aspects of the role played by multinational firms in international trade, and on certain structural effects of globalisation on international trade. Consequently, much of the chapter is devoted to indicators on intra-firm trade and some complementary and experimental methods for evaluating the trade balances of countries on the basis of the ownership of their firms rather than their geographical borders. Other indicators are provided on shifts in the structure of international trade, such as intra-industry trade, trade in intermediate goods, the import content of exports, and intra-regional trade.

Target audience of the *Handbook*

15. The *Handbook* is intended first and foremost for those who collect basic data and are responsible for constructing and disseminating indicators. It also aims indirectly at other categories of statistics users, who will be able to find useful information concerning basic concept definitions, data availability, and construction of indicators. As for the countries concerned, the *Handbook* is designed in the first instance solely to cover data originating

from OECD-based data compilers. However, given the economic importance in world markets of countries outside the OECD area and the nature of the subject, the country coverage of the *Handbook* will possibly have to be enlarged in a future version in order to take into account the specificities and priorities of non-OECD economies.

Limitations of the existing *Handbook* and future work

16. This is only an initial foray into a vast area and does not pretend to provide answers to all questions. The *Handbook* rather seeks to provide an initial foundation which can serve as a basis for further work. Notwithstanding these shortcomings, notably certain problems relating to data comparability which largely reflect the need to harmonise the definitions of the concepts used in this field, it was the belief of the contributors to the *Handbook* that progress on these issues would benefit from experience gained through the use of this initial version. Given this, and the changing nature of what constitutes "globalisation", this *Handbook* is intended to be dynamic rather than static. It will have to be revised at regular intervals and enriched with the most recent experience and trends by incorporating the suggestions of the users and producers of basic data.

ISBN 92-64-10808-4
OECD Handbook on Economic Globalisation Indicators

Chapter 1

The Concept of Economic Globalisation and its Measurement

1.1. The concept of economic globalisation[1]

17. As noted in the Introduction, the term "globalisation" has been widely used to describe the increasing internationalisation of markets for goods and services, the financial system, corporations and industries, technology and competition.

18. Three major forces have contributed importantly to the globalisation process: *i)* the liberalisation of capital movements and deregulation, of financial services in particular; *ii)* the further opening of markets to trade and investment, spurring the growth of international competition; and *iii)* the pivotal role played by information and communication technologies (ICT) in the economy. In each of these cases, market forces and specific public policies have played important roles as determinants of these changes. In important respects, globalisation could be seen mainly as a microeconomic phenomenon, driven by the strategies and behaviour of firms that have responded to these changes. Government, through international organisations, has also played an important role. For example, first GATT, then the WTO (see list of acronyms at the back of this *Handbook*) has helped extend the process of globalisation and market opening by regularly reducing tariff barriers through various rounds of trade negotiations, whilst the IMF has worked to ensure the smooth operation of the international monetary system. The OECD, too, has played a leading role in liberalising capital movements through the "Codes of Liberalisation of Capital Movements", including direct investment, and the "Codes of Liberalisation of Invisible Operations", covering services.[2] In addition, the deregulation policies adopted by some OECD countries and the unilateral liberalisation of the economy and opening up of the market undertaken by a number of developing countries – particularly in East Asia – have also helped to accelerate the globalisation process. Furthermore, the demise of central planning in Eastern Europe and the former Soviet Union has contributed to the globalisation process as the economies in question have gradually integrated themselves into the world economy.

19. The globalisation of *trade in goods and services* is opening up new and increasingly vast markets. The globalisation of *financial markets* has triggered sharp growth in investment portfolios and large movements of short-term capital, with borrowers and investors interacting through a more and more unified market. The globalisation of *competition* heralds the emergence of new strategic considerations for enterprises. The globalisation of *technology* stems from the speed with which innovations are propagated, with international networks linking to public and private research centres, as well as from converging standards. Lastly, the globalisation of *corporations and industries* was led by sharp increases in foreign direct investment and relocation of enterprises heavily driven by joint ventures, co-operation agreements and strategic alliances, and mergers and acquisitions. One consequence of these changes is the fragmentation of production processes, where different stages of production for a given product are carried out in different countries.

20. In a globalising economy, distances and national boundaries have substantially diminished with the removal of obstacles to market access. The markets and the production of different countries have become increasingly interdependent through the

 OECD HANDBOOK ON ECONOMIC GLOBALISATION INDICATORS – ISBN 92-64-10808-4 – © OECD 2005

changes induced by the dynamics of trade and capital flows and transfer of technology – changes of which the primary vehicles are multinational enterprises (MNEs). Thanks to ICT, firms are organising themselves into transnational networks in response to intense international competition and the increasing need for strategic interactions. Despite the fact that economic integration is a dominant feature, as mentioned in the Introduction, other dimensions of globalisation are also important, such as its social, cultural, political and institutional aspects. Across all of these dimensions, MNEs are perceived to be a key vector through which globalisation has occurred and continues to evolve. For this reason, much of the work on globalisation undertaken by the OECD to date has focused on MNEs.

21. One feature is the growing *interdependence* of the various *facets* of globalisation. In many cases, direct investment flows generate exports of goods and services from the investor countries and in most cases are accompanied by transfers of technology and know-how, along with movements of capital (equity, international loans, repatriation of profits, interest, royalties, etc.). Similar interconnections could be recorded using factors other than direct investment as the starting point (*i.e.* exports generate technology transfers and new FDI flows). Empirical analysis of these interdependencies is still incomplete. However, the work available, concerning trade links and direct investment targeted at manufactures in particular, would suggest that there tends to be complementary, particularly at the macroeconomic level.[3]

22. Another feature involves patterns of international trade. The creation of many foreign-based affiliates by national firms, and of host country affiliates by foreign parent companies, has been conducive to *intra-firm* trade. For such trade, as will be seen in Chapter 5, the prices that are charged between firms belonging to the same group (*i.e.* transfer prices) may not correspond to market prices.

23. The acceleration in capital movements and greater mobility of factors of production has significantly changed countries' traditional specialisation models. These changes are prompting many firms in the developed countries to seek to strengthen their competitive advantages by specialising in differentiated products with an increasingly large technological content. This form of specialisation concerning firms is conducive to *intra-industry* trade between OECD countries. Abandoned activities are often acquired by other firms in the same industry that are seeking to strengthen their positions. To this end, many firms, in all industries and in different countries, also establish *co-operation agreements* or adopt strategies of *mergers and acquisitions* and *network organisation*, and this has contributed to the surge in *direct investment* over the past decade or so. This movement has been further accelerated as the capital of public enterprises has opened up (via total or partial privatisation) and foreign investors have made acquisitions or equity investments.

24. The expansion of trade and liberalisation of capital movements, combined with advances in communications technology, has resulted in a strengthening of "global competition" – a term that suggests the need for firms to tackle their competitors in all markets and in a large number of areas. In order to contend with this competition, firms are obliged to harness a range of skills simultaneously. In this environment, competitiveness increasingly depends on the synergy generated by a broad range of specialised industrial, financial, technological, commercial, administrative and cultural skills located in different regions or even on different continents. Henceforth, a growing number of firms are competing in their own markets as well as in foreign ones, with new players from around the globe.

25. Box 1.1 summarises some of the important features of globalisation which form the basis for developing indicators that measure the phenomenon and that will be presented in the following chapters of this *Handbook*.

Box 1.1. **Important features of globalisation (summary)**

General aspects

- Reduction of barriers to trade.
- The high integration of financial markets is increasingly impacting on the conduct and performance of the industrial sector.
- Foreign direct investment is becoming a crucial factor in the world-wide process of industrial restructuring and the development of genuinely global industries.
- Multinational firms constitute one of the main vectors of economic internationalisation.
- Close linkages between trade and direct investment.
- Evolving multilateral frameworks for trade and investment (*e.g.* TRIMS, TRIPS, GATS, etc.)
- Internationalisation of production: multinational origin of product components, services and capital often characterised by co-operation or subcontracting agreements among firms.
- Location strategies for the activities of multinational firms are strongly influenced by the comparative advantages of countries and regions.
- A significant proportion of world trade has become intra-firm.
- Accelerating international dissemination of technology and simultaneous shortening of the cycle of production and technological innovation.
- Simultaneous competition in markets between numerous new competitors from all over the world, places acquired positions at risk, necessitating extremely rapid structural adjustments in numerous areas.
- Substantial interdependence of the various dimensions of globalisation (trade, direct investment flows, technology transfers, capital movements, etc.). High degree of integration of national economies, but also significant risks of contagion following economic and financial shocks in certain regions, which may spread to other regions not directly involved.
- Compression of time and distance in international transactions and reduction of transaction costs.
- Multiplication of regional free-trade agreements.

Microeconomic aspects inter-state

- Global strategies adopted by firms may include:
  - Global conception of markets.
  - Multi-regional integration strategy.
  - Changes in external organisation of multinational firms (*e.g.* mergers and acquisitions rather than greenfields, cooperation agreements and alliances, international subcontracting, worldwide network structure).
  - Changes in internal organisation (*e.g.* just-in-time flows, outsourcing, smaller average production units, individualisation of tasks and pay, less emphasis on hierarchical relationships, need for greater transparency, and for corporate governance regulations, etc.).

1.2. Why does measuring economic globalisation matter?

26. Globalisation challenges and places new demands on statistics and indicators designed to help public authorities and firms to assess developments and formulate appropriate policies. The existing traditional economic statistics and indicators were developed largely in an era where most economic activity, with the exception of trade, occurred domestically. These measures need to be reinterpreted or readjusted in this new context to take into greater account influences from abroad, many of which are intra-firm and as such are more difficult to value.

27. For example, many analyses focusing on competitiveness see international trade as a key indicator of globalisation and market conquest. This focus does not adequately reflect the fact that other forms of globalisation such as direct investment can be complementary or provide alternative strategies. When a firm decides to expand abroad, whether by setting up "greenfield investments" or via acquisitions of existing firms, it could influence economic activity in various ways. For example, output may fall if foreign affiliates act as local subcontractors and produce the same products at lower costs, or it may increase if the affiliates' products are complementary to the products being manufactured at home. In the latter case, the parent company's additional production might be exported essentially to its affiliates, while part of the affiliates' production might be imported by the parent company (*intra-firm trade*).[4]

28. Better accounting for the role of foreign affiliates also helps to better understand the nature of the service sector that dominates all OECD member countries in terms of value added or employment. Given the nature of certain services and the sector's scant degree of international liberalisation, accessing foreign markets often requires a foreign presence since a relatively limited share of the sector's production is tradable.

29. The role of MNEs is also prominent in the realm of technology. Measurements of what is called the "*national research effort*" may be affected when research centres, rather than production facilities, are shifted abroad. Reductions in some countries' R&D expenditure have been attributed to the fact that a number of major companies have moved R&D laboratories abroad. These companies have also acquired foreign R&D laboratories through mergers and acquisitions. At the same time, a significant part of domestic R&D is funded from abroad and is performed for enterprises located abroad while other foreign enterprises located abroad perform R&D for domestic enterprises. To these developments may be added R&D co-operation agreements and joint ventures located in third countries, making it difficult to get a precise idea of the meaning of "national R&D effort" and of its impact on the technological potential of one country.[5]

30. Indicators corresponding to economic globalisation should generally respond to the following questions:

- To what extent can the intensity of the globalisation process be measured?
- How can the impact of globalisation on economic performance be evaluated?
- How can we measure the impact of structural policy reforms designed to get national economies to benefit more from globalisation?

31. However, the *Handbook* is devoted to measures concerning almost exclusively the first question that corresponds to the extent and intensity of globalisation. There were two reasons for this: first, the need to have better tools and more realistic evaluation and analysis of the extent and intensity of the economic activity in a global market; also, the

need to harmonise these tools across the OECD countries to achieve reliable analysis for policy recommendations, decision making and other analytical work. Second, the impact of globalisation and structural policies on economic performance are generally the results of analytical studies that are complex and not readily amenable to a manual of this type.

1.3. A "core" set of indicators of economic globalisation

32. This *Handbook* is above all a methodological work having the particularity that it begins by identifying a set of relevant indicators that collectively provide insight into the globalisation process (see Box 1.2), while these indicators (combinations of basic statistics) are then broken down into their constituent variables. In a second phase, the definitions and concepts corresponding to these basic statistics (variables) are presented, and specific recommendations formulated, with some recommendations drawing inspiration from other existing manuals. By adopting this approach, the *Handbook* integrates parts of other relevant manuals into one source. These indicators provide a partial, but fairly concrete and coherent response to the need to assess the extent and intensity of globalisation by examining the role of MNEs in three areas that have played a driving role in the process of globalisation: international trade, foreign direct investment and various forms of technological dissemination.

Box 1.2. **Classification of economic globalisation indicators**

The economic globalisation indicators proposed in this *Handbook* are classified into three categories which were developed as a guide to OECD members to prioritize their work in improving their statistical systems. These categories are:

a) Reference indicators.

b) Supplemental indicators.

c) Experimental indicators.

The usefulness of all categories of indicators is greatly enhanced when they are available in all countries under review.

Reference indicators are the most commonly used indicators, and are necessary for any analysis of economic globalisation in all or parts of the world economy. All member countries are encouraged to produce these indicators as first priority. In practice, a significant share of these indicators is currently available in most OECD countries even if further harmonisation is necessary. Statistical authorities of member countries are invited to fill in the data gaps in their statistical systems.

Supplemental indicators are, in principle, developed to provide additional information. In the present context, they also include indicators which are, in theory, desirable but may be difficult or costly to implement in practice (*e.g.* activity of MNEs abroad). Consequently, supplemental indicators have lower priority as compared to reference indicators.

Experimental indicators address issues that exhibit a growing importance in the context of globalisation but where statistical concepts and methods require further work (*e.g.* new forms of international economic alliances). Countries are encouraged to participate in the work of international organisations on such issues and are invited to share their experiences. Experimental indicators are discussed briefly in the *Handbook* to stimulate further research and development.

33. Some of the main questions related to the activity of multinational firms that the reference indicators seek to address are:

- What is the FDI position (inward and outward) as a share of GDP?
- What is the balance of inflows and outflows of direct investment for a given country?
- What is the propensity to reinvest earnings (earnings/income) from direct investment?
- What is the share of foreign-controlled affiliates in economic output (*e.g.* GDP, value added, gross output) and employment in the compiling country?
- What is the share of parent companies' economic output, gross fixed capital formation, employment, and employee compensation in their own compiling country?
- What is the share of foreign-controlled R&D in the overall R&D of the host country?
- What is the ratio of controlled affiliates abroad R&D to the overall R&D of the host country?
- What is the role and importance of MNEs in trade?
- What is the importance of trade between parent companies and their affiliates (intra-firm trade)?
- How important are affiliates controlled abroad in delivering goods and services to international markets?

34. In this chapter, only the reference indicators are presented while all three categories are described in greater detail in certain thematic chapters.

1.3.1. *Scope, coverage and interpretation of the reference indicators*

35. Economic globalisation indicators are statistical tools that measure the extent and intensity (degree) of economic globalisation based on different types of analysis:

a) Geographical analysis in countries, regions or the world as a whole.

b) Industry sector analysis in one or more sectors of the economy.

c) Type of economic variable.

36. The indicators are constructed to standardize the most relevant measurement of the economic globalisation. They allow for a sound comparison of the elements of globalisation over time and across countries and industry sectors.

37. As stated above, the indicators proposed in this *Handbook* are mostly ratios expressed as percentages, which facilitates comparability between countries. As such, the trend of these indicators over time usually corresponds to an increase or a decrease in the extent and/or intensity of economic globalisation. For example, an increase in the share of employment in enterprises under foreign control might suggest that an economy's foreign dependence (intensity) is increasing. A concentration index such as the Herfindahl Index[6] is an inverse measure of the extent of geographic diversification (globalisation). Thus, it indicates a higher degree of globalisation when ratios are lower.

38. The measuring techniques allow, as much as possible the construction of variables that are additive across countries and/or industries, allowing the computation of regional and international indicators. For example, affiliates under foreign control are defined in such a way that related variables can be summed up across the countries of a region, without duplication, to compute regional economic globalisation indicators.

39. The proposed "core" set of reference indicators (Box 1.3) characterising globalisation therefore cover the following areas:

- Foreign direct investment.
- The economic activity of multinational firms.
- The international dissemination of technology.
- The globalisation of trade.

40. These indicators are designed primarily to reflect each country's overall economy, (*i.e.* at the aggregate level). However, many could also be constructed at the sectoral level and, in respect of certain types of trade, at product level as well. Each of the indicators is described in more detail in the subsequent chapters of the *Handbook*.

1.3.2. Reference indicators of foreign direct investment

41. There are mainly three types of FDI-linked reference indicators. First, the *extent of globalisation of an economy* is widely measured by cross-country comparisons based on the relative importance of FDI financial flows, income flows and FDI positions as a percentage of GDP. Each ratio indicates the relative importance of globalisation for the reporting economy either for total investments or for investments by economic sector. Comprehensive and timely GDP series are available in all OECD countries which together with FDI statistics allow complete coverage of the OECD area. Such ratios based on FDI positions are structural indicators which reflect the interdependence of economies and the extent of sustained foreign presence in home and host economies.

42. The *contributions of investing and host economies and of economic sectors to globalisation* can be measured by ratios that show the relative share of individual economies or economic sectors in comparison to total investments. Ratios based on outward investments relate to the economy of the direct investor while those based on inward investments relate to the economy of the direct investment enterprise. When the ratios relate to economic sectors, the results allow measuring the relative contribution of different economic sectors through foreign direct investment to globalisation. The increase of either one of these indicators implies greater contribution to globalisation of the host or investing economy or of individual economic sectors.

43. *Return on FDI* indicators provide preliminary information on the profitability of direct investment enterprises. If FDI income increases as a percentage of total inward FDI stocks, it is likely that the profitability of resident direct investment enterprises has increased, thus making them more and more attractive to investors. If the share of reinvested earnings, as compared to dividends and distributed branch profits, tends to increase in the long term, it suggests a desire to expand investment in the host country through this means. Nevertheless, to fully confirm these observations would require other information on such aspects as overall business strategy for direct investment and policy towards shareholders.

1.3.3. Reference Indicators of the economic activity of multinational firms

44. Indicators concerning the economic activity of multinational firms (such as production, employment, R&D or exports) are available for a more limited number of countries than are indicators of direct investment flows. Efforts to collect this type of data are more recent and not all the concepts and basic definitions are as yet the same for all countries. Even in the service sector, for which the main guidelines were defined in

Box 1.3. **Proposed reference indicators**

Foreign Direct Investment concerning a compiling country's inward and outward FDI (Chapter 2)

i) Degree of globalisation via FDI

- FDI financial flows as a percentage of GDP.
- FDI income flows as a percentage of GDP.
- FDI positions as a percentage of GDP.

ii) Contributions of investing and host countries by economic sector

- Relative share of FDI financial flows by partner country as a percentage of total FDI flows.
- Relative share of FDI positions by partner country as a percentage of total FDI stocks.
- Relative share of FDI financial flows by economic sector as a percentage of total FDI flows.
- Relative share of FDI positions by economic sector as a percentage of total FDI stocks.

iii) Returns on inward and outward FDI

- FDI income as a percentage of FDI positions (rate of return for total FDI or by economic sector or investing country) in a compiling economy.

Economic Activity of Multinational Enterprises (Chapter 3) *(By country and by industry)*

- Foreign CAs' share of value added, turnover or gross output, and gross fixed capital formation.
- Foreign CAs' share of employment.
- Foreign CAs' share of compensation of employees.
- Parent enterprises' share of value added, turnover or gross output, employment and compensation of employees.
- A compiling country's MNEs' (parent companies and foreign CAs) share of that country's value added, turnover or gross output, employment and compensation of employees.

International dissemination of Technology (Chapter 4) *(By country and by industry)*

iv) Degree of internationalisation of the R&D of multinational firms in the compiling country

- Share of R&D expenditure and of the number of researchers of foreign-controlled affiliates.
- Share of industrial R&D expenditure financed from abroad.
- Share of value added, turnover and employment attributable to foreign-controlled affiliates whose main activity is R&D.
- Share of parent companies in R&D expenditure and the number of researchers.

v) Degree of internationalisation of the diffusion of technology in the compiling country (total and by industry)

- Technology payments and receipts as a percentage of GDP.
- Technology payments and receipts as a percentage of R&D expenditure.

vi) Degree of internationalisation of trade in technology-intensive products in compiling countries (total and by industry)

- Share of foreign-controlled affiliates' high-technology manufacturing exports in high-technology manufacturing output.
- Share of foreign-controlled affiliates' and parent companies' high-technology manufacturing exports and imports in total high-technology exports and imports.

Box 1.3. **Proposed reference indicators** *(cont.)*

Globalisation of Trade (Chapter 5)

vii) Aggregate trade of a compiling country

- Share of total exports in GDP.
- Average of exports in GDP.
- Share of domestic final demand met by imports.
- Share of GDP generated by total exports.

viii) Trade of foreign-controlled affiliates

- Foreign-CAs' share of the compiling country's total exports.
- Foreign-CAs' share of the compiling country's total imports.
- Intra-firm exports of goods by foreign-CAs in the host (compiling) country's total exports of goods.
- Intra-firm imports of goods by foreign-CAs in the host (compiling) country's total imports of goods.

connection with the *Manual on Statistics of International Trade in Services*, they are not yet applied by all countries.

45. The proposed reference indicators on the economic activity of multinational firms focus on host countries, given that not as many countries have information available about the activities of their affiliates abroad.

46. The first three proposed indicators concerning the economic activity of multinational firms answer the following questions:

- What contribution do foreign-controlled firms make to value added turnover or gross production and fixed capital formation in host countries?
- What share of employment is supplied by foreign-controlled firms in host countries?
- What is the share of compensation (*e.g.* earnings per hour) under foreign control in host countries?

47. The next indicator concerns the parent companies' role in the compiling countries. The last indicator proposes to measure the share of total multinational enterprise activities in the compiling country concerning affiliates under foreign control as well as parent companies. In this case and in order to avoid double counting, it is important to take into account only parent companies controlled by residents.

48. The indicators can be used to make an overall assessment of the role of foreign-controlled firms in the economic activity of the host countries. Exceptions concern many aspects of trade and technology – areas that are dealt with separately.

49. Indicators corresponding to the activities of parent companies in their home countries would fill a gap which now exists since the data compiled on multinational firms refer to the activities of either foreign-controlled firms in host countries or of affiliates controlled by residents abroad. The activity of parent companies in their home countries is not contained in surveys on either inward or outward investment insofar as it involves firms located in those countries and controlled by residents. The only collected

 OECD HANDBOOK ON ECONOMIC GLOBALISATION INDICATORS – ISBN 92-64-10808-4 – © OECD 2005

information, which concerns them indirectly, deals with intra-firm trade (see Chapter 5). Data on parent company activity exist in practically all countries, but they have not to date been systematically collected by international organisations like the OECD.

1.3.4. *Reference indicators of the international diffusion of technology*

50. While the dissemination of information and communication technologies has been one of the most decisive factors in accelerating the process of globalisation, the diffusion of technology at the global level may not have advanced at as swift a pace as international trade or direct investment. To develop their technology and innovate, global firms derive their knowledge from a variety of information centres located in different countries. It is a phase dominated by the setting up of numerous research and innovation laboratories outside the countries of origin, or the acquisition of existing laboratories. The greater the extent to which the role of these laboratories is to produce new technologies for world markers, the more it advances the globalisation stage of the firms and industries concerned.

51. The proposed reference indicators of the international diffusion of technology concern a number of aspects that are characteristic of research and development (R&D) activities, trade in disembodied technology in the form of patents, licences, know-how, technical assistance, R&D studies (technology balance of payments) and trade in high-tech products.

52. To assess the extent to which R&D has been globalised in the compiling countries, four main categories of indicators are proposed: 1) R&D expenditure (and number of researchers) by foreign-controlled firms as a proportion of the host country's total industrial R&D; 2) share of R&D expenditure financed by foreign sources; 3) share of value added, turnover or gross production, and employment of affiliates under foreign control with R&D as a main activity; and 4) the share of R&D expenditure and number of researchers of parent companies in compiling countries.

53. The first group of indicator corresponds to R&D activity of foreign affiliates is associated with inward investment. These indicators, which are compiled for a large number of countries, show that R&D activities are less internationalised than production activities, but that they are continuing to expand. They also show that in a majority of cases R&D activity is linked closely to the other productive activities of affiliates in the host countries, and that it is rarely totally independent.

54. To elucidate this more clearly, it is important to collect information on the aims of the R&D activities of multinational firms. The greater the extent to which research is aimed at customising affiliates' products for local markets, the closer the linkages between R&D and local production. On the other hand, if the goal of affiliates' R&D is to develop new technologies of relevance to all of the world's markets, ties will be just as close with the parent company abroad, which will play a more active role in steering R&D and exploiting the results. Although they are important to understanding and analysing the role of foreign firms' R&D laboratories, these indicators have not been incorporated in the list of reference indicators because now they are available in only one or two countries but it is proposed in Chapter 4 that they be developed in the future.

55. Globalisation puts pressure on firms to concentrate their activities in areas in which they are more competitive, and to purchase all of the technologies they need but are unable to produce on their own. The sale and purchase of such technologies give rise to

commercial trade in patents, licensing and know-how contracts, technical assistance and industrial R&D. Purchases of such forms of disembodied technology correspond to what has been called "technology payments", and sales of them to "technology receipts".

56. These indicators are traditionally broken down by industrial sector and by geographic area (of origin and destination). Another important distinction concerns affiliated *versus* unaffiliated firms, since empirical data show that a majority of technology transfers of this kind take place between parent companies and their affiliates. Unfortunately, few countries at the present time collect these data and for this reason they are excluded from the list of reference indicators. The economic interpretation of these indicators cannot be carried out independently without taking into account, simultaneously, the links not only with international trade, R&D efforts, direct investment and co-operation agreements, but also with other economic aggregates.

57. Trade in high-tech products constitutes the most widespread form of dissemination of technology embodied in goods and services. The common interest displayed by governments in high technology may thus be justified because of its increasing contribution to growth, the strengthening of a country's technological and innovation potential and industrial competitiveness, and the creation of highly skilled jobs.

1.3.5. *Reference indicators of the globalisation of trade*

58. The oldest form of internationalisation of economic activities is trade. In quantitative terms, trade is still the most substantial form of integration into the global economy. Indicators involving trade can be designed at the level of a country, industry as a whole (manufacturing and services), a sector (manufacturing or services), a firm or a product.

59. The chosen indicators in the restricted list correspond to some major features of international trade. The first four reflect the scale of globalisation and the last four correspond to trade involving foreign-controlled affiliates.

60. It may be considered that a compiling country or a sector, for example, is more highly internationalised if a larger proportion of its domestic production is exported. However, this simple ratio, particularly when applied to the entire economy (total exports to GDP), must be interpreted cautiously since it reflects developments in prices as well as volumes, and does not reflect the import content of exports.

61. International trade involving multinational firms is covered by the last four of the proposed indicators, namely exports and imports of foreign affiliates in the host countries and intra-firm trade (exports and imports) of host countries. As a generalisation, in host countries foreign affiliates export more than the average for firms controlled by residents, but they also import more. That said, it depends on the nature of the investment, from when it dates, the sector concerned and the commercial strategy of the group to which the affiliates belong.

62. Intra-firm trade is an important indicator of the degree of globalisation. In general, the indicator takes four forms, depending on whether it refers to exports or imports from each country's inward or outward investment. More specifically, this indicator measures trade between foreign affiliates and their parent companies and among other affiliates belonging to the same group, and trade between the parent companies of domestic firms and their affiliates abroad, or among affiliates of the same group located in different countries. Only the first two indicators are proposed as reference indicators.

63. The ratio of intra-firm exports to a sector's total exports naturally depends on the number and size of affiliates abroad, whether the product is an intermediate or final one, and how firms are organised. It could be assumed that in a majority of cases the ratio might be higher in the case of vertical integration and less so in the case of horizontal organisation.

1.4. A conceptual framework for the analysis and development of economic globalisation indicators

64. The above list of reference indicators as well as supplementary and experimental indicators presented in the thematic chapters refer to concepts either already explored and analysed in other manuals or are based on new material provided in this *Handbook*.

65. The present *Handbook* draws as much as possible on existing methodological standards and recommendations included in the System of National Accounts 1993 (SNA 93); IMF Balance of Payments Manual 5th edition (BPM 5) and companion manuals; and the OECD *Benchmark Definition of Foreign Direct Investment*, 3rd edition (*Benchmark Definition*).

66. Consequently the definitions of notions such as FDI financial flows, direct investment position, direct investment income, dividends, equity capital, reinvested earnings, etc. are simply repeated in this *Handbook* with the appropriate references to the previous sources. However, other new concepts relating to core globalisation issues had to be developed and links between these various concepts were made when appropriate. All these concepts together form the framework for globalisation indicators. These new concepts are developed particularly in Chapter 3 on economic activities of multinational enterprises. Here, attention is paid to notions of *ownership* and *control* of an enterprise and particularly the forms of *direct and indirect control* of affiliates are analysed. Chapter 3 also defines the term *parent company* and its relationship with its affiliates, as well as the notion of *parent group* and the difficult task of identifying the owner of the *enterprise of ultimate control*. Chapter 3 discusses the role of enterprises controlled by residents and non-residents in compiling countries or abroad and the issues concerning the comparability between indicators of multinational enterprises with indicators referring to national total. This problem is linked to the more general issue of statistical units which is also discussed in Chapter 3. The definition of concepts and their measurement is essential for data collection, and for this reason each chapter and particularly Chapter 3 provides recommendations to compilers and users. Given the breadth of the topic and its evolving nature, not all of the concepts directly linked to globalisation have been presented and discussed in this first edition of the *Handbook*.

1.5. Areas for future investigation

67. As was mentioned in the introduction, the present version of the *Handbook* does not pretend to provide answers to all questions linked to economic globalisation. Some important issues that it was not possible to incorporate into this edition include:

- The role of financial markets, and particularly portfolio investment.
- The international migration of persons.
- The treatment of intellectual property, such as patents.
- The impact of e-business processes, such as electronic commerce.

68. In addition, some important aspects concerning the driving forces of economic globalisation which are already presented in thematic chapters were not developed in the present *Handbook* because for some of them, no consensus was obtained concerning the definition of concepts and their measurement. For this reason most of these concepts are not defined in the *Handbook* and no specific recommendations are made.

69. The main areas for further investigation in the future could be related to:

- Mergers and acquisitions.
- Greenfield investments.
- Investment of extension of existing capacities.
- Relocation of activities.
- Enterprise group statistics.
- Co-operation agreements.
- Strategic alliances.
- International sub-contracting (outsourcing).

70. Some of these issues may be addressed through the revision of other statistical manuals which future revisions of this *Handbook* could reference.

71. The areas mentioned above could not be incorporated into this version of the *Handbook* for three additional reasons. The first is that they entailed collaboration with other working groups or international organisations more specialised in the areas in question. In particular, this involves the role of *capital markets* and *portfolio investments*, the regime for *intellectual property*, including *patents*, and statistics on *enterprise groups*. Work on these three themes is fairly far along and might be incorporated into the *Handbook*'s next revision if the groups and international organisations concerned (the IMF and Eurostat in particular) wish to contribute.

72. A second reason why some of the above areas are absent from the *Handbook* is a lack of sufficient progress in collecting the relevant data, or the fact that data collection still raises difficulties that preclude the proposal of practical recommendations. This applies in particular to *international migration* of individuals, and especially of skilled labour (such as researchers), *international electronic commerce* and *international outsourcing*.

73. The third reason stems from the difficulties involved in defining and measuring basic concepts. This category includes *relocations*, *co-operation agreements* and *strategic alliances*, and *mergers and acquisitions*. In respect of the last two categories a large volume of data is already available, largely from private sources, but they are fairly heterogeneous. Extensive methodological work will therefore be indispensable before this information can be incorporated into future editions of the *Handbook*.

Notes

1. Many of the features of globalisation are also described in Globalisation of Industry: Overview and Sector Reports, OECD, 1996.
2. See "OECD Codes of Liberalisation of Capital Movements and Current Invisible Operations: User's Guide" (OECD, 2003). In addition, the "OECD Declaration on International Investment and Multinational Enterprises" (OECD, 2000) contain the relevant instruments. For a more detailed description, see Chapter 2, Box 2.7 and *www.oecd.org/daf/investment*.

3. See also the following OECD internal working documents by Lionel Fontagné:
   - "The Links between Foreign Direct Investment and International Trade" (1995).
   - "The Links between Foreign Direct Investment and Trade: Empirical Evidence for US and French industries" (1996).
   - "Trade Competition and Foreign Direct Investment: A New Assessment" (1998).
   - "Links between Direct Investment and Trade: Short- and Long-term Effects" (1999).
4. These flows are significant. Of all exports coming from manufacturing affiliates under foreign control, between 35 and 60% are intra-firm. The ratio for imports for countries where this data is available is even higher, ranging from 50 to 80%.
5. For example, the amount of manufacturing R&D expenditure under foreign control has grown by nearly 90% between 1993 and 1999 (current prices) with the United States being the destination for nearly half of this investment. For many countries, including Canada, Ireland, Hungary, the Netherlands, Spain, Sweden, and the United Kingdom, foreign affiliates account for 30% or more of manufacturing R&D.
6. See Chapter 2, Annex 5, Box 1.

ISBN 92-64-10808-4
OECD Handbook on Economic Globalisation Indicators

Chapter 2

Foreign Direct Investment

2.1. Introduction

74. Liberalisation of exchange controls and market access have led to increasing competitive pressures in financial markets. As the latter rapidly integrated into a global framework, new financial instruments with broad market access and fewer transaction costs were developed, attracting investors of multiple nationalities and residences. At the same time, the expansion of cross-border financial flows was further accelerated by technological innovations in communications and data processing. Against this background, foreign investment in equities rose significantly, spurred, at times, by spectacular cross-border enterprise link-ups.

75. The present chapter focuses on foreign direct investment (FDI), which remains a key element in the rapidly evolving globalisation process and, as such, of international economic integration. FDI provides a means for creating direct, stable and long-lasting links between economies. It can serve as an important vehicle for local enterprise development, and it may also help improve the competitive position of the recipient ("host") economy. In particular, FDI encourages the transfer of technology and know-how between countries, and it provides an opportunity for the host economy to promote its products more widely in international markets. FDI has acted as an important additional source of capital in a range of host and home countries. FDI also has a positive effect on the development of international trade.[1]

76. The significant growth of FDI in recent decades and its international pervasiveness reflect an increase in the size and in the number of individual transactions as well as their growing diversification across countries and sectors. Large multinational enterprises (MNEs) are traditionally the dominant players in such cross-border transactions. This development coincided with an increased propensity for MNEs to participate in foreign trade. Moreover, in recent years small and medium-sized enterprises (SMEs) have become increasingly involved in foreign direct investment.

77. The removal of legal and regulatory restrictions on cross-border operations in many countries has complicated the task of statistical systems that depend largely on reports from national financial institutions. In some cases, these modifications even had an adverse impact on the coverage and the quality of national statistics. Overall, the globalisation of activities implies that data compilers can no longer rely solely on domestic information about investment activities, as investors have increasing recourse to overseas intermediaries. These developments have reinforced the need for improving the *ad hoc* data collection procedures and for adopting and implementing a harmonised analytical framework for constructing meaningful, comprehensive and internationally comparable statistics on cross-border investments. In this context, FDI compilers should pursue efforts at the international level for sharing information on company ownership. However, due to strict confidentiality rules applied in many countries, information sharing could only be limited to publicly available information on companies.

 OECD HANDBOOK ON ECONOMIC GLOBALISATION INDICATORS – ISBN 92-64-10808-4 –

78. Harmonised statistical indicators of FDI flows and positions are necessary to assist policymakers in dealing with the challenges of globalisation and monitoring the developments of FDI and other cross-border financial flows. The usefulness of such statistics depends on their compliance with several quality parameters:

a) Avoiding inconsistencies between countries.

b) Achieving consistent statistical series over time.

c) Allowing a meaningful exchange of data between partner countries.

d) Reducing global discrepancies in FDI and other balance of payments statistics at the world level.

79. Importantly, the timeliness and the reliability of the statistics are also crucial elements if they are to serve as a useful tool for policy makers and would-be investors.

80. Most of the conceptual framework with regard to statistics on international financial flows, financial assets and liabilities and on foreign direct investments statistics has largely been defined and elaborated already by other international manuals. The present chapter focuses on foreign direct investment and limits itself to broad concepts and definitions to avoid repeating the details elaborated in these manuals. Frequent references are made to existing material, such as:

a) *IMF Balance of Payments Manual*, 5th edition, 1993 [IMF BPM5].

b) *OECD Benchmark Definition of Foreign Direct Investment*, 3rd edition, 1995 [OECD *Benchmark Definition*].

c) *IMF Balance of Payments Compilation Guide, 1995* [IMF *BOP Guide*].

d) *IMF Balance of Payments Textbook, 1996* [IMF *BOP Textbook*].

e) *IMF Financial Derivatives: A Supplement to the Fifth Edition (1993) of the Balance of Payments Manual, 2000 [IMF BOP Derivatives]*.

f) *IMF Recommended Treatment of Selected Direct Investment Transactions, 2002*.

81. For a detailed discussion of the underlying concepts and definitions, the reader should refer to the reference material listed above.

82. Moreover, it should be noted that the OECD, in close co-operation with experts from member countries, IMF and EC institutions, is conducting further methodological work on specific FDI items. The work is organised together with the network of experts of the OECD Workshop on International Investment Statistics. This work will result in the development of a practical guide on foreign direct investment statistics to provide additional practical guidance to national compilers, as well as a practical aid to the users of the statistics in interpreting the FDI statistics.

83. The present chapter is divided into two sections (and supplemented by four annexes):

i) Proposed indicators and core statistics.

ii) Concepts and methods.

84. The chapter also includes a number of text boxes which recall main concepts and definitions for the convenience of the reader. It should however be noted that these are *not* new methodologies but refer to existing international standards set out by the *IMF Balance of Payments Manual*, 5th edition (and companion documents) and the OECD *Benchmark Definition of Foreign Direct Investment*, 3rd edition.

2.2. Proposed FDI indicators to measure globalisation and core statistics

2.2.1. Rationale

85. Foreign direct investment statistics can be used to derive indicators that are most frequently used to monitor the global market. The growing role of the OECD countries in the overall FDI activity, accounting for a large share of such investments, and the accompanying analytical requirements have influenced the development of statistical systems in member countries. The implementation of international standards for comprehensive and comparable statistics to measure foreign investments are, however, not completely fulfilled by OECD countries even if notable progress was made over the past decade or so. The reliability of FDI indicators is closely related to the reliability of the underlying statistics compiled by each country as well as their conformity with international standards. Due to methodological deviations, there are usually asymmetries in bilateral comparisons of the data. Detailed methodological information on national practices of OECD countries can be accessed on the OECD Web site at *www.oecd.org/daf/simsdi*.

86. Indicators relating to FDI[2] are divided into *i) reference indicators and ii) supplemental indicators*. Most of the statistical series required for calculating both sets of indicators are currently available for the OECD countries.

87. The rationale behind these indicators can be summarised as:

i) The role of FDI in international economic integration and the extent of globalization.

ii) The contribution to globalisation by the host and investing economy for foreign investment.

iii) The significance of globalisation for individual economic sectors.

iv) The geographical concentration of FDI.

v) The competitiveness and attractiveness of economies or economic sectors.[3]

88. The following sub-sections describe briefly the content of each category of indicators listed in Box 2.1.

2.2.2. Reference indicators

i) Extent of globalisation through FDI

89. These indicators are the most commonly used measurement of the globalisation of an economy. They measure the extent of cross-border investments realised with the objective of a lasting interest to and from an economy. They also allow cross-country comparisons based on the relative importance of FDI, *i.e. i)* financial flows; or *ii)* income flows; or *iii)* FDI positions as a percentage of GDP. Each ratio indicates the relative importance of globalisation for the reporting economy either for total investments or for investments by economic sector. An increase of the ratio implies a greater share of foreign investment, thus an increase in the relative share of globalisation. It is, however, to be noted that FDI flows and FDI positions and GDP are not fully compatible measurements. Nevertheless, in the absence of other more meaningful cross-country comparisons of the relative size of globalisation, GDP remains as the best common reference. In addition, comprehensive and timely GDP statistics are available in all member countries, thus allowing complete coverage of the OECD area.

90. As a complement to these indicators, it is recommended to review the aggregate FDI series (variables) listed in Box 2.2: FDI flows and positions. These time series can be very

informative and useful for both short and long-term analysis. Timely estimates of the FDI activity allow the monitoring of recent developments. On the other hand, longer series contribute to the measurement of the attractiveness of the reporting economy within the global market and the competitiveness of the economic agents, *i.e.* foreign direct investors and foreign direct investment enterprises.

91. An increase in inward investments by foreign direct investors implies additional capital injected into the economy (the domestic market) and, thus, is likely to have an impact on its economic performance. On the other hand, the size of outward investment transactions indicates the extent of penetration of the resident direct investor in other markets. FDI flows (FDI financial flows and FDI income flows) provide information for a given time period while FDI positions data indicate the levels at a given point in time. The results obtained from FDI flows[4] and FDI positions may be quite different.

92. FDI financial flows (inward and outward) as a percentage of GDP indicate the degree of globalisation of an economy based on the economic framework for a given time period, *i.e.* the changes between two periods. This indicator provides preliminary information on the relative attractiveness of economies (both domestic and foreign) and industries for new investments after allowing for the withdrawal of investments (disinvestment) during the period. FDI flows are compiled in many countries on a quarterly basis or on a monthly basis, with a view to allowing a timely monitoring of the FDI activities.

93. FDI income flows (inward and outward) as a percentage of GDP provide information on the relative importance of the earnings of direct investment enterprises both in the reporting economy and abroad.

94. FDI positions (inward and outward) as a percentage of GDP indicate the extent of globalisation at a given point in time. These structural indicators designate the interdependence of economies. The ratio for inward FDI positions indicates the extent of foreign ownership (of foreign presence) in an economy. The ratio for outward investment indicates the degree of ownership (of presence abroad) of economic agents in other markets. They also illustrate, respectively, the level of dependence of the domestic economy on foreign economies and their capacity of penetration in foreign markets. A comparison of the results obtained for inward and outward FDI will designate the comparative importance of the country as an exporter or recipient of FDI.

ii) Contribution of investing and host economies and of economic sectors to globalisation

95. Expressed as ratios (as percentage of totals within each category of FDI), the results reflect the process of globalisation of the economies by their level of financial expansion abroad and their dependence to financing from abroad. The indicator related to investing and host economies shows the evolution of the share of individual economies as origin of direct investment (outward investment by reporting economy) or as host of direct investment (inward investment by non-residents to the reporting economy). The ratio based on FDI flows allows an analysis of the changes between two periods while the ratio based on positions indicates the structural developments over time. The geographical analysis can be further deepened by measuring the share of the sub-component FDI equity capital in such investments by partner country (see also the list of variables in Box 2.1). An increase of this ratio could indicate a greater contribution to globalisation by the host or investing economy.

96. The indicator based on economic sectors is similar to the previous indicator (by partner country) but the focus this time is on the economic sector for both inward and

Box 2.1. **Proposed globalisation indicators related to FDI**

Reference indicators

i) Extent of globalization through FDI (total FDI or by economic sector)[1]

- Inward FDI financial flows as a percentage of GDP.
- Outward FDI financial flows as a percentage of GDP.
- Inward FDI income flows as a percentage of GDP.
- Outward FDI income flows as a percentage of GDP.
- Inward FDI positions as a percentage of GDP.
- Outward FDI positions as a percentage of GDP.

ii) Contribution of host and investing economies or of economic sectors to globalisation through FDI[2]

- Relative share of inward FDI financial flows by partner country as a percentage of total inward FDI flows.
- Relative share of outward FDI financial flows by partner country as a percentage of total outward FDI flows.
- Relative share of inward FDI positions by partner country as a percentage of total inward FDI positions.
- Relative share of outward FDI positions by partner country as a percentage of total outward FDI position.
- Relative share of inward FDI financial flows by economic sector as a percentage of total inward FDI flows.
- Relative share of outward FDI financial flows by economic sector as a percentage of total outward FDI flows.
- Relative share of inward FDI positions by economic sector as a percentage of total inward FDI position.
- Relative share of outward FDI positions by economic sector as a percentage of total outward FDI position.

iii) Return on FDI

- Inward FDI equity income debits [debits for *a)* dividends/distributed branch profits, plus *b)* reinvested earnings/undistributed branch profits] as a percentage of inward FDI position [rate of return for total inward FDI or by economic sector or investing country].
- Outward FDI equity income credits [credits for *a)* dividends/distributed branch profits, plus *b)* reinvested earnings/undistributed branch profits] as a percentage of outward FDI position [rate of return for total outward FDI or by economic sector or investing country].

Supplemental indicators

iv) Degree of concentration of FDI (for total FDI or by economic sector or by geographical distribution)

- Herfindhal index of inward FDI financial flows.
- Herfindhal index of outward FDI financial flows.
- Herfindhal index of inward FDI positions.
- Herfindhal index of outward FDI positions.

OECD HANDBOOK ON ECONOMIC GLOBALISATION INDICATORS – ISBN 92-64-10808-4 – © OECD 2005

Box 2.1. **Proposed globalisation indicators related to FDI** *(cont.)*

v) Dynamics of FDI in reporting economy

- Inward FDI positions as a percentage of total liabilities of the domestic economy (balance sheet totals).
- Outward FDI positions as a percentage of total assets of the domestic economy (balance sheet totals).

vi) Share of FDI by category [by i) partner country and ii) economic sector]

- Inward equity capital flows as a percentage of inward FDI flows.
- Inward reinvested earnings as a percentage of inward FDI flows.
- Inward other capital flows as a percentage of inward FDI flows.
- Outward equity capital flows as a percentage of outward FDI flows.
- Outward reinvested earnings as a percentage of outward FDI flows.
- Outward other capital flows as a percentage of outward FDI flows.
- Inward position of equity capital and reinvested earnings as a percentage of FDI positions.
- Inward other capital positions as a percentage of inward FDI positions.
- Outward positions of equity capital and reinvested earnings as a percentage of FDI positions.
- Outward other capital positions as a percentage of outward FDI positions.

1. GDP for the entire economy.
2. This indicator relates to statistics *a)* by partner country; or *b)* by economic sector depending on the type of analysis. The indicator does not relate to a matrix type partner country and economic sector data although an analysis of such statistics would be of additional value.

outward investments. This indicator describes the relative contribution of different economic sectors to the international economic system by the measurement of the share of FDI positions by economic sector abroad or by the measurement of the dependence of the economic sectors on investments from abroad. An increase of this ratio indicates a greater contribution to globalisation by individual economic sectors. Furthermore, the analysis can be refined by examining the statistics by partner country and economic sector of the reporting country. However, such statistics, although of analytical interest, are still quite scarce within the OECD countries.

iii) Return on FDI

97. The indicator, based on FDI equity income, provides information regarding the profitability of the direct investment enterprises. For example, when the rate of return of inward FDI [FDI equity income debits – *i.e.* debits for *a)* dividends and distributed branch profits, plus *b)* debits for reinvested earnings and undistributed branch profits – as a percentage of total inward FDI positions] increases, it implies that the resident direct investment enterprises are more profitable and increasingly attractive for investors. However, observations based purely on the results of the statistical ratios are not sufficient to draw conclusions on the competitiveness of enterprises (or an economy). Many other factors should also be taken into account such as cyclical or structural factors, variation of stock

value developments in the sector of economic activity as well as other factors related to the global strategy of the investing enterprise(s).

2.2.3. Supplemental indicators

i) Degree of concentration of FDI

98. This indicator is based on the Herfindahl index to measure the geographical concentration of FDI or the concentration of FDI by economic sector. It is "obtained by squaring the market share of the various players, and then summing those squares".[5] It measures the extent of diversification of the investments *a)* by home and host countries; and *b)* by economic sectors. A decrease in the ratio implies a higher degree of globalisation. In other words, *e.g.* the more investments are diversified geographically the greater is the extent of globalisation.

ii) Dynamics of FDI in reporting economy

99. This indicator measures the share of foreign capital in the reporting economy. First of all it compares, at a specific point in time, the positions of FDI enterprises (inward FDI) to the overall liabilities (balance sheet totals) of the domestic sector as reported in the national financial accounts.[6] Likewise, it also compares the positions of direct investors (outward FDI) to total assets (balance sheet totals) of the reporting economy. In the first case, an increase of the ratio could imply a higher foreign presence through FDI, thus a higher attractiveness of the reporting economy. In the latter indicator, an increase implies the opposite, *i.e.* increasing presence in foreign markets which may be more attractive.

Box 2.2. **Variables required for globalisation indicators related to FDI**[1]

Variables	Type of breakdown					
	Inward			Outward		
	Total aggregates	By partner country	By economic sector	Total aggregates	By partner country	By economic sector
1. FDI income flows[2]	√	√	√	√	√	√
Income on equity	√	√	√	√	√	√
Dividends and distributed branch profits	√	√	√	√	√	√
Reinvested earnings and undistributed branch profits	√	√	√	√	√	√
Income on debt (interest)	√	√	√	√	√	√
2. FDI financial flows[2]	√	√	√	√	√	√
Equity capital	√	√	√	√	√	√
Reinvested earnings	√	√	√	√	√	√
Other capital	√	√	√	√	√	√
3. FDI positions[2]						
Equity capital and reinvested earnings	√	√	√	√	√	√
Other capital	√	√	√	√	√	√
4. Memo item[3]						
Assets and liabilities of the domestic economy (balance sheet totals)	√	√	√	√	√	√
GDP	√	√	√	√	√	√

1. These variables are available in most of the OECD countries.
2. Source: International direct investment statistics database, OECD.
3. Source: National accounts database, OECD.

iii) Share of FDI by category: cross-country and sectoral analysis

100. This indicator provides detailed information on the relative share of categories of FDI flows and positions for both inward and outward investment. The information is based on aggregate data by sub-components of FDI (equity capital, reinvested earnings and other capital) and by geographical distribution or by economic sector. The focus is specific markets or economies. The patterns of contribution to the market, in its broad definition, will vary across the countries or economic sectors depending on the degree of globalisation and the competitiveness of economies or economic sectors. As the ratio increases, the contribution to globalisation will be more important.

2.3. International comparability of FDI statistics and data availability

2.3.1. International comparability

101. Foreign direct investment statistics should be compiled as a part of balance of payments statistics. Nevertheless, some countries do not have a full data reporting system based on international standards. In some cases, FDI statistics are derived from administrative sources such as the information on investment approvals. These statistics provide only an approximation as they reflect investment intentions. The methods for compiling such data do not usually follow the recommended standards. The majority of OECD countries compile their statistics largely in accordance with international guidelines set out in the IMF *BPM5* and the OECD *Benchmark Definition*. However, the extent of the implementation of these standards varies across the countries.

102. The IMF and OECD closely monitor the methodologies used in their member countries for compiling FDI statistics. To maximise the benefit of such an effort, the IMF and OECD launched a common review exercise in 1997. To this end, a joint survey was organised to assess the type of data sources and data collection and dissemination methods used by national compilers as well as the methodologies they apply to their FDI statistics (see Box 2.3).

Box 2.3. The *Survey of Implementation of Methodological Standards for Direct Investment* (SIMSDI)

SIMSDI is a comprehensive study of methodological practices as well as data sources, collection and dissemination methods for foreign direct investment statistics. It is also intended to facilitate the exchange of information between reporting countries. It provides information on the methods used by partner countries that, to some extent, may help explain the discrepancies in the bilateral comparison of national statistics.

SIMSDI was conducted for the first time in 1997 jointly by IMF and OECD and covered 114 countries. The exercise was repeated in 2001 for 61 countries. The results of the 1997 and 2001 SIMSDI surveys have been analysed in reports prepared by IMF and OECD secretariats. Main results of the study measuring the progress since the 1997 survey are outlined in Box 2.4.* A further survey of all IMF and OECD members is planned for late 2003.

* See *Foreign Direct Investment Statistics – How countries measure FDI*, IMF/OECD, 2003.

Note: Information for OECD countries is updated as required and can be viewed on the OECD Web site at: *www1.oecd.org/daf/simsdi/.*

Box 2.4. Summary of the results of 2001 compared with 1997 of the *Survey of Implementation of Methodological Standards for Direct Investment* (SIMSDI)*

Areas where there have been marked improvements since 1997:

a) Availability of FDI statistics, particularly:

- Position data.
- Income data (including reinvested earnings).
- Geographic and industrial sector breakdowns.

b) Coverage of the FDI statistics, particularly the inclusion of:

- Non-cash acquisitions of equity.
- Inter-company loans and financial leases.
- Real estate owned by non-residents.
- Activities of Special Purpose Entities (SPEs).
- Activities of offshore enterprises in the outward FDI statistics.
- Expenditure on natural resource exploration.

Areas where more than 75% of countries surveyed follow the international standards applicable to their economy:

- Use of the 10% ownership rule as the basic criterion for defining FDI relationships.
- Equity capital transactions between affiliated banks and between affiliated financial intermediaries.
- Recording of reverse investment equity transactions when two FDI relationships have been established.
- Inclusion of data on real estate owned by non-residents.
- Inclusion of data on activities of SPEs.
- Inclusion of data on activities of offshore enterprises.

Areas where, despite improvements, the majority of countries do not yet follow the international standards:

- Inclusion of indirectly owned direct investment enterprises – the Fully Consolidated System.
- Use of the Current Operating Performance Concept to measure direct investment earnings.
- Time of recording FDI income on equity and income on debt.
- Recording of reverse investment transactions when the FDI relationship is in one direction only.
- Inclusion of data on quasi-corporations involving construction enterprises and mobile equipment.
- Valuation of FDI positions (assets and liabilities).

* See *Foreign Direct Investment Statistics – How countries measure FDI*, IMF/OECD, 2003. Information for OECD countries is updated as required and can be viewed on the OECD Web site at: *www1.oecd.org/daf/simsdi/*.

2.3.2. Data availability

103. FDI statistics are compiled and disseminated annually and quarterly by the IMF and other international institutions as a part of the overall balance of payments (BOP) and international investment position (IIP) statistics. These aggregate statistics are classified according to the standard components.

104. FDI statistics aggregated according to the standard BOP and IIP aggregates cannot, however, meet all types of user needs depending on the extent of the analytical requirements. More detailed FDI breakdowns are needed to complement these aggregate data to analyse:

a) The geographical distribution of FDI: components of FDI by partner country or economic zone/region.

b) The penetration of FDI into individual economic sectors: FDI components by sector of economic activity.

c) The penetration of FDI into individual economic sectors by country: FDI components by combination of main partner country or economic zone/region and sector of economic activity.

d) The return on FDI: investment income distribution from FDI by partner country or economic sector.

105. The OECD and EUROSTAT annually collect detailed FDI statistics from their member countries based on a common questionnaire. Statistics are compiled according to a standard framework and using the concepts and definitions recommended by the IMF and the OECD. Both institutions have well established databases and disseminate the FDI statistics regularly to the public at large.

106. According to this common framework, the OECD and EUROSTAT collect the following FDI components:

1) FDI income flows

a) FDI Income: in reporting economy.

- *i)* Income on equity.
  1. Dividends and distributed branch profits.
  2. Reinvested earnings and undistributed branch profits.
- *ii)* Income on debt (interest).

b) FDI Income: abroad.

- *i)* Income on equity.
  1. Dividends and distributed branch profits.
  2. Reinvested earnings and undistributed branch profits.
- *ii)* Income on debt (interest).

2) FDI financial flows

a) Direct investment in the reporting economy:

- *i)* Equity capital (claims, liabilities).
- *ii)* Reinvested earnings (net).
- *iii)* Other capital (claims, liabilities).

b) Direct investment abroad:

i) Equity capital (claims, liabilities).

ii) Reinvested earnings (net).

iii) Other capital (claims, liabilities).

3) FDI positions

a) Direct investment in the reporting economy:

i) Equity capital and reinvested earnings (claims, liabilities).

ii) Other capital (claims, liabilities).

b) Direct investment abroad.

i) Equity capital and reinvested earnings (claims, liabilities).

ii) Other capital (claims, liabilities).

Note: Each component of FDI flows and positions is further broken down separately by:

a) Country or economic zone.

b) Economic sector.

c) Country or economic zone and economic sector (this breakdown is not yet fully developed for many countries).

107. The geographical and industry classifications of FDI statistics are available for most OECD member countries according to the full set of breakdowns listed above:

- Geographical classification for OECD countries: by partner country and regions covering all countries of the world.
- Industry classification for OECD countries according to ISIC revision 3 (and NACE) which is standard classification established by the United Nations (see Annex 2.4 for the classification used by the OECD/EUROSTAT FDI data collection questionnaire).

2.3.3. FDI data sources and collection methods

108. Data sources used for compiling FDI statistics have a direct impact for determining the ability of compilers to implement the standard methodology. Data sources are generally:

a) Enterprise surveys.

b) International transactions reporting systems (ITRS).

c) Exchange control authorities.

d) Investment approval authorities.

e) Debt registers.

f) Bilateral sources.

g) Press reports.

h) Other published and administrative sources.

109. In general, OECD countries rely on either an ITRS or an enterprise survey for FDI transactions. However, OECD countries are increasingly using enterprise surveys to supplement the information from an ITRS, given that reinvested earnings cannot be calculated when the ITRS is the only source of information. As to FDI position statistics, most OECD countries use enterprise surveys and only a very few countries rely on ITRS.

Box 2.5. International transactions reporting system (ITRS)

An **ITRS** measures individual balance of payments cash transactions passing through the domestic banks and may also measure individual transactions passing through the foreign bank accounts of enterprises and non-cash transactions and positions (for "closed ITRS" to reconcile positions and flows). Statistics are compiled from forms submitted by domestic banks to the compilers and may also be compiled from forms submitted by enterprises to the compilers.

110. When an ITRS is used as data source, FDI positions are compiled using the "perpetual inventory method" which consists of deriving stocks from transactions data. Accordingly, the value of a stock at the end of the period will be considered to be equal to the value of the stock at the beginning of the period, plus the impact of transactions and other changes in the value of the stock during the period.

111. FDI statistics can be compiled from total aggregate amounts or from individual transactions reported by respondents to national compilers. Data reporting by respondents is in many countries compulsory whereby there is a legally binding obligation for respondents to report the requested statistical information to national authorities. On the other hand, reporting requirements on a voluntary basis may have some impact on the degree of reliability and the completeness of the statistics.

2.4. Scope and coverage: A common framework to record cross-border investments

2.4.1. Balance of payments and international investment position

112. *Balance of payments* (BOP) provides a comprehensive conceptual framework for an internationally harmonised presentation and analysis of cross-border transactions. They represent the only commonly agreed methodology for undertaking a meaningful and consistent aggregation of economic transactions in order to analyse effectively the financial flows between economies.

113. Closely linked to BOP statistics is the *international investment position (IIP)* statement, which is conceptually similar to a balance sheet. IIP records the stock of external financial assets and liabilities of an economy at a particular point in time (such as at the end of a quarter or the end of a calendar year).

2.4.2. Financial account

114. Financial flows are recorded under the financial accounts[7] of the balance of payments which is a sub-category of the ***capital and financial account***. The ***financial account*** analyses the financing of a country's balance of payments transactions which are classified according to five functional categories:

- Direct investment (see Section 2.5 of the present chapter on concepts and methods).
- Portfolio investment is subdivided into *equity securities* and *debt securities*.
  - *Equity securities* "cover all instruments and records acknowledging, after the claims of all creditors have been met, claims to the residual values of incorporated enterprises" (IMF *BPM5* §388).[8]

Box 2.6. Balance of payments statistics and international investment position

The Balance of Payments Manual, 5th *edition (BPM5)* issued by the International Monetary Fund (IMF) provides a guide on international standards for compiling the balance of payments and the international investment position statistics of an economy.

The balance of payments is a statistical statement that systematically summarises, for a specific time period, the economic transactions of an economy with the rest of the world. Transactions, for the most part between residents and non-residents, consist of those involving goods and services and income; those involving financial claims on, and liabilities to, the rest of the world; and those (such as gifts) classified as transfers, which involve offsetting entries to balance – in an accounting sense – one-sided transactions. A transaction itself is defined as an economic flow that reflects the creation, transformation, exchange, transfer or extinction of economic value and involves changes in ownership of goods and/or financial assets, the provision of services, or the provision of labour and capital (§13 BPM5).

International investment position. Compiled at a specific date such as year end, this investment position is a statistical statement of: i) the value and the composition of the stock of an economy's financial assets, or the economy's claims on the rest of the world, and ii) the value and the composition of the stock of an economy's liabilities to the rest of the world (§14 BPM5).[*]

Conceptually, balance of payments accounts and related data on the international investment position are closely linked to a broader system of national accounts, which provides a comprehensive and systematic framework for the collection and presentation of the economic statistics of an economy. The international standard for such a framework is the System of National Accounts (SNA), which encompasses transactions, other flows, stocks and other changes affecting the level of assets and liabilities from one accounting period to another (BPM5 §34).

* See also IMF Balance of Payments Textbook, Chapter 13.

Source: (See IMF Balance of Payments Manual, 5th edition, and companion manuals.)

- *Debt securities* "cover *i)* bonds, debentures, notes, etc; *ii)* money market or negotiable debt instruments" (IMF *BPM5* §389).[9]

- Financial derivatives: "A *financial derivative contract* is a financial instrument that is linked to another specific financial instrument or indicator or commodity and through which financial risks (such as interest rate risk, foreign exchange risk, equity and commodity price risks, credit risk, etc.) can, in their own right, be traded in financial markets.

  Transactions in financial derivatives are treated as separate transactions rather than as integral parts of the values of the underlying transactions to which they are linked. The value of financial derivatives derives from the price of an underlying item such as an asset or index. No principal amount that must be repaid is advanced and no investment income accrues. Financial derivatives are used for a number of purposes – risk management, hedging, arbitrage between markets, and speculation, for example." (FDI IMF *BOP Derivatives*).

- Other investment is a residual category that includes all financial transactions not included in direct investment, portfolio investment, or reserve assets (§411 IMF *BPM5*).[10]

- Reserve assets "consist of those external assets that are readily available to, and controlled by, monetary authorities for direct financing of payments imbalances, for indirectly regulating the magnitude of such imbalances through intervention in exchange markets to affect the currency exchange rate, and/or for other purposes" (§424 *IMF BPM5*).

115. The above definitions of equity securities, debt securities, financial derivatives and other investment are also consistent with the definitions used in the OECD *Code of Liberalisation of Capital Movements* (see Box 2.7).

116. In the balance of payments "the financial account is defined as comprising all transactions (actual and imputed) in the external financial assets and liabilities of an economy. (...) Three criteria must be met for a transaction to be included in the financial account. These criteria are:

- A transaction involves a change of ownership, including the creation or liquidation of an asset or liability (...).
- An asset or liability must represent actual claims that are legally in existence...
- A transaction involves an external financial asset or liability... The important determinants for classifying financial items (assets or liabilities) as external are the identities of the creditor and debtor. The creditor and debtor must be residents of two different economies..." (see §446 and §447 of IMF BOP *Textbook*).

117. The financial account is expressed in terms of net credit or net debit, designating net financial inflows and net financial outflows, respectively (see Box 2.8 for standard components of the financial account).

118. "The international investment position is the balance sheet of the stock of external financial assets and liabilities" (§461 IMF *BPM5*). The harmonisation of the presentation of IIP along the lines of the financial account provides to the user the ability to relate financial flows and positions. There are also factors other than the actual transactions, such as price changes, that affect the alterations in the stocks of investment. Such non-transaction adjustments are included in the IIP, as the position data measure the value of the assets and liabilities at a specific point in time, but not just transactions during a period of time.

119. The financial account is also closely related to the sub-component *income* of the current account. In the balance of payments "income covers two types of transactions between residents and non-residents *i)* those involving compensation of employees, which is paid to non-resident workers, and *ii)* those involving investment income receipts and payments on external financial assets and liabilities. Included in the latter are receipts and

Box 2.7. **OECD Codes of Liberalisation***

OECD supports the liberalisation of trade in goods and services and capital movements between member countries. *OECD Codes of Liberalisation* are legal instruments which establish rules of conduct for the governments of OECD member countries. The OECD Codes have a binding legal status on all its members

There are two codes of liberalisation:

i) *Code of Liberalisation of Capital Movements* which also covers direct investment and establishment.

ii) *Code of Liberalisation of Current Invisible Operations.*

* See also *User's Guide to the OECD Codes* (OECD, 2003), also available at *www.oecd.org/daf/investment*, and *Forty Years of Experience with the OECD Code of Liberalisation of Capital Movements*, OECD, 2002.

Box 2.8. **Balance of payments: Current account, and capital and financial account**

Current account	Capital and financial account
A. Goods and Services	A. Capital account
1. Goods	1. Capital transfers
2. Services	2. Acquisition/disposal of non-produced non-financial assets
B. Income	B. Financial account
1. Compensation of employees	1. Direct investment
2. Investment income	2. Portfolio investment
2.1. Direct Investment	3. Financial derivatives
2.2. Portfolio investment	4. Other Investment
2.3. Other Investment	5. Reserve assets
C. Current transfers	
1. General government	
2. Other sectors	

Note: For this revised presentation of standard components listedabove,see Financial Derivatives: A Supplement to the Fifth Edition (1993) of the Balance of Payments Manual.

payments on direct investment, portfolio investment and other investments and receipts on reserve assets" (see §267 IMF *BPM5*).

120. To distinguish cross-border transactions from a purely domestic operation it is necessary to apply the same criteria across the countries to ensure comparability. In consequence, economic units involved in cross-border transactions are defined according to the residence criteria. The concept of residence does not necessarily correspond to the nationality of the transactor or to other legal boundaries, such as those established for political purposes (see Box 2.9 for definitions related to residence). The underlying concepts of residence used for the balance of payments are in line with the concepts used in the *System of National Accounts, 1993* (SNA93).

121. Within this general framework, there is also a need for a uniform basis for calculating aggregate cross-border transactions and the related stock of assets/liabilities. The recommended *method of valuation* for balance of payments and IIP is the use of *market values* (see also §534 of the IMF *Balance of Payments Textbook*). This methodology is fully consistent with SNA93. For FDI transactions it is recommended to use the market prices agreed upon by the transactors and for assets and liabilities the principle is the market values prevailing at the time the positions are recorded in FDI statistics.

122. These principles are not questioned in terms of their analytical value. However, at the same time, it is recognised that there are deviations in the application of this recommendation due to difficulties in identifying all the elements required to establish the corresponding market prices. In practice, book values from the balance sheet of the direct investment enterprises are generally utilised to determine the value of the stock of direct investment. As a guide to the practical implementation of the recommendation, the compiler would find it useful to refer to alternative approaches provided in various methodological documentations cited in the introduction to this chapter.

123. Closely related to the valuation concept is *the time of recording* the transactions. According to the balance of payments, which is a double entry system, for each transaction

Box 2.9. Definition of residence[1]

"**The concept of residence** is not based on nationality or legal criteria, although it may be similar to concepts of residence used for exchange control, tax and other purposes in many countries. The concept of residence is based on a sectoral transactor's centre of economic interest. (...) It is necessary to recognise the economic territory of a country as the relevant geographical area to which the concept of residence is applied. An institutional unit is a resident unit when it has a centre of economic interest in the economic territory of a country." (BPM5§58)

"**Economic territory** of a country consists of the geographic territory administered by a government; within this territory, persons, goods and capital circulate freely." (BPM5§59)

"An institutional unit has a **centre of economic interest** within a country when there exists some location – dwelling, place of production, or other premises – within the economic territory of the country on or from which the unit engages and intends to continue engaging, either indefinitely or over a finite but long period of time, in economic activities and transactions on a significant scale. The location need not be fixed so long as it remains within the economic territory." (BPM5§62)

1. For a detailed discussion of the concept of residence, see also *Balance of Payments Textbook*, IMF, 1996, Chapter 2.

Note: (See IMF Balance of Payments Manual, 5th edition).

two entries must be recorded on the same date. Determining the date of recording must follow the international standards. Hence, the registration is made when the underlying transaction occurs, as recommended by BPM5 and SNA93. For the income component, the concept of accrual accounting applies whereby the underlying transactions are recorded when they accrue.[11] For financial assets/liabilities the date of the booking or the date of payment should be used.

2.5. Concepts and methods

2.5.1. FDI statistics according to international standards: Concepts and methods

2.5.1.1. Definition of FDI

124. Comprehensive methodological and practical recommendations are available to guide national compilers who have the responsibility for assembling the FDI statistics of their respective countries. National data collection and dissemination authorities have the responsibility for transmitting these guidelines to their respondents who are the providers of the underlying information necessary for compiling the statistics. The authorities also have a responsibility for regularly disseminating the data series and informing the users and the public at large.

125. International standards and guidelines for compiling FDI statistics are set out in the IMF *BPM5* (and companion manuals) and the OECD *Benchmark Definition*. Therefore the present text will relate only to selected features. The reader is referred to the reference documents[12] for complete coverage of the statistical treatment of FDI.

i) Direct investment and major players

126. Although FDI represents a large share of cross-border investments, not all foreign investments are in the form of direct investment. Therefore, it is necessary, first of all, to identify the type of transaction and the characteristics of the entities involved. The underlying motivation of the investor provides the initial criteria to distinguish between direct investment and other types of cross-border investments, in particular as compared

Box 2.10. OECD *Benchmark Definition of Foreign Direct Investment*, 3rd edition (the *Benchmark Definition*)

The OECD ***Benchmark Definition*** covers the main statistical concepts and definitions of FDI including valuation of FDI flows and stocks and a broad range of related issues. It is consistent with the concepts in the IMF BPM5. The *Benchmark Definition* provides operational guidance to statisticians and proposes practical solutions based on concrete examples, wherever possible.

By setting a standard for FDI statistics, the *Benchmark Definition* serves three objectives:

a) It provides a clear orientation for individual countries as they develop or change their statistical system for recording FDI.

b) It improves the basis for economic analysis of FDI, especially in international comparisons, to the extent that progress is made in reducing national deviations from the standard.

c) It offers an objective standard for measuring remaining methodological differences between national FDI data that need to be taken into account for cross-country analysis of FDI.

The OECD *BenchmarkDefinition* was first published in 1983 as an OECD Council Recommendation. The latest revision, the third edition, was approved by the OECD Council in 1995.

to portfolio investment. FDI relationship may be a simple straightforward structure but it may also represent very complex combinations which exhibit more and more complex FDI structures.

127. "*Foreign direct investment* reflects the objective of obtaining a lasting interest by a resident entity in one economy (direct investor) in an entity resident in an economy other than that of the investor (direct investment enterprise). The lasting interest implies the existence of a long-term relationship between the direct investor and the enterprise and a significant degree of influence on the management of the enterprise" (§5, OECD *Benchmark Definition*). The numerical guideline of ownership of 10% of ordinary shares or voting stock of the enterprise by the direct investor determines the existence of a direct investment relationship. If the percentage share of equity investment is less than 10%, the transaction will be classified as *portfolio investment* where the motivation of the investor, not seeking a continued relation with the enterprise, is different: "... portfolio investors are primarily concerned about the safety of their capital, the likelihood of appreciation in value, and the return generated" (§361, IMF BPM5) (See also Sub-section 3.1.2 iv) *Reclassification of portfolio investments as FDI*). Direct investment involves both the initial transactions between the two entities and all subsequent capital transactions between them and among affiliated enterprises, both incorporated and unincorporated.

128. A *foreign direct investor* is an entity that has a direct investment enterprise operating in a country other than the economy of residence of the foreign direct investor. A direct investor could be either one of the following:

a) Individuals.

b) A group of related individuals.

c) Incorporated or unincorporated enterprises.

d) Public or private enterprises.

e) A group of related enterprises.

OECD HANDBOOK ON ECONOMIC GLOBALISATION INDICATORS – ISBN 92-64-10808-4 – © OECD 2005

f) A government or government agencies.

g) Estates, trusts and other organisations that own a direct investment enterprise.

(See §367 IMF *BPM5* and §6 OECD *Benchmark Definition*.)

129. A *direct investment enterprise* is an incorporated (subsidiary or an associate) or an unincorporated enterprise (branch) in which a foreign investor owns 10% or more of the ordinary shares or voting power of an incorporated enterprise or the equivalent of an unincorporated enterprise. Once a direct investment link is established according to the 10% ownership, other enterprises that are related to the first enterprise are also considered as direct investment enterprises. Accordingly, "inward and outward direct investment statistics should, as a matter of principle, cover all directly and indirectly owned subsidiaries, associates, and branches" (§14 OECD *Benchmark Definition*). These statistics are referred to as based on the fully consolidated system (FCS) as defined by the OECD *Benchmark Definition* (see also Sub-section 3.1.1., *ii) Direct investment relationship*). Applying a numerical standard across the countries facilitates international comparability.

130. The ownership of at least 10% implies that the direct investor has a voice in the management and is able to influence or participate in the management of an enterprise. An effective voice in the management does not require control by the foreign investor which is a different concept, relating for the purpose of statistics described in Chapter 3, to the ownership of more than 50% of the equity of the enterprise. Therefore, direct investment enterprises controlled by the direct investor represent in principle a sub-category of the population of overall direct investment enterprises. The economic activities of such enterprises are discussed in Chapter 3 (Box 3.6).

131. It is argued by some compilers that in practice there are cases whereby the ownership of 10% of the ordinary shares or voting power may not lead to the exercise of any significant influence while, on the other hand, a direct investor may own less than 10% but have an effective voice in the management. These considerations are usually based on one or more factors such as:

a) Representation on the board of directors.

b) Participation in policy-making processes.

c) Material inter-company transactions.

d) Interchange of managerial personnel.

e) Provision of technical information.

f) Provision of long-term loans at lower than existing market rates.

(See §10 OECD *Benchmark Definition*.)

132. The *Benchmark Definition* as well as *BPM5* strictly recommend against this alternative approach. Nonetheless, some countries, including several OECD members, still consider it necessary to treat the 10% cut-off point flexibly and prefer to make adjustments under certain circumstances. Consequently, they deviate from both IMF and OECD recommendations.

133. There may be relationships between enterprises in different economies which exhibit the characteristics of FDI even if there is no formal link with regard to shareholding. For example, two enterprises, each operating in different economies, may have a common board and common policy making and may share resources including funds but with neither having a shareholding in the other of 10% or more. These enterprises do not have a direct investment relationship (see Annex 2.1 for some examples of borderline cases).

Box 2.11. **Foreign direct investment: definitions and criteria**

Foreign direct investment "reflects the objective of obtaining a lasting interest by a resident entity in one economy ('direct investor') in an entity resident in an economy other than that of the investor ('direct investment enterprise'). The lasting interest implies the existence of a long-term relationship between the direct investor and the enterprise and a significant degree of influence on the management of the enterprise. Direct investment involves both the initial transaction between the two entities and all subsequent capital transactions between them and among affiliated enterprises, both incorporated and unincorporated" (§5 OECD *Benchmark Definition*).

A ***foreign direct investor*** "is an individual, an incorporated or unincorporated public or private enterprise, a government, a group of related individuals, or a group of related incorporated and/or unincorporated enterprises which has a direct investment enterprise – that is, a subsidiary, associate or branch – operating in a country other than the country or countries of residence of the foreign direct investor or investors" (§6 OECD *Benchmark Definition*).

A ***foreign direct investment enterprise*** is "defined as an incorporated or unincorporated enterprise in which a foreign investor owns 10% or more of the ordinary shares or voting power of an incorporated enterprise or the equivalent of an unincorporated enterprise.

The numerical guideline of ownership of 10% of ordinary shares or voting stock determines the existence of a direct investment relationship. An effective voice in the management, as evidenced by an ownership of at least 10%, implies that the direct investor is able to influence or participate in the management of an enterprise; it does not require absolute control by the foreign investor" (§7 and §8 OECD *Benchmark Definition*).

International standards recommend against the use of other or additional thresholds and/or other qualifications. *Direct investment enterprises* are entities that are either directly and indirectly owned by the direct investor: In other words, a direct investment enterprise may be:

a) A *subsidiary:* an enterprise of which more than 50% is owned by a non-resident investor;

b) an *associate:* an enterprise of which 10 to 50% is owned by a non-resident investors; and

c) a *branch*: an unincorporated enterprise wholly or jointly owned by a non-resident investor.

Note: (See *IMF Balance of Payments Manual*, 5th edition, and *OECD Benchmark Definition of Foreign Direct Investment*, 3rd edition.)

134. To achieve international harmonisation, it is recommended that countries which deviate from the standard treatment should provide additional statistics on the amounts corresponding to the 10% criterion.

ii) Direct investment relationship

135. Direct investment enterprises may have *subsidiaries* (an incorporated enterprise in which a non-resident owns more than 50%), *associates* (an incorporated enterprise in which a non-resident owns between 10% and 50%) and *branches* (an unincorporated enterprise wholly or jointly owned by a non-resident investor) in one country or in several countries. The OECD *Benchmark Definition* defines these enterprises as follows:

1. *Subsidiary companies*

   a) Company X is a subsidiary of enterprise N if, and only if

   enterprise N either

i) is a shareholder in or member of X and has the right to appoint or remove a majority of the members of X's administrative, management or supervisory body; or

ii) owns more than half of the shareholders' or members' voting power in X; or

b) company X is a subsidiary of any other company Y which is a subsidiary of N.

2. *Associate companies*

Company R is an associate of enterprise N if N, its subsidiaries and its other associated enterprises own not more than 50% of the shareholders' or members' voting power in R and if N and its subsidiaries have a direct investment interest in R. Thus company R is an associate of N if N and its subsidiaries own between 10 and 50% of the shareholders' voting power in R.

3. *Branches*

A direct investment branch is an unincorporated enterprise in the host country that:

i) is a permanent establishment or office of a foreign direct investor; or

ii) is an unincorporated partnership or joint venture between a foreign direct investor and third parties; or

iii) includes land, structures (except those structures owned by foreign government entities), and immovable equipment and objects, in the host country, that are directly owned by a foreign resident. Holiday and second homes owned by non-residents are therefore regarded as part of direct investment, though few, if any, countries actually include such investment in their direct investment statistics; or

iv) includes mobile equipment (such as ships, aircraft, gas and oil drilling rigs) that operates within an economy for at least one year if accounted for separately by the operator and is so recognised by the tax authorities. This is considered to be direct investment in a notional enterprise in the host country.

(§14 OECD *Benchmark Definition*.)

136. According to international standards, inward and outward direct investment statistics should cover all directly and indirectly owned incorporated and unincorporated enterprises that meet the specific criteria, *i.e.* all subsidiaries, associate companies and branches. The application of the full coverage of the direct investment relationships referred to as FCS in the paragraphs above is illustrated in Figure 2.1 Application of the Fully Consolidated System.

137. According to the Fully Consolidated System the statistical treatment of the example in Figure 2.1 is as follows:

- Company A is a subsidiary of N. Company B is a subsidiary of A and thus a subsidiary of N even though only 33% of B is indirectly attributable to N.
- Company C is an associate of B and, through the chain of subsidiaries A and B, of N as well, even though only 4%of C is indirectly attributable to N.
- Company D is an associate of N, Company E is a subsidiary of D and thus an associate of N even though only 6% of E is indirectly attributable to N.
- Company F is an associate of N and G is an associate of F, but G is not an associate of N.
- Company H is a subsidiary of N and Company J is an associate of H and thus an associate of N.

Figure 2.1. **Application of the Fully Consolidated System**

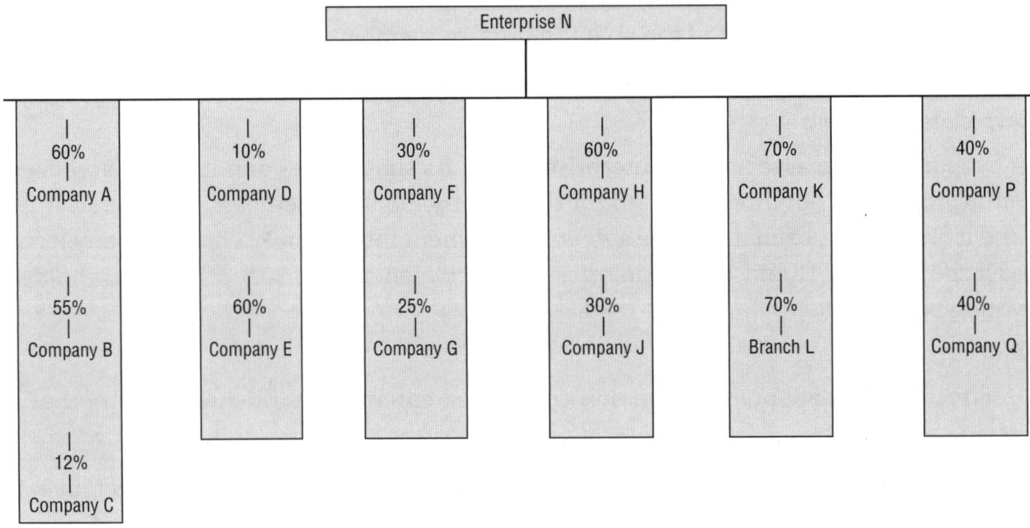

- Company K is a subsidiary of N and L is a branch of K and thus of N.
- Company P is an associate of N and Q is an associate of P, but Q is not an associate of N.

In conclusion, FDI statistics based on the Fully Consolidated System would cover enterprises A, B, C, D, E, F, H, J, K, L and P but will exclude G and Q.

(See §12 to §19 OECD *Benchmark Definition.*)

Box 2.12. **Direct investment relationship**

International standards recommend the use of the Fully Consolidated System to identify an indirectly owned direct investment relationship.* Recognising the practical difficulties compilers may experience in the application of this method, some countries have chosen alternate methods, slightly different from the one recommended by the methodology, which, as a result, restricts the coverage of the FDI relationships. This alternate method which is most frequently used is referred as the "US Method – USM" of which the differences from the FCS can be described as follows:

The USM and the FCS system differ in two ways in defining which indirectly-held companies are direct investment enterprises:

i) The USM excludes, and the FCS may include, foreign enterprises in which the direct investor has less than a 10% equity interest, and

ii) the USM includes, and the FCS excludes, associates (minority-owned affiliates) of associates in which direct investor has 10% or more equity interest.

According to the presentation in Figure 2.1, USM will:

a) Exclude companies C and E,

b) include Q.

* While the IMF BPM5 and the companion manuals do not specifically refer to the FCS by name, the documents are deemed to be consistent with the OECD *Benchmark Definition.*

Note: (See *IMF Balance of Payments Manual*, 5th edition, and Annex I of *OECD Benchmark Definition of Foreign Direct Investment*, 3rd edition.)

138. Regarding inter-company transactions between affiliated banks and affiliated financial intermediaries, only those transactions associated with permanent debt and equity capital should be recorded as FDI. Deposits and other claims and liabilities related to the usual banking activities of depository institutions and claims and liabilities related to usual financial intermediation activities of other financial intermediaries should be excluded from the FDI statistics. Transactions between direct investment enterprises that are not financial intermediaries and affiliated financial intermediaries (including SPEs) should be included in the direct investment data.

iii) Special cases

139. The so-called special cases in FDI statistics are:

a) Special purpose entities.

b) Off-shore enterprises.

c) Quasi-corporations.

d) Land and buildings.

e) Natural resources exploration.

140. *Special purpose entities.*[13] "As multinational enterprises mature, they diversify their investments geographically, through adequate organisational structures. These include certain special purpose entities (SPEs) which facilitate financing of investments for the group from sources both internal and external to the multinational enterprises. Additionally, such SPEs also serve other functions such as sale and regional administration including management of foreign exchange risks and other activities aimed at profit maximisation. 'Special purpose entity' is a generic label applicable to such organisational structures which are also variously referred to as financing subsidiaries, conduits, holding companies, base companies and regional headquarters. In some instances, multinational enterprises use existing operational companies to perform functions usually associated with SPEs. Since these SPEs are an integral part of the organisational structure of a multinational enterprise, their transactions that arise from direct investment relationships [except as noted in paragraphs 39 and 40 c of the *Benchmark Definition*)] should be reflected in the statistics and, if possible, shown as a sub-component" (§70 OECD *Benchmark Definition*). If the SPEs meet the 10% ownership criteria, all transactions should be included. If the SPE serves as a financial intermediary, transactions with affiliated banks and financial intermediaries should be excluded with the exception of transactions in equity capital and permanent debt.

141. Recourse to holding companies for FDI transactions has grown substantially over recent years. A significant number of transactions are effectively transferred through holding companies which are entities having the main function of holding assets. According to international standards, transactions of holding companies which meet the criteria, with the exception of the cases described above, are included in FDI statistics. However, the economic value of FDI including such transactions may be questioned from a purely analytical view point, on the grounds that many of the holding companies do not have an economic activity (in the economy of residence) or employees or turnover but are used as purely investment vehicles.

142. *Off-shore enterprises.* The residency of off-shore enterprises is attributed to the economies in which the enterprises are located, disregarding the special treatment they

Box 2.13. **Transactions between affiliated financial intermediaries**

Financial transactions *between affiliated financial intermediaries* should be excluded from FDI except for transactions in the form of equity capital or permanent debt. This recommendation also applies to investment income.

Financial intermediaries are defined in the *SNA 93* and *BPM5* as:

a) Other depository institutions (banks, other than the central bank);

b) other financial intermediaries, except insurance companies and pension funds; and

c) financial auxiliaries.

Special purpose entities (SPEs) principally engaged in financial intermediation for a group of related enterprises are included in this definition. Transactions of such SPEs with enterprises belonging to the above defined categories of financial intermediaries should be excluded from FDI *except* for transactions in the form of equity capital or permanent debt. In contrast, financial transactions between units that are not financial intermediaries and affiliated financial SPEs abroad should be recorded under FDI.

Note: (See *Recommended Treatment of Selected Direct Investment Transactions*, IMF, 2002, and *OECD Benchmark Definition of Foreign Direct Investment*, 3rd edition.)

may receive from local authorities, such as exemptions from taxes, tariffs or duties. These enterprises may be engaged in:

a) Trade and financial operations.

b) The assembly of components manufactured elsewhere.

c) The processing of re-exported goods.

143. There are a number of companies incorporated in one country with their management office in another country which do not trade in their country of incorporation. The management office holds all the assets of the company and the only transaction with the country of incorporation is that the management office pays dividends on behalf of the company to any resident shareholder of the company in the country of incorporation. These companies may also have direct investment in third countries, the dividend and capital flows then being between the third countries and the country of the management office. The third country will probably assume in its statistics that these transactions are with the country of incorporation, while the management office's country will probably show the transactions as being between it and the third countries. An added complication is that the company owning the management office may itself be a subsidiary of an enterprise in another country" (§68 OECD *Benchmark Definition*). Transactions between off-shore enterprises and their direct investors should be included in FDI statistics (see also §79 and §381 *IMF BPM5*).

144. *Quasi-corporations* are enterprises that produce goods and services in an economy other than their own, but do not establish separate legal corporations in the host country. They are mostly involved in construction or the operation of mobile equipment and are considered as a part of the direct investment relationship if:

a) Production is maintained for one year or more.

b) A separate set of accounts is maintained for the local activities.

c) Income tax is paid in the host country.

145. *Land and buildings* which are located within the boundaries of an economy are considered as being owned by residents with the exception of those owned by foreign governments (*e.g.* embassies). If the proprietor is a non-resident, it is considered that the ownership is transferred to a resident *notional enterprise*. The non-resident entity has a financial investment in this notional unit which is, in this case, a direct investment enterprise (see also §51 *IMF BPM5*).

146. *Exploration of natural resources* may involve the establishment of a direct investment enterprise:[14]

a) Inward direct investment flows provided by a non-resident direct investor to the direct investment enterprise should be recorded as FDI equity capital.

b) There may be cases of a bonus payment to a government by direct investors for the right to undertake a direct investment in the host economy, typically for concession rights related to the extraction of natural resources. Such bonus payments should be treated as direct investment, equity capital, when there is a clear intention to establish a direct investment enterprise (such as in the case of a contractual agreement between the investor and the government).

c) No transactions should be recorded in the balance of payments statistic for the shutdown of an FDI enterprise established for natural resources exploration. The reduction in direct investment assets will be shown in the international investment position/*other adjustments*.

2.5.1.2. Methodology for recording FDI

i) Direct investment capital

Basic principle

147. FDI capital transactions are recorded on a directional basis: *i)* resident direct investment abroad; and *ii)* non-resident direct investment in the reporting economy while other types of cross-border investments are recorded on a asset/liability basis.[15] FDI is composed of three types of direct financing: *equity capital, reinvested earnings* and *other capital.*

Standard components

148. *Equity capital* "covers equity in branches, all shares (whether voting or non-voting) in subsidiaries and associates, and other capital contributions in kind (for example, the provision of machinery – which constitutes a part of the capital of the direct investment enterprise – by a direct investor to a direct investment enterprise). Equity capital also covers the acquisition by a direct investment enterprise of shares in its direct investor" (§520 IMF *BOP Textbook*). However, non-participating preference shares are not part of equity capital but are treated as debt securities and classified as "other direct investment capital".

149. *Reinvested earnings* are considered to be additional capital of the direct investment enterprises. "Reinvested earnings are the direct investors' shares (in proportion to equity held) of the undistributed earnings of the direct investment enterprises. They are recorded as income with an offsetting capital transaction" (§520 IMF *BOP Textbook*).

150. *Other capital* (or inter-company debt transactions) "covers the borrowing and lending of funds, including debt securities and trade credits, between direct investors and direct investment enterprises and between two direct investment enterprises that share the

same direct investor. Debt claims on the direct investor by the direct investment enterprise are also included as direct investment capital" (§521 IMF *BOP Textbook*).

Recording principles (directional principle)

151. As stated above, direct investment is recorded on a directional principle as opposed to straight asset/liability basis used for other posts of the financial account. Two directions of FDI are considered whatever the type of underlying transaction or the type of assets or liabilities: resident direct investment abroad and non-resident direct investment in the reporting economy (see also §369 of IMF *BPM5*).

Box 2.14. **Recording FDI transactions**

FDI is recorded on a directional basis as resident direct investment abroad and non-resident direct investment in the reporting economy. If a direct investment enterprise makes capital investments in its direct investor, this is considered as reverse investment (disinvestment) and should be recorded according to the directional principle.

Direct investment abroad	***Direct investment in reporting economy***
Equity capital	Equity capital
Claims on affiliated enterprises	Claims on direct investor
Liabilities to affiliated enterprises	Liabilities to direct investor
Reinvested earnings	Reinvested earnings
Other capital	Other capital
Claims on affiliated enterprises	Claims on direct investor
Liabilities to affiliated enterprises	Liabilities to direct investor

Note: (See IMF Balance of Payments Manual, 5th edition, the IMF Balance of Payments Textbook, and OECD Benchmark Definition of Foreign Direct Investment, 3rd edition.)

152. A direct investment enterprise may acquire financial claims on its direct investor. Such transactions are referred to as *reverse investments*, which can be established as one or two independent FDI relationships.

a) When the equity participation is at least 10% in both directions, *two direct investment relationships* are established. In such cases, equity and other capital transactions between enterprises are recorded as direct investment claims and liabilities in both directions, as appropriate:

- Assets are recorded as *direct investment abroad* (outward investment, claims on affiliated enterprises).
- Liabilities are recorded as *direct investment in reporting economy* (inward investment, liabilities to direct investor).

b) When the equity participation (claims) is *not sufficient to establish a separate direct investment relationship on its own right*, the reverse investment (disinvestment) should be recorded according to the direction of the original direct investment relationship. Hence, reverse investment is considered as an offset to the capital invested in the direct investment enterprise by the direct investor and its related enterprises:

- For the statistics of the economy in which the direct investment enterprise is resident – as direct investment in reporting economy (inward investment), claims on direct investor.
- For the statistics of the economy in which the direct investor is resident – as *direct investment abroad* (outward investment), *liabilities to affiliated enterprises.*

ii) Direct investment income

153. The components of FDI income include *income on equity* – dividends and distributed branch profits and reinvested earnings – and *income on debt (interest)*.

- *Dividends* comprise all dividends that, in an accounting period, are declared payable to the direct investor, less dividends declared payable by the direct investor to the direct investment enterprise.
- *Distributed branch profits* are earnings that branches and other unincorporated enterprises remit to their direct investors.
- *Reinvested earnings* and undistributed branch profits comprise the direct investors' share – in proportion to equity held – of 1) earnings that foreign subsidiaries and associated enterprises do not distribute as dividends and 2) earnings that branches and other unincorporated enterprises do not remit to direct investors.
- *Income on debt* comprises the interest accrued during the accounting period by the enterprise to the direct investor, less the interest accrued during the same period and owed by that direct investor to that enterprise.

(See §276 to §279, §288, §321 *IMF BPM5.)*

Box 2.15. **Recording direct investment income**

Components	Time of recording
Direct investment income	
• Income on equity	
i) Dividends and distributed branch profits	*i)* As of the day they are declared payable
ii) Reinvested earnings and undistributed branch profits	*ii)* In the periods which the underlying profits are earned
Income on debt (interest)	*iii)* On an accrual basis

Recommended method for recording earnings: Current Operating Performance Concept (COPC)

Earnings should

Include: Provisions for depreciation of capital and Income and corporation taxes.

Exclude: Exchange *rate* gains and losses, realised and unrealised capital gains and losses, write-offs (*e.g.* inventory write-offs, write-off for intangibles, write-offs for bad debt, or expropriations without compensation).

Note: (See *IMF Balance of Payments Manual*, 5th edition, *IMF Balance of Payments Textbook* and *OECD Benchmark Definition of Foreign Direct Investment*, 3rd edition.)

154. Dividends should be recorded as of the date they are declared payable. The time of accrual for dividends depends on the date selected by the enterprise to distribute income. Reinvested earnings should be recorded during the periods in which the underlying profits are earned. Recording interest income on an accrual basis allows matching the cost of capital with the provision of capital.

155. International standards recommend the *Current Operating Performance Concept* (COPC) to measure earnings.[16] "Operational earnings of the direct investment enterprise should be reported after deducting provisions for depreciation and for income and corporation tax charged on these earnings. Depreciation should, in principle, be measured at current replacement cost, particularly if market values are available for stock figures. If the latter and depreciation data are available only on a book value or historical cost basis, those values should be used. Direct investment earnings should not include any realised or unrealised

capital gains or losses made by either the direct investment enterprise or the direct investor. However, for many countries data are available only on an all-inclusive basis. Therefore, so as to promote comparability of data across countries, those countries that report earnings on either an operating basis or all-inclusive basis should collect and publish supplementary information on capital gains and losses. This data will also allow reconciliation of movements in the net asset value of the stock of direct investment between the beginning and end of the period" (§32 OECD *Benchmark Definition*). On an *ad hoc* basis, one may also try to exclude the most significant components with an exceptional character from the profit and loss accounts from major enterprises in order to approximate the COPC value.

156. "The earnings of the direct investment enterprise which are reported using the 'current operating performance concept', should not include any realised or unrealised capital gains or losses made by the enterprise or include any gains or losses arising from valuation changes such as inventory write-offs; gains or losses on plant and equipment from the closure of part or all of a business; writing-off intangibles, including goodwill, because of unusual events or developments during the period; writing-off research and development expenditure; abnormal charges for bad debts; abnormal provisions for losses on long-term contracts; and exchange rate gains and losses incurred by the direct investment enterprise both from its trading activities and from its holdings of foreign currency assets and liabilities. Unrealised gains or losses from the revaluation of fixed assets, investments and liabilities, as well as any realised gains or losses made by the enterprise from the disposal of assets or liabilities should be excluded from direct investment earnings, *i.e.* gains should not be added in and losses should not be deducted. This exclusion of all classes of realised and unrealised gains and losses is applicable to all direct investment enterprises, including those such as banks and securities dealers for whom the making of such gains is an important or even the main part of their business" (§33 OECD *Benchmark Definition*).

157. "The direct investor also incurs gains and losses arising from the sale of the direct investment enterprises; revaluations of the market value of the enterprise due to unforeseen obsolescence, falls or rises in stock markets, etc., amounts written off for bad debts owed to the direct investor; expropriation of assets without compensation; war damage, etc. These should not be taken into account in direct investment earnings" (§34 OECD *Benchmark Definition*).[17]

iii) Valuation of assets

158. Direct investment assets and liabilities should be valued at the market prices prevailing as at the date of recording. Nevertheless, there are many departures from this principle. Amounts recorded in the balance sheets of direct investment enterprises (book values) are generally used to determine the value of the stock of direct investment. If these balance sheet values are recorded on the basis of market prices prevailing as at the balance sheet date, such values are in general in accordance with the market valuation principle. If balance sheet values are based on historical cost or on interim, but not current revaluations, such balance sheet values do not conform with the principle (see §467 IMF *BPM5*) (See also Chapter 5, Section 5.3.2.5: Transfer Pricing).

159. "Transactions between affiliated enterprises integrated under the same management cannot necessarily be taken as market transactions because of the lack of independence among the parties to the exchange. Whether or not the transactions portrayed in the books of the enterprises actually reflect market values can only be judged for each individual

enterprise. To the extent that a group of affiliated enterprises desires to allocate its gross earnings in a realistic fashion among its separate units, bookkeeping practices would have to reflect market related pricing for all purchases and sales by the units. In that situation the view might reasonably be taken that pricing adopted for bookkeeping purposes, often referred to as transfer pricing, is no different from, or equivalent to, market valuation. On the other hand, transfer pricing not based closely on market considerations could be expected to be common among affiliated enterprises conducting business across national boundaries because disparities between taxes and regulations imposed by different governments are a factor in management decisions on the optimum allocation of profits among units. In those circumstances, it cannot be presumed that the mode of valuation adopted will accurately reflect economic relationships (*e.g.* the ratio of income to capital). When the distortions are large, replacement of book values with market value equivalents is desirable in principle" (§97 IMF *BPM5*). "In view of practical difficulties involved in substituting imputed or notional market value for an actual transfer value, substitution should be the exception rather than the rule" (§102 IMF *BPM5*).[18]

Box 2.16. **Methods of valuation of assets/liabilities**

Valuation of assets/liabilities

The IMF *BPM5* and the OECD *Benchmark Definition* recommend the use of market prices for asset/liabilities prevailing at the time of the FDI position. Many countries deviate from this recommendation and book values were applied by two-thirds of OECD countries in 2001.* Furthermore, different results may be obtained depending on the type of book value applied which could be based on either one of the following methods:

a) Current market prices.

b) Fair market value.

c) An interim adjusted price.

d) Historical cost.

e) Replacement cost.

* For a detailed example on revaluation methods of the United States FDI positions, see "Valuation of the US net international investment position" by J.S. Landefeld and A.M. Lawson, *Survey of Current Business*, May 1991.

Note: (See IMF *Balance of Payments Manual*, 5th edition, and OECD *Benchmark Definition of Foreign Direct Investment*, 3rd edition.)

iv) Reclassification of portfolio investments as FDI

160. Non-resident equity holdings representing less than 10% of the shares or voting stock of an enterprise are classified as portfolio investments. A non-resident investor may acquire additional shares of a company in which the investor already has an equity stake of less than 10%. If the equity holdings of the investor are more than 10% consequent to the additional acquisition, there is a need to adjust the IIP statistics accordingly. The balance of payments statistics should only take into account the purchase of the additional shares during the recording period. However, in the IIP data, the holdings acquired previously will be reclassified from portfolio investment into FDI (see also Annex 2.3 for standard components of balance of payments and international investment position).

v) Geographic classification of FDI

161. The method used for determining the geographical classification of inward and outward FDI will play an important role, particularly in the bilateral comparison of the data. There are two methods whereby compilers may apply for the geographical allocation of FDI transactions to and from their economies:

- The *debtor/creditor principle* allocates FDI transactions to the country of the direct investment enterprise or direct investor, even if the amounts are paid to or received from another country.
- The *transactor principle* allocates FDI transactions to the country to which the funds are paid or the country from which the funds are received, even if this is not the country of the direct investment enterprise or of the direct investor.

(See also §482 of IMF *BPM5*.)

162. "Any country analysis is complicated by holding companies where the ultimate parent enterprise's[19] investment in Country C is held through another subsidiary in Country B. Further, long chains of subsequent direct investment enterprises could be analysed in different ways in function of the level considered as the direct investor. Therefore information is often required on two bases:

a) By ultimate host country/ultimate investing country.

b) By immediate host country/immediate investing country.

163. "The immediate host/investing country system looks, for outward FDI, only to the country of the directly owned subsidiaries, associates and branches. For inward FDI, it is the country directly owning the domestic enterprises that is of interest. In this approach, the consolidated earnings and consolidated net assets cover the directly owned enterprise and all its subsidiaries and associates in its country and any other country, all of them being allocated for outward FDI to the country of the directly owned enterprise, and in the case of inward FDI to the country directly owning the enterprise" (§41 OECD *Benchmark Definition*).

164. "For outward direct investment although it may be possible in some instances to compile earnings and the stock of net assets on either basis, it is often very difficult to obtain data on outward direct investment flows by the ultimate host country; funds received by the ultimate host country may bear no relationship to the outward direct investment flows by the ultimate parent company" (§42 OECD *Benchmark Definition*).

165. "For inward direct investment it is possible to estimate earnings and the stock of net assets due to the immediate investing country and to reanalyse this by country of ultimate control. The share of the earnings and net assets attributable to the ultimate parent company will not normally be known. This is because the host country does not know the percentage shareholdings in the various intermediary companies between it and the ultimate parent" (§43 OECD *Benchmark Definition*).

166. Following the international standards:

- "Total direct investment flows be compiled only in respect of the immediate host or investing country.[20] Any figures in respect of the ultimate host or controlling country would be artificial.[21] Changes in the stock of outward direct investment will, however, give some indication of investment flows to the ultimate host countries" (§46 OECD *Benchmark Definition*).

 OECD HANDBOOK ON ECONOMIC GLOBALISATION INDICATORS – ISBN 92-64-10808-4 – © OECD 2005

- "The stock of direct investment net assets be compiled in respect of the immediate host or investing country and in respect of the ultimate host or controlling country" (§45 OECD *Benchmark Definition*).
- "Inward and outward direct investment earnings be compiled in respect of the immediate host or investing country. Ideally, outward FDI earnings should also be recorded with respect to the ultimate host country. This would enable investing countries to see where their overseas earnings originate. However, in practice, recording earnings on the basis of the ultimate host country would appear more appropriate in the case of operating data of affiliates, for those countries that collect such data" (§47 OECD *Benchmark Definition*).

(See also Chapter 3 of this *Handbook*.)

Box 2.17. **Geographic classification**

Basic principles:

1. The debtor/creditor principle allocates transactions resulting from changes in the financial claims of the compiling economy to the country or residence of the non-resident debtor; and transactions resulting in changes in the financial liabilities of the compiling economy to the country of residence of the non-resident creditor, even if the amounts are paid to or received from a different country.
2. The transactor principle allocates transactions resulting from changes in the financial claims and liabilities of the compiling economy to the country of residence of the non-resident party to the transaction (the transactor), even if this is not the country of residence of the direct investment enterprise or direct investor.

International manuals do not specifically recommend the basis to be used for the geographic allocation of FDI transactions data. The BPM5 allows for transactions to be allocated using either the debtor/creditor principle or the transactor principle. However, it recommends that position data be allocated using the debtor/creditor principle.

Country identification

1. "Total direct investment flows be compiled only in respect of the immediate host or investing country" (§46 OECD *Benchmark Definition*).
2. "The stock of direct investment net assets be compiled in respect of the immediate host or investing country and in respect of the ultimate host or controlling country" (§45 OECD *Benchmark Definition*).
3. "Inward and outward direct investment earnings be compiled in respect of the immediate host or investing country" (§47 OECD *Benchmark Definition*).

Note: (See *IMF Balance of Payments Manual*, 5th edition, and *OECD Benchmark Definition of Foreign Direct Investment*, 3rd edition.)

vi) Industry classification of FDI

167. Classifying cross-border financial transactions by economic activity is not a part of the general recommendations for balance of payments statistics. On the other hand, this is a recommendation of the *OECD Benchmark Definition* for FDI statistics as there is a wide interest in such analytical information provided both for direct investment enterprises and the direct investor.[22]

168. Industrial sector breakdowns are usually compiled on an aggregate basis primarily for reasons of confidentiality. In addition, classification of enterprises may at times be difficult keeping in mind that the large majority of FDI enterprises are incorporated enterprises involved in a range of activities as opposed to one establishment with one specific economic activity. An investor may conduct all its cross-border investments through a single subsidiary established for this purpose or it may invest through its domestic subsidiaries each specialised in a different sector of activity (see also Chapter 3 for a discussion on statistical units, Section 3.3.7). The results of classification in either one of these structures will be different in the absence of additional guidelines. "OECD recommends that the economic activity should be the main activity of the direct investor and all its subsidiaries and related companies in its country of residence. This avoids distortions due to different organisational arrangements" (§50 *OECD Benchmark Definition*).

Box 2.18. **Industry classification**[1]

a) OECD recommends that, where feasible, the direct investment enterprise be analysed both by its industrial activity in the host country and by the industrial activity of its direct investor. This recommendation applies both to inward and outward investments. Furthermore, OECD recommends that the economic activity should be the main activity of the direct investor and all its subsidiaries and related companies in its country of residence.

b) The industrial classification should be based at least on main categories identified by the *United Nations International Standard Industrial Classification of All Economic Activity*. for disseminating FDI statistics are: 1) Agriculture and fishing, 2) Mining and quarrying 3) Manufacturing, 4) Electricity, gas and water, 5) Construction, 6) Trade and repairs, 7) Hotels and restaurants, 8) Transport and communications, 9) Financial intermediation, 10) Real estate and business activities, and 11) Other services.

(§50 OECD *Benchmark Definition*.)

1. See also Annex 2.4 of this chapter and tables 3.1 and 3.2 of Chapter 3.

Note: (See *IMF Balance of Payments Manual*, 5th edition, and OECD *Benchmark Definition* of Foreign Direct Investment, 3rd edition.)

169. Another issue which may create discrepancies is the type of reference used for identifying the economic activity of the enterprise, *i.e.* the economic activity of the enterprise in the host country or that of the direct investor in the home country. Depending on the method, the industrial classification will be different. OECD recommends that, where feasible, statistics be compiled on both bases to allow for bilateral comparison.

2.5.2. Future methodological work

170. Currently there are no comprehensive and comparable data compilations according to type of direct investment which can be of three types:

a) Cross-border mergers and acquisitions (M&A).

b) Greenfield investments (creation of a firm from scratch).

c) Changes in output capacity (*i.e.* the extension or increase of the existing capacity of an enterprise).

171. These additional breakdowns are not required by the balance of payments statistics. Likewise, they are not included in the recommendations of the OECD *Benchmark Definition*

for compiling FDI statistics. Nevertheless, these breakdowns could be usefully developed within the framework of FDI statistics. It should be kept in mind that FDI statistics use concepts and definitions of the balance of payments as well as the guidelines for recording such investments. However, FDI statistics are more detailed (*e.g.* industrial classification is not a requirement of the balance of payments statistics). Within this framework, FDI statistics could be supplemented by additional information that would provide a valuable analytical dimension to these statistics.

172. *Mergers and acquisitions* relate to the combination of two or more companies belonging to the same legal entity or not to achieve strategic and financial objectives. Companies involved in the operation may come from different economic sectors. The success of M&A operations depends, to a large extent, on how well the companies and their organisations can be integrated. Shareholders and managers of the companies have a crucial role in the successful realisation of M&As.

173. Several private databank companies collect and disseminate statistics on M&As. These data are compiled for various purposes but not as a part of FDI statistics. Therefore, the data are not based on the standards recommended for compiling FDI statistics. The differences in methodologies do not allow integrating and analysing these data as a part of the regular FDI statistics. Any further discussion on the breakdown of FDI statistics into M&As and greenfield investments in the present document would be premature.

174. The OECD Workshop on International Investment Statistics has started work on the feasibility for compiling statistics by type of FDI. The initial focus of the study is on data collection for M&As. Currently very few OECD countries compile M&A statistics according to international standards that apply to FDI statistics. The exercise is intended not only to cover data collection as a part of FDI but also to examine the harmonisation of statistical recording of such transactions (in particular the operations which are not cash payments). The results of this work will be incorporated in the "OECD Practical guide to FDI statistics". Developing additional indicators and their relevance to globalisation will be determined at a later time depending on the results of the feasibility study.

175. The OECD Workshop is also preparing a report on Special Purpose Entities (SPE) and off-shore economies [see also Sub-section 2.5.1.1. *iii)* Special cases].

Notes

1. See also Chapter IV, *Foreign Direct Investment for Development – Maximising Benefits, Minimising Costs*, OECD, 2002, and the following OECD internal working documents by Lionel Fontagné:
   - "The Links between Foreign Direct Investment and International Trade" (1995).
   - "The Links between Foreign Direct Investment and Trade: Empirical Evidence for US and French industries" (1996).
   - "Trade Competition and Foreign Direct Investment: A New Assessment" (1998).
   - "Links between Direct Investment and Trade: Short- and Long-term Effects" (1999).
2. A third category, "Experimental indicators" are defined in Chapter 1. This category is not included for FDI indicators as the developmental work is still in very preliminary stages.
3. Although competitiveness and attractiveness cannot be concluded from purely statistical information on FDI activity, the statistics may provide preliminary elements regarding the competitiveness and the attractiveness of markets or specific sectors of the economy.
4. FDI Flows relate to FDI financial flows and FDI income flows. The terms financial flows and financial transactions are used interchangeably in the present document.

5. See Annex 2.5, Box 1.
6. "Transactions in financial assets and liabilities arising from the provision of, or receipt of, direct foreign investment are to be recorded under the appropriate categories listed above ..., shares and other equity, loans, and other accounts receivable/payable. However, the amounts of direct foreign investment included within each of these categories should also be recorded separately as memorandum item." §11.102 SNA93.
7. For the coverage of financial accounts, see also BPM5 §313-316.
8. See also *Co-ordinated Portfolio Investment Survey Guide, 2nd edition,* IMF, 2002.
9. See also *Co-ordinated Portfolio Investment Survey Guide*, IMF, *2nd edition*, 2002.
10. See also *The OECD Code of Capital Movements* provides a further breakdown of this residual category.
11. In spite of this agreement on the basic principle, there are difficulties and differences in the interpretation of the SNA93 and BPM5 recommendations. It is expected that the Inter-secretariat Working Group on National Accounts (ISWGNA), will provide clarifications on the interpretation of the accrual principle. See also "Income from Bonds: the 1993 SNA treatment", March 2002, Lucie Laliberté (IMF).
12. See methodological documentation cited in the introduction of this chapter.
13. For more detailed description and examples see OECD *Benchmark*, Annex 3 "Special Purpose Entities". See also IMF *BPM5* §365 and *BOP Textbook* §542, and *Recommended Treatment of Selected Direct Investment Transactions, IMF,* 2002.
14. See *Treatment of Selected Direct Investment Transactions, IMF,* 2002.
15. In the International Investment Position statement, FDI in the reporting economy (inward direct investment) is treated as a liability, while FDI abroad (outward direct investment) is treated as an asset.
16. The alternative method to measure earnings is the "*All-inclusive Concept*" whereby income is the amount remaining after all items (including capital gains and losses) that cause any increase or decrease in the shareholders' or investors' interests during the period are allowed for. Although not recommended by international standards, this method is used by a significant number of direct investment enterprises to measure earnings.
17. See also IMF BPM5 §285 and §286.
18. For more information on "transfer pricing" see also the IMF *BPM5,* Chapter V. and *BOP Compilation Guide*, Chapter 11, and Chapter 5, Section 5.3.2.5.
19. In this chapter, the "ultimate parent enterprise" corresponds to the "ultimate control parent company" or "ultimate control unit" defined in Chapter 3 (Box 3.7).
20. Reporting basis used in the joint OECD-EUROSTAT questionnaire for collecting data on foreign direct investment.
21. However, concerning data on the activity of multinationals presented in Chapter 3, a majority of OECD countries are able to provide figures according to the country of ultimate control enterprise in the case of inward investment.
22. OECD database on FDI statistics includes industrial classification for main FDI components and sub-components for inward and outward investments.

ANNEX 2.A1

Borderline Cases to be Excluded from FDI for Statistical Purposes

(§11, OECD Benchmark Definition)

176. Some examples of cross border transactions may, in a global framework, give the impression that they qualify as direct investment even if they do not meet the criteria. The *Benchmark* cites the following examples:

a) An enterprise undertakes to build for a foreign client, usually a government, a complete manufacturing plant, to provide technical know-how, and to manage and operate a plant for a number of years, without an ongoing on-site managerial presence and without other criteria for existence of a direct investment enterprise being met. It has complete control over day-to-day operations and receives a management fee, paid either in cash or in goods produced by the plant. However, the enterprise has no equity stake in the plant and is performing a cross-border service.

b) An enterprise has a long-term contract with a foreign company, provides it with technical know-how, and has considerable influence over the quality and quantity of output. The enterprise may provide a loan to the foreign company and sometimes will have a member on the company's board. However, there is no equity stake. It is once again a cross-border service.

c) Some host countries have made agreements with a number of foreign enterprises where the host country supplies factory accommodation, electricity, staff accommodation, administration and labour. The foreign enterprise supplies all production machinery, fixtures and fittings for the building and production materials, and is responsible for the initial training of the labour force. The foreign enterprise then pays an agreed piecework rate for each item produced. Where the production machinery and fixtures and fittings remain the property of the foreign enterprise, there is technically a direct investment branch, though the branch's profits will be zero. There is no direct investment interest if the machinery becomes the property of the host country.

d) Some professional firms operate much like a multinational firm, but do not hold equity in one another. For example, unaffiliated (in an equity sense) accounting or management consulting firms may operate globally under a single name, refer business to one another and receive fees in return, share costs (or facilities) for such items as training or advertising, and may have a board of directors to plan business strategy for the group. This is not direct investment, and would be difficult or impossible to account for as such, but it does have much in common with direct investment.

e) Other cases might include foreign sales and representative offices, as well as foreign stations, ticket offices and terminal or port facilities of domestic airlines or ship operators. Such offices or activities can be treated as direct investment only if they meet the requirements of residence and the attribution of production in an economy.

177. The OECD Code of Liberalisation of Capital Movements has recognised non-resident investor's credit to a resident enterprise (not necessarily qualifying for an inter-company loan) of a maturity of five years of more as qualifying for FDI, subject to certain other conditions. Such transactions are not to be included in FDI statistics.

ANNEX 2.A2

FDI Data Sources

(Source: *IMF Balance of Payments Guide*)

Table 2.A2.1. **Sources of information on direct investment (DI)**

Advantages	Disadvantages
International transactions reporting system (ITRS)	
A large part of the necessary information is often readily available from banking records. Use of an ITRS avoids the expense of developing alternative collections for countries already using this method for compilation of BOP statistics.	In general, only cash transactions are measured. DI often involves non-cash transactions, such as reinvested earnings; equity provided in the form of machinery, etc; and inter-company indebtedness. Supplementary collections will be required to measure these transactions properly. The concept of direct investment (and therefore appropriate treatment of particular transactions) is difficult to explain on a generalised foreign exchange/banking report form. As a result, there are often problems with classification. The level of detail that can be obtained on DI is often limited. An ITRS may not readily provide information on levels of investment. Transactions in domestic currency or through accounts with non-resident banks are difficult to measure, although these difficulties can be overcome through the development of sound collection procedures.
Enterprise surveys (ES)	
ES provide for complete recording of direct investment transactions and stocks of investment by each enterprise surveyed. Information on other economic activity relating to DI can be easily collected for analytical purposes and for quality control. ES provide the best opportunity to explain to data providers the concept of direct investment and the treatment of particular transactions.	It may be difficult to maintain comprehensive lists of enterprises with direct investment transactions. Countries that do not normally use enterprise surveys for BOP measurement will incur costs in developing and implementing specialised direct investment surveys.
Information from approvals	
Information is often readily available as a by-product of the approval process.	Approval processes are rarely set up with BOP requirements in mind. Therefore, the range of information available for use in BOP compilation is generally limited. There could be significant time lags between approval and actual investment, or approved investment may never actually take place.
Information from approvals	Information on income (including reinvested earnings) and on withdrawals of investment may not be available. Information on non-equity transactions, such as lending by the direct investor and inter-company accounts, is generally limited. Information on stocks of investment valued at market price is typically not available The approval process may relate only to investment in particular industries or to investment greater than thresholds. Generally, approvals relate only to direct investment in the reporting economy and not to direct investment abroad.

ANNEX 2.A3

Standard Foreign Direct Investment Components (IMF BPM5)

Table 2.A3.1. **Balance of payments**

Direct investment income (page 44, IMF *BPM5*)	Credit	Debit
Income on equity		
Dividends and distributed branch profits		
Reinvested earnings and undistributed branch profits		
Income on debt (interest)		
Direct investment financial flows (pages 44-45 IMF *BPM5*)	Credit	Debit
Abroad		
Equity capital		
Claims on affiliated enterprises		
Liabilities to affiliated enterprises		
Reinvested earnings		
Other capital		
Claims on affiliated enterprises		
Liabilities to affiliated enterprises		
In reporting economy		
Equity capital		
Claims on direct investors		
Liabilities to direct investors		
Reinvested earnings		
Other capital		
Claims on direct investors		
Liabilities to direct investors		

Table 2.A3.2. **International investment position** (pages 108 and 110 IMF BPM5)

	Position at beginning of year	Changes in position reflecting: Transactions	Price changes	Exchange rate changes	Other adjustments	Position at end of year
Assets						
*Direct investment abroad**						
Equity capital and reinvested earnings						
Claims on affiliated enterprises						
Liabilities to affiliated enterprises						
Other capital						
Claims on affiliated enterprises						
Liabilities to affiliated enterprises						
Liabilities						
*Direct investment in reporting economy**						
Equity capital and reinvested earnings						
Claims on direct investors						
Liabilities to direct investors						
Other capital						
Claims on direct investors						
Liabilities to direct investors						

* Because direct investment is classified primarily on a directional basis – abroad under the heading **Assets** and in the reporting economy under the heading **Liabilities** – breakdowns of claims/liabilities are shown for the components of each, although these sub-items do not strictly conform to the overall headings of **Assets** and **Liabilities.**

ANNEX 2.A4

ISIC/NACE Codes Used in OECD-EUROSTAT Questionnaire for Industrial Activities

Table 2.A4.1. **ISIC/NACE codes used in OECD-EUROSTAT Questionnaire for industrial activities**

	ISIC Rev. 3	NACE Rev. 1	OECD/ EUROSTAT
AGRICULTURE AND FISHING	Sections A et B	Sections A et B	0595
MINING AND QUARRYING	Section C	Section C	1495
of which: Extraction of petroleum and gas	Division 11	Division 11	1100
MANUFACTURING	Section D	Section D	3995
of which: Food products, beverages and tobacco	Divisions 15, 16	Sub-section DA	1605
Textiles and wearing apparel	Divisions 17, 18	Subsection DB	1805
Wood, publishing and printing	Divisions 20, 21, 22	Sub-sections DD and DE	2205
Total textile and wood activities*			**2295**
Refined petroleum products and other treatments	Division 23	Division 23	2300
Chemicals and chemical products	Division 24	Division 24	2400
Rubber and plastic products	Division 25	Division 25	2500
Total petroleum, chemical, rubber, plastic products*			**2595**
Metal products	Divisions 27, 28	sub-section DJ	2805
Mechanical products	Division 29	Division 29	2900
Total metal and mechanical products*			**2995**
Office machinery and computers	Division 30	Division 30	3000
Radio, TV, communication equipment	Division 32	Division 32	3200
Total machinery, computer, RTV, communication*			**3295**
Motor vehicles	Division 34	Division 34	3400
Other transport equipment	Division 35	Division 35	3500
Total vehicles and other transport equipment*			**3595**
ELECTRICITY, GAS AND WATER	Section E	Section E	4195
CONSTRUCTION	Section F	Section F	4500
TRADE AND REPAIRS	Section G	Section G	5295
HOTELS AND RESTAURANTS	Section H	Section H	5500
TRANSPORTS, COMMUNICATION	Section I	Section I	6495
of which: Land transport	Division 60	Division 60	6000
Sea and coastal water transport	Group 611	Group 61.1	6110
Air transport	Division 62	Division 62	6200
Total land, sea and air transport*			**6295**
Telecommunications	Group 642	Group 64.2	6420
FINANCIAL INTERMEDIATION	Section J	Section J	6895
of which: Monetary intermediation	Group 651	Group 65.1	6510
Other financial intermediation	Group 659	Group 65.2	6520
of which: Financial holding companies	Part of class 6599	Part of class 65.23	6524
Insurance and activities auxiliary to insurance	Division 66 and group 672	Division 66 and group 67.2	6730
Total other fin. intermediation + insurance activities*			**6795**
REAL ESTATE AND BUSINESS ACTIVITIES	Section K	Section K	7395
Real estate	Division 70	Division 70	7000
Computer activities	Division 72	Division 72	7200
Research and development	Division 73	Division 73	7300
Other business activities	Division 74	Division 74	7400
of which: Business and management consultancy	Group 741	Group 74.1	7410
of which: Management holding companies	Part of class 7414	Class 74.15	7415
Advertising	Group 743	Group 74.4	7440
OTHER SERVICES	Sections L, M, N, O, P, Q	Sections L, M, N,O, P, Q	9995
UNALLOCATED			9996
SUB-TOTAL			9997
PRIVATE PURCHASES AND SALES OF REAL ESTATE			9998
TOTAL			9999

* OECD-EUROSTAT classification.

ANNEX 2.A5

Herfindahl Concentration Index

Box 2.A5.1. **Herfindahl concentration index**

One way to measure the degree of concentration of international investment, in terms of flows or stocks, is to use the Herfindahl index. This is easy to compile and offers the advantage that the information necessary to compute it is in most cases available. For example, to compare the degree of geographic concentration of stocks of foreign direct investment by a compiling country, it is necessary to add the squares of the country's market share of FDI for each of the countries (markets) in which that country has invested. In other words, the Herfindahl index for Country A (H_A) would be equal to:

$$H_A = \left(\frac{FDI_1}{\sum_{i=1}^{n} FDI_i} \right)^2 + \left(\frac{FDI_2}{\sum_{i=1}^{n} FDI_i} \right)^2 + .. + \left(\frac{FDI_n}{\sum_{i=1}^{n} FDI_i} \right)^2 = \sum_{i=1}^{n} \left(\frac{FDI_i}{\sum_{i=1}^{n} FDI_i} \right)^2$$

where:

FDI_i = the value of Country A's stock of foreign direct investment in each destination country i.

$\sum_{i=1}^{n} FDI_i$ = the sum of Country A's stocks of foreign direct investment in all countries i.

If Country A had invested the same value in terms of stocks in each host country, *i.e.* if:

$FDI_1 = FDI_2 = \ldots FDI_n$

then the value of the Herfindahl index would be equal to $\frac{1}{n}$.

It is easy to deduce that the lower Country A's market shares are, the more negligible their values would be, and the calculations could disregard them. Herfindahl indices can be calculated to measure the geographic concentration of foreign direct investment (stocks or flows) between two or more countries, between different sectors of a given country or between different countries in respect of a particular sector. Countries or sectors having a low Herfindahl index will be less geographically concentrated and thus more highly internationalised. The indices can be adjusted to factor in the geographic distance between the investing Country A and the countries *i* in which Country A makes its investments. The more distant the countries in which Country A invests, the greater the degree of globalisation may be.

ISBN 92-64-10808-4
OECD Handbook on Economic Globalisation Indicators

Chapter 3

The Economic Activity of Multinational Enterprises

3.1. Introduction

178. An important feature of the increasing globalisation of the world economy is the prominent role of multinational enterprises (MNEs). Two broadly defined types of data are relevant to understanding the role of multinational enterprises in the world economy. The first type, described in detail in Chapter 2, covers data on *direct investment flows and related positions* (FDI statistics). FDI statistics track the value of transactions that occur between direct investors and the direct investment enterprises (affiliates) they own in other countries, and the stock value of their investment in those affiliates. The second type, concerning data on the *activities of multinational enterprises* (AMNE or activity data) discussed in this chapter, provides measures such as turnover (sales), employment, and value added that reflect the overall operations of MNEs, whether or not financed by the direct investor.

179. This chapter presents indicators of economic globalisation based on AMNE data, discusses the variables to be collected that underlie the said indicators, and considers conceptual and methodological issues that arise in developing and using those indicators and variables. This chapter focuses primarily on economic activities of MNEs occurring within countries (*e.g.* employment in foreign control affiliates in the compiling country) but also gives certain recommendations concerning the activities of these enterprises outside the borders of the compiling country. Chapters 4 and 5 are concerned, respectively, with international technology transfers and trade flows involving MNEs.

180. FDI statistics are used extensively to measure movements of capital between direct investors and affiliates, as well as receipts and payments of income. As measures of direct investment-related financial flows and positions between countries, FDI statistics are integral components of investing and host (compiling) countries' international transactions accounts, international investment positions, and national income and product accounts.

181. By covering only transactions and positions between direct investors and their affiliates, FDI statistics do not measure other sources of funds, such as borrowing from unaffiliated persons, which help finance the overall operations of affiliates. FDI statistics cover direct investment transactions and positions of all affiliates, including those in which the direct investor does not necessarily have control (*i.e.* those in which the investor has only an influence since he owns between 10% and 50% of the capital). Also, because FDI flows and positions are usually attributed to the country of immediate rather than ultimate ownership (for inward investment), and to the immediate rather than ultimate country of destination (for outward investment), the data cannot identify either the ultimate beneficiary or the ultimate location of affiliate operations, particularly for those affiliates that are indirectly held.

182. AMNE data cover the overall operations of affiliates and parent companies. As will be proposed later in this chapter, AMNE data should be compiled, as a first priority, for affiliates in which the direct investor has unambiguous control and should be attributed to

the country of the investor of ultimate control (for inward investment) and the country in which the operations actually take place (for outward investment). As a result, AMNE data can provide information about the operations of affiliates – for example, the number of people employed by foreign-controlled affiliates in a given country that are essential to a more complete understanding of the role played by MNEs in host and home countries. In the case of a compiling country, AMNE data concern *foreign-controlled affiliates* (foreign-CAs), *parent companies* (controlled by residents or by foreign investors), and *affiliates abroad* controlled by this country.[1]

183. From a practical point of view, this chapter recognises that, for most compiling countries, it is easier to collect AMNE data on inward investment and on parent companies resident in the compiling country than on affiliates located abroad, because the first two categories of firm are located within the territory of the compiling country. AMNE data on controlled affiliates located abroad (CAs abroad) are generally available in fewer compiling countries and frequently with less detail. Because data collection authority of a compiling country typically does not extend beyond its national borders, data on affiliates abroad usually must be collected through surveys of parents (institutional units controlling affiliates abroad) in the compiling country. From an analytical point of view, however, data on affiliates abroad are very important to have a full picture of the activity of multinational enterprises. They also add clear analytical value to the data on the activity of parent companies. In an effort to balance practical and analytical aspects, this chapter focuses primarily on development of AMNE data for affiliates under foreign control and parent companies located in the compiling country. While giving guidance for the compilation of data on the activity of affiliates abroad controlled by the compiling country, it recognises that their development on an internationally comparable basis is a longer term process.

184. This chapter has several important objectives. First, by identifying useful indicators of the economic globalisation process, it hopes to assist policymakers and analysts in the use and interpretation of currently available AMNE data. Second, by providing clear, practical, and consistent guidance on the collection of AMNE data on inward and (secondarily) outward investment, it seeks to encourage compilers to both expand their data collection efforts and to promote improved comparability within compiling countries of AMNE data accompanied by comparable national totals. Finally, by recognizing the utility for international and regional organisations of aggregation of AMNE data across countries, and by identifying data issues that currently limit the aggregation especially for data on affiliates abroad, the chapter seeks to promote development, over the longer term, of internationally comparable data.

185. In attempting to meet these objectives, this chapter, like the present *Handbook* in general, relies on, and to the extent possible is consistent with, existing statistical standards. For example, the System of National Accounts (SNA 1993), provides a concept central to the collection of AMNE data – that of the "*foreign-controlled enterprise*". The IMF's Balance of Payments Manual, 5th edition (IMF *BPM5*) and the OECD's *Benchmark Definition of Direct Investment*, 3rd edition (OECD *Benchmark Definition*), provide guidelines on the definition of direct investment; because AMNE data are predicated on the existence of a direct investment relationship between investor and affiliate, these guidelines, discussed in detail in Chapter 2, are central to the issues discussed in this chapter. Finally, the Manual on Statistics of International Trade in Services (MSITS), which is a joint product of the United Nations, European Commission, IMF, OECD, UNCTAD, and WTO and was recently approved for international use, provides, in its Chapter 4, extremely useful and relevant

guidance on collection of AMNE data (termed foreign affiliate trade in services, or FATS, statistics in the Manual on Statistics of International Trade in Services, or MSITS). Although guidance in this chapter on collection of AMNE data extends to businesses outside the service sector, they are fully consistent with the guidance in Chapter 4 of the MSITS. (Some passages in what follows are drawn, in part or in full, from Chapter 4 of the MSITS.)

3.2. Proposed indicators

3.2.1. *Rationale*

186. A set of reference, supplemental and experimental indicators, based on AMNE data, are proposed to examine questions deemed of interest to analysts and policy-makers such as the following:

3.2.1.1. *Reference indicators*

- What is the share of a foreign-controlled affiliate *(foreign-CAs)* in economic output (*e.g.* GDP, value added, sales or turnover) in the compiling country?
- What is the share of foreign-CAs in total employment and employee compensation in the compiling country?
- What is the share of foreign-CAs in gross fixed capital formation in the compiling country?
- What is the share of parent companies' economic output, value added, turnover, gross fixed capital formation, employment, and employee compensation in the compiling country?
- In the compiling country, what are the number and operating characteristics of foreign-CAs, and parent companies?

3.2.1.2. *Supplemental indicators*

- What are the output and employment generated by investment ensuring control of the capital in CAs abroad in relation to output and employment in the compiling country?
- What is the importance of sales of CAs abroad in relation to total exports of the investing country's domestic enterprises?
- How much of these sales derive from the production of the CAs abroad and how much from their imports (particularly from their parents)?
- How much of the sales of CAs abroad is sold to the home country (compiling country)?

187. Box 3.1 lists the proposed reference and supplemental indicators to be derived from AMNE data.

3.2.1.3. *Measuring and interpreting indicators based on shares*

188. As with many measures of globalization that are ratios of AMNE data to country totals, care must be exercised to ensure that the numerator and denominator of the ratio are reasonably comparable. For example, value added based on enterprise surveys of foreign-CAs, if calculated appropriately, would be very close in concept and content to a country's estimate of GDP for all of its enterprises, and can be compared with confidence to that aggregate. However, if the country's estimates of GDP by industrial sector are based on data at the establishment (or plant) level, comparisons by industry with data for foreign-CAs may not be appropriate because there may be significant differences in the

Box 3.1. **Proposed indicators for measuring the extent of globalisation related to MNEs**

(For indicators of technology and trade, see chapters 4 and 5 respectively)

1. Reference indicators

Extent of foreign control in the compiling country (total and by industry)

- Foreign-CAs' share of value added.
- Foreign-CAs' share of turnover (sales) or gross production.
- Foreign-CAs' share of gross fixed capital formation.
- Foreign-CAs' share of employment.
- Foreign-CAs' share of compensation of employees.
- Foreign-CAs' share of the number of (consolidated) enterprises.

Extent of parent companies' activities in the compiling country (total and by industry)

- Parent companies' share of value added.
- Parent companies' share of turnover (sales).
- Parent companies' share of gross fixed capital formation.
- Parent companies' share of employment.
- Parent companies' share of compensation of employees.

Extent of MNEs' activities in the compiling country (total)

- MNEs' share of value added.
- MNEs' share of gross fixed capital formation.
- MNEs' share of employment.
- MNEs' share of compensation of employees.
- MNEs' share of number of consolidated enterprises.

2. Supplemental indicators

a) Outward activities of compiling country

Extent of CAs' activities abroad (total and by industry)

- CAs' abroad share of employment in the total of parent companies in the compiling country and their CAs abroad.
- CAs' abroad share of turnover done by parent companies in the compiling country and their CAs abroad.

Degree of geographical diversification of CAs' activities abroad (total and by industry)

- Herfindahl index of employment.
- Herfindahl index of sales or turnover.

b) Inward activities of compiling country

Extent of foreign control in the compiling country (total and by industry)

Foreign CAs' and parents' share of:

- Gross operating surplus.
- Taxes on income.
- Assets (financial and non-financial).

Box 3.1. **Proposed indicators for measuring the extent of globalisation related to MNEs** *(cont.)*
(For indicators of technology and trade, see chapters 4 and 5 respectively)

Degree of geographic diversification of foreign control (total and by industry)

- Herfindahl index of value added.
- Herfindahl index of sales or turnover.
- Herfindahl index of employment.

distribution by industry between establishment and enterprise data. This issue is presented in more detail in Section 3.3.7.

189. Furthermore, changes over time in ratios of AMNE data to compiling country totals must be interpreted with care because AMNE data reflect changes in ownership of firms – from resident ownership to foreign ownership, and *vice-versa* – while the country totals do not. For example, period-to-period change in value added of foreign-CAs has three components: 1) change in value added of firms that were foreign-CAs in both periods, 2) addition of value added of firms that were foreign-CAs in the second period but not in the first, and 3) subtraction of value added of firms that were foreign-CAs in the first period but not in the second. If changes in ownership are very significant from period to period, analysis of foreign-CAs' contribution to growth in the value added of all of a country's enterprises ought preferably to be confined to the first of these components.

190. Ideally, measures of AMNE data should be broken down into the three components of change to better isolate contributions of foreign-CAs to a country's economy, absent the impact of ownership changes. This may be possible in countries where AMNE data are available on an establishment level, or on a deconsolidated enterprise level (a concept which will be developed below), where firms, or components of firms, that have undergone ownership change can be separately identified. However, if AMNE data are available only on a fully consolidated enterprise basis (see also Chapter 2), it may not be possible to track the impact of ownership change that involves components of the fully consolidated enterprise, rather than the enterprise itself. In large industrial economies, when merger and acquisition activity is high, significant ownership changes occur within consolidated enterprises.

3.2.2. Reference indicators

191. The reference indicators related to MNEs measure the extent of foreign-CAs' and parent companies' activities in the compiling country. The sum of these two categories of business indicators provides therefore an estimate of the extent of economic activities related to MNEs in the compiling country.

3.2.2.1. Extent of foreign control in the compiling country

192. The reference indicators related to foreign-CAs' activities measure the degree of foreign control (presence) in the compiling country.

Foreign-CAs' share of value added in the compiling country

193. Value added, the portion of an enterprise's output that originates within the enterprise itself, is perhaps the most comprehensive measure of economic activity that

can be derived from AMNE data and a particularly useful measure from the perspective of globalisation analysis. Value added concerning all the components of a country's economy adds up to its gross domestic product (GDP), the most widely available aggregate measure of the size of an economy and its growth. Thus, the share of GDP, in a given country's total GDP, and by industrial sector, that is accounted for by foreign-CAs, is an important indicator for measuring the extent to which economic globalisation has taken place in a domestic economy.

Foreign CAs' share of turnover (sales) or gross output

194. While it is true that in some cases value-added is not available, almost all enterprises collect data concerning turnover (sales) or gross production. While value-added is the preferred measure, gross output can be used to reflect the value of the economic activity being generated. As discussed below, gross output includes the purchases of intermediate output and as such when summed across countries includes considerable double counting, limiting its utility as an economy-wide measure.

Foreign-CAs' share of gross fixed capital formation (GFCF) in the compiling country

195. Available figures show that in a majority of OECD countries, the share of gross fixed capital formation by foreign-CAs in the manufacturing sector corresponds to the proportion of those enterprises' gross output in the respective national totals. However, in some countries, these shares are proportionately greater than those CAs' share of gross output in their respective compiling countries' manufacturing industries. In view of this, it could be interesting, to identify the sectors concerned. If fixed capital investment is greater in certain sectors, it could also be useful to analyse the reasons and measure, for example, productivity, export capacity and contribution to growth of these enterprises and sectors. However, the *Handbook* gives lower priority to these calculations.

Foreign-CAs' share of employment in compiling country

196. For employment in foreign-CAs, which must be defined in the same way as total industrial employment, the relevant ratio may reflect the importance of foreign investment in maintaining or creating employment in a compiling country. However, this information is not sufficient to evaluate the net job creation by foreign investment in the compiling countries.

Foreign-CAs' share of compensation of employees in compiling country

197. These ratios are of particular interest since they can show: *a)* if average pay in foreign-CAs is higher or lower than pay levels in enterprises controlled by the residents of the compiling country, and *b)* if average pay in foreign-CAs in the same sector differs significantly between countries of control. In most countries, average pay in foreign-CAs is higher than in enterprises controlled by residents of the compiling country, essentially for two reasons: 1) foreign-CAs tends to be larger than enterprises controlled by residents, which include many SMEs, and 2) because of the choice of sectors in which foreign control is concentrated. In many cases these are high-tech or medium-high-tech sectors that are very capital-intensive and use mostly high-skilled labour. Pay differentials associated with country of foreign control for foreign-CAs in the same sector can be attributed to the same causes, notably differences in enterprise size, pattern of organisation, productivity levels and workforce skills.

Foreign-CAs' share of the number of (consolidated) enterprises in compiling country

198. In the case of inward investment, the number of foreign-CA enterprises is of interest when compared with the total number of enterprises in a country mainly at the sectoral level. The two numbers should therefore be expressed in the same statistical unit (see Section 3.3.7). Likewise, the level of enterprise consolidation may significantly affect comparisons of the number of enterprises.

199. The analytical relevance of the number of foreign-CAs enterprises when compared with total turnover or employment is that it can provide some indication of the average size of foreign-CAs (turnover/number of affiliates or total employment/number of affiliates). These comparisons, even if rather approximate, may show that in most countries the average size of foreign-CAs is considerably larger than that of enterprises controlled by the residents of the compiling country. From this standpoint, it is interesting to identify whether foreign investors prefer to control enterprises of medium size or to concentrate their investment on a few big enterprises and also whether there are significant differences across sectors. However, finer analysis of such tendencies necessitates a breakdown by enterprise size.

3.2.2.2. *Extent of parent companies' activities in the compiling country*

200. The reference indicators related to parent companies' activities measure the importance, in the compiling country, of foreign direct investment enterprises located in this country (see definition, Section 3.3.3) and controlling enterprises abroad. These enterprises are in principle controlled by the residents of this country, but some may be under foreign control.

201. Indicators of parent companies' activity in compiling country are important for two reasons. First, because strategic decisions for a corporate group are usually taken by the parent companies who exercise close supervision of certain strategic activities such as finance, R&D and innovation. The second reason is that parent companies are a useful group for comparison, constituting a population which can be more readily compared with foreign-CAs than other categories of enterprises controlled by residents of the compiling country. In host countries, the performances of affiliates under foreign control are generally better than the average. On the other hand, when the performances of these affiliates are compared with those of parent companies controlled by residents of the compiling country, most of the differences tend to diminish because of the relatively similar profiles of the two categories of enterprises in terms of size, economies of scale and organisation in world markets.[2]

202. These reference indicators – total and by industry – should be published for all parent companies (regardless of their country of control). It is also important to produce separately at least indicators concerning the aggregate total for parent companies controlled by residents of the compiling country and under foreign control in order to be able to compute aggregated indicators for all MNEs in the compiling country. (See discussion on "target population", Section 3.3.1).

203. The description of the reference indicators related to parent companies in the compiling country is similar to those related to foreign-CAs and is therefore much shorter.

Parent companies' share of value added in the compiling country

204. The share of value added, in total and by industrial sector, that is accounted for by enterprises controlled by residents with CAs abroad, is a powerful measure of the extent to which enterprises controlled by residents of the compiling country have globalised their economic activity abroad.

Parent companies' share of turnover (sales) in the compiling country

205. Sales or turnover are very similar to gross output in terms of interpretation. The double-counting issue affects this variable. Moreover, shares based on sales tend to give more weight to wholesale enterprises than would gross output or value added, as only the wholesale margins are included in these latter concepts. Industry level analysis is therefore recommended for the shares based on this variable.

Parent companies' share of gross fixed capital formation (GFCF) in the compiling country

206. The data for parent companies on GFCF could help assess their fixed investment propensity. It would therefore be very interesting to analyse this issue once more member countries publish this indicator.

Parent companies' share of employment in compiling country

207. The share of employment accounted for by parent companies in the compiling country could go up as these companies increase their activities as a result of acquiring control of other enterprises or increase their market shares inside and outside the compiling country. Comparing this indicator with the share of value added accounted for by parent companies can reveal the labour productivity of these companies relative to others.

Parent companies' share of compensation of employees in compiling country

208. As for employment, this share measures the degree of "outward" globalisation of multinational enterprises controlled by residents. It could go up as the size of these enterprises grows and they increase their world market shares. The analytical value of this indicator is enhanced when compared to the corresponding employment share, as it reveals information about relative average pay. For example, if the share of compensation of employees accounted for by parent companies grows faster than the corresponding ratio for employment, it shows that average compensation grows faster in enterprises with CAs abroad than for all compiling country enterprises.

3.2.2.3. Extent of MNEs' activities in the compiling country

209. These more global reference indicators are simply the summation of the corresponding indicators for foreign-CAs and parent companies. They represent the share of economic activity in the compiling country that is accounted for by multinationals located in this country.

210. The importance of MNEs' (parent companies and foreign CAs) in a compiling country's economic activity is an indicator which is available in most countries at total industry level. This indicator is not so easy to obtain by sector for two reasons. First, statistics by industry on parent companies do not distinguish between resident-controlled and foreign-controlled parent companies, raising certain double-counting problems which are discussed in Section 3.3.1.2. Publishing these data separately for each sector would

cause confidentiality problems for many countries inasmuch as the number of foreign CAs in a particular sector is generally extremely low.

211. Second, data at the industry level might not be consistent across the different populations. For example, the number of foreign-CAs might be measured at the establishment level while parent companies are usually consolidated. Countries that could provide industrial statistics that were consistent across all these categories of enterprise would greatly increase the usefulness of these statistics.

212. The description of the reference indicators related to MNEs in the compiling country is not necessarily as they are constructed as the simple aggregation of indicators related to foreign-CAs and parent companies.

3.2.3. Supplemental indicators

213. In addition to these reference indicators, there are supplementary indicators which are not currently available in all countries but which nevertheless provide useful complementary information.

a) Outward activities

Extent of CAs' activities abroad (total and by industry)

214. The indicators of the extent of CAs' activities abroad measure the extent of foreign activities (globalisation) of parent companies in the compiling countries. More specifically, these indicators are shares of the economic activities related to both the parent companies and their CAs abroad that are controlled by the former.

215. These indicators are relevant both at the total and industry levels. It is also useful, for several reasons, to analyse separately data for CAs abroad and parent companies controlled by residents in the compiling country:

i) The parent companies that are controlled by residents of the compiling country plus their CAs abroad constitute the world wide activity of MNEs controlled by residents of a compiling country. In the few cases where the parent companies in the compiling country is also a foreign-CAs there is a part of the world wide activities of the MNEs they belong to that is not accounted for.

ii) CAs abroad share of both parent companies controlled by residents and foreign-controlled parent companies in the total for these two categories of company in the compiling country could be misleading. For example, if foreign-controlled parent companies in the compiling country are small financial or administrative holdings, they could be controlling affiliates abroad that have much larger operations.

CAs abroad share of employment in the total of parent companies in the compiling country and their CAs abroad

216. This indicator is particularly interesting because it is more readily available than value added and does not suffer from double-counting as sales do.

CAs abroad share of sales or turnover achieved by the parent companies in the compiling country and their CAs abroad

217. This share is more readily available than value added but, as mentioned above, suffers from double-counting. This double-counting is particularly important when the CAs

OECD HANDBOOK ON ECONOMIC GLOBALISATION INDICATORS – ISBN 92-64-10808-4 – © OECD 2005

abroad are distributing products produced in the compiling country. For example, a parent company could be distributing all its products via a wholesale arm established in a foreign country. In this case, the CAs abroad share of sales could be 50% while it is in fact selling the whole of its parent company's production.

Degree of geographic diversification of CAs' activities abroad

218. The greater the number of countries and regions in which the affiliates of a multinational enterprise are located, the more globalised is this multinational. In order to measure the geographical diversification of the location of affiliates abroad, it is useful to measure the degree of geographical concentration of these affiliates. The Herfindahl index is a good indicator for this evaluation.

219. The three proposed Herfindahl indexes measure the degree of geographic concentration (diversification) of the economic activities of CAs abroad. A lower Herfindahl index means that the parent companies in the compiling country have activities outside the country that are more globalised in terms of country coverage. These indicators are particularly useful when comparing countries that have similar degree of parent companies' activities abroad. In this situation, countries with a lower Herfindahl index have diversified their activities abroad to other countries to a greater extent (less concentrated). These indicators can be computed for the total and by industry.

220. It should be noted that Herfindahl indexes based on the summation of activity data for foreign-CAs and CAs abroad could be computed. The following description of the three Herfindahl indexes focuses on specificities of these indexes for CAs' activities abroad and builds on the related paragraphs above.

Herfindahl index of employment and turnover (sales)

221. The Herfindahl index based on employment in CAs abroad measures the degree of geographic concentration (diversification) of parent companies abroad in terms of foreign workers experiencing their "influence" and potentially benefiting it.

222. The drawbacks related to sales or turnover mentioned previously also affect the Herfindahl index on CAs' activities abroad. First, parent companies often establish wholesaling facilities abroad. Second, the sales of CAs abroad can be consolidated at the country level but it is much more difficult to net out intra-group sales across countries, which would avoid the double-counting issues. This variable is however more readily available for CAs abroad.

b) Inward activities

Extent of foreign control in the compiling country (total and by industry)

223. These supplementary indicators are similar to the reference indicators on MNEs' activities in the compiling country in terms of construct and broad interpretation. They are however based on different variables. Their specific interpretation is therefore related to the economic analytical value of the variables.

224. The variables used for these supplementary indicators add new insights to the analysis of the extent and intensity of globalisation related to the economic activities related to MNEs. But, more importantly they are crucial variables required in understanding the impact of MNEs on domestic economies. First, these variables in addition to those used for the reference indicators can be used to derive key economic performance indicators such

as productivity and profitability. Second, these variables are necessary to study links between control status (control by residents *versus* foreign control, part of MNE or not, country of control, etc.) and performance indicators.

225. The following description applies to total MNEs (foreign CAs and parent companies in the compiling country).

Share of gross operating surplus

226. This measure of income arising from the economic activities of enterprises is an important dimension in the analysis of MNEs in the compiling countries. The analytical value of the share of gross operating surplus accounted for by MNEs in a compiling country increases significantly when it is analysed in relation to other indicators. For example, if the share of gross operating surplus attributed to foreign-CAs is higher than the corresponding value added share, then one can conclude that these enterprises generate proportionally more profits than their domestic counterparts. This could be due to several factors such as a higher capital intensity, profitability or productivity.

Share of taxes on income

227. The share of taxes on income reflects the importance of MNEs to the government revenue in compiling country. For example, a higher share for this variable relative to the corresponding value added share would be indicative that these firms contribute relatively more to government revenues than non-MNE firms. Depending on the country, this indicator should be interpreted with care as it reflects other factors than globalisation per se, such as differences in tax regime, industrial structure, etc.

Share of assets (financial and non-financial)

228. The share of assets controlled by MNEs is a broad measure of the importance of their holdings in the compiling country. This share can shed light on financial performances of these firms when analysed in conjunction with other financial variables such as gross operating surplus, sales, etc.

Degree of geographic diversification of foreign control

229. These indicators measure the degree of geographic concentration of the origins of foreign control. A lower Herfindahl index means that the compiling country has a more diversified (globalised) source of foreign control (ownership), which is an indicator of the degree of inward globalisation of resident enterprises. These indicators are particularly useful when comparing countries that have a similar degree of foreign control. In this situation, countries with a lower Herfindahl index have a more diversified source of foreign control and can be considered more globalised than countries with a higher index. These indicators can be computed for the total and by industry.

230. This *Handbook* proposes to focus on three variables only. These three variables should be sufficient to measure the geographic diversification. They are also the most available variables for CAs abroad, allowing for comparison between inward and outward globalisation of resident MNEs.

Herfindahl index of value added

231. The Herfindahl index of value added is probably the most relevant and reliable measure of geographic concentration (diversification). Value added is a relevant measure of production and reliable because it is not affected by double-counting.

Herfindahl index of sales or turnover

232. Herfindahl indexes based on sales or turnover suffer from two drawbacks. First, sales related to foreign-CAs that only act as wholesaling-arms of foreign-controlled MNEs give a much higher weight to these firms than value added or employment would. Second, there might be some double-counting if sales are not consolidated for CAs belonging to the same MNE or if CAs of different MNEs sale products to each others with little value added. Analysis at the industry level would not suffer as much from these problems.

Herfindahl index of employment and turnover (sales)

233. The Herfindahl index based on employment measures the degree of geographic concentration (diversification) that workers of the compiling country experience and potentially can benefit from. Employment is as relevant and reliable as value added but focus on the labour dimension of economic activity.

3.2.4. General considerations when interpreting indicators

234. When looking to measure the degree of globalisation of the whole of a country's industrial sector, or of a particular sector, it is important to keep two questions in mind:

i) Changes over time concerning the share of economic activity attributed to multinational enterprises.

ii) The difficulties involved in reaching a conclusion on the basis of a set of available indicators.

235. In order to better understand the impact of changes over time concerning the share of economic activity attributed to multinational enterprises, it could be useful to identify the underlying causes: for example, the consequences of an increase in the share of foreign-controlled firms in employment are different in the case of a new acquisition or a greenfield investment. Three underlying reasons could be identified for such an increase (reduction):

- Greenfield investment in new production units (or, conversely, plant closures).
- The acquisition of a resident-controlled firm which may become foreign-controlled (or, conversely, a foreign-controlled firm may shift to resident ownership); and
- The increased capacity of existing firms under foreign control (or, conversely, a reduction in the capacity of the said firms).

236. As reported in the first chapter, this information is not for the moment available so we would not be able to gauge the implications, for example, of an increase in foreign-controlled value added in the economic activity of the reporting country (host country), that are due to the nature of the foreign investment. If, for example, the change were due simply to a change in ownership, this would not necessarily have a significant impact on a possible increase in the host country's overall industrial value added. The situation would be different if the increase in foreign-controlled value added were the result of foreign investors setting up new production units (greenfield investment).

237. The second problem concerns the indicators available, but is probably also a methodological and analytical problem related more to the industrial sectors concerned. Whenever, in the case of one or more countries, the object is to identify which of two industrial sectors is the more globalised, and assuming that all the indicators proposed in this *Handbook* are available (*i.e.* those for trade, direct investment and technology transfers), what is difficult is to make an overall assessment on the basis of all the said indicators. Taking the automobile and aviation industries as an example, clearly, the automobile industry exports a lot, has production units located in numerous countries and also has research laboratories in a large number of countries; the aviation industry, on the other hand, has a higher export rate but its factories and research laboratories are not widely dispersed throughout the world. Yet it would be wrong to conclude from this that the automobile industry is more globalised than the aviation industry.

238. The fact is that, because the aviation sector is very concentrated geographically and involves very substantial investment, it does not need to be located in a lot of different countries, yet its aircraft are sold throughout the entire world. Conversely, even if automobile production units are located in numerous countries, the models sold are often different since they are adapted to the requirements of each regional market, while the aviation industry sells the same types of aircraft everywhere in the world. From that point of view, the automobile industry could be said to be more multi-regional, while the aviation industry is truly a world industry. These examples show the difficulty of assessing an industry's degree of globalization and the need for information in addition to the proposed indicators, such as the level of competition, the nature of the goods and services sold throughout the world (if they are the same or regionalised, the links with international sub-contracting, co-operation agreements or strategic alliances between firms, etc. Such additional indicators and the method to be used to consolidate them are doubtless outside the scope of the *Handbook*, but readers should be aware that these problems exist.

3.2.5. *Variables required, availability, priority and definition*

3.2.5.1. *Variables required and their current availability*

239. The complete list of basic data to be collected, the great majority of which correspond to the basic indicators collected by the OECD and Eurostat on the AMNE, is given in Box 3.2. with the current availability in OECD countries.

240. The indicators and data proposed above are necessary in order to be able to cater for, formulate, back up and monitor compiling countries' domestic and international economic policies.

241. The development of the indicators listed in the previous section depends on a broad spectrum of economic variables. The choice of variables to be collected should be based on their relevance to the process of globalisation and the needs of the *General Agreement on Trade in Services* (GATS) with regard to services. While many OECD countries collect most of the basic data, the variables collected through national surveys tend to differ both in coverage and in definition. The purpose of this section is to address this problem by providing guidelines. In most cases, these recommendations are based on already existing methodological standards such as SNA 1993 and MSITS.

Box 3.2. Data required to construct globalisation indicators related to MNEs

Variables by target population[1]	Availability in the OECD countries	
	Available in most countries	Available in some countries
I) AMNE in the compiling country		
a) Foreign-CA activities, total, with and without CA abroad, by industry and country of ultimate control[1]		
Value added	X	
Gross output	X	
Sales or turnover	X	
Gross fixed capital formation	X	
Number of people in employment	X	
Compensation of employees	X	
Number of establishments or enterprises	X	
Number of consolidated enterprises		X
Gross operating surplus		X
Taxes on income	X	
R&D expenditure*	X	
Number of researchers*		X
Technological payments and receipt*	X	
Total exports and imports**	X	
Intra-firm exports and imports**		X
b) Parent companies' activities, total, by industry[1]		
Value added		X
Gross output		X
Sales or turnover		X
Gross fixed capital formation		X
Number of people in employment		X
Compensation of employees		X
Number of establishments or enterprises		X
Number of consolidated enterprises		X
Gross operating surplus		X
Taxes on income		X
R&D expenditure*		X
Number of researchers*		X
Technological payments and receipt*		X
Total exports and imports**		X
Intra-firm exports and imports**		X
II. Activities of all enterprises, by industry		
Value added	X	
Gross output	X	
Sales or turnover	X	
Gross fixed capital formation	X	
Number of people in employment	X	
Compensation of employees	X	
Number of establishments or enterprises	X	
Number of consolidated enterprises		X
Gross operating surplus	X	
Taxes on income	X	
Assets (financial and non-financial)	X	
R&D expenditure*	X	
Number of researchers*	X	
Technological payments and receipt*	X	
Total exports and imports**	X	
Intra-firm exports and imports**		X

Box 3.2. **Data required to construct globalisation indicators related to MNEs** *(cont.)*

Variables by target population[1]	Availability in the OECD countries	
	Available in most countries	Available in some countries
III) AMNE abroad		
a) CAs activities abroad, total and by industry and country of location[1]		
Value added		X
Sales or turnover		X
Number of people in employment		X
R&D expenditure*		X
Number of researchers*		X
Technological payments and receipt*		X
Total exports and imports**		X
Intra-firm exports and imports**		X

* Variables relating to indicators discussed in Chapter 4.

** Variables relating to indicators discussed in Chapter 5.

1. See discussion on target population in Section 3.3.1.

3.2.5.2. *Priority for data collection*

242. This section primarily focuses on the key variables that need to be collected so as to construct the reference indicators, but prior to doing so it is useful to provide broad guidance as to the relative priorities assigned to data compilation based on the nature of the activity of the multinational enterprise. A **first priority**, based on both availability which minimises respondent burden and its analytical importance is placed on variables that describe the activity of foreign-CAs – enterprises under foreign control in compiling countries. A **second priority** is placed on variables that describe the activities of parent companies in the compiling country. A **third priority** is placed on variables that describe activities of CA' abroad – enterprises controlled by parent companies in the compiling country. The various methods for collecting these different categories of AMNE data are described in Section 3.3.1.

3.2.5.3. *Variables definition*

243. This section provides brief but comprehensive definitions for the variables required to construct the globalisation indicators. References to the relevant manual are also provided to guide national statisticians if further readings are necessary.

244. AMNE data, in accordance with SNA 1993, should theoretically be recorded on the basis of current year accounting data. Variables for flows such as output and value added should relate to the reference year. Variables for stocks ought to correspond to those for the end of the reference period, which as far as possible should coincide with the calendar year. Countries that can gather and compile data only on a fiscal or accounting year basis are invited to submit notes explaining their practice, specifying the difference between the fiscal year and the calendar year.

OECD HANDBOOK ON ECONOMIC GLOBALISATION INDICATORS – ISBN 92-64-10808-4 – © OECD 2005

Value added

245. SNA 1993 defines "the gross value added of an establishment, enterprise, industry or sector" as "the value of output less the value of intermediate consumption"; the "net value added" is defined as "the value of output less the values of both intermediate consumption and consumption of fixed capital" (SNA 1993, §6.222). "Gross value added can provide information about the contribution of foreign affiliates to host-country gross domestic product, both in the aggregate and in specific industries. For this reason, and because it may often be easier to compute (because it does not require estimation of capital consumption) and is thus more widely available, the higher priority should be accorded to the gross measure of value added" (MSITS Chapter 4, §4.58).

246. Gross value added may be obtained by associating different price vectors with a given vector of input and output quantities. "Gross value added at basic prices is defined as output valued at basic prices less intermediate consumption valued at purchaser's prices..." (SNA 1993, §6.226). "Gross value added at factor cost is not a concept used explicitly in the SNA. Nevertheless, it can easily be derived from either of the measures of gross value added by subtracting the value of any taxes, less subsidies, on production payable out of gross value added as defined... Gross value added at factor cost can therefore be derived from gross value added at basic prices by subtracting "other taxes, less subsidies, on production. The conceptual difficulty with gross value added at factor cost is that there is no observable vector of prices, such that gross value added at factor cost is obtained directly by multiplying the price vector by the vector of quantities of inputs and outputs that defines the production process. By definition, other taxes and subsidies on production are not taxes or subsidies on products that can be eliminated from the input and output prices. Thus, despite its traditional name, gross value added at factor cost is not strictly a measure of value added. Gross value added at factor cost is essentially a measure of income and not output..." (SNA 1993, §6.229-6.231).

247. "... Although it is defined in terms of outputs and intermediate inputs, value added also is equal to the sum of primary incomes generated in production (compensation of employees, profits, etc.). In some cases, depending on the particular data that are available, this equivalence may be exploited in deriving estimates of value added. This alternative might be chosen, for example, if data on intermediate consumption were lacking but information on the various incomes generated in production were available" (MSITS, Chapter 4, §4.59).

Gross output (production)

248. "The gross output value measures the amount actually produced by the enterprise, based on sales, including changes in stocks and the resale of goods and services. The gross output value is defined as turnover, plus or minus the changes in stocks (finished products, work-in-progress and goods and services purchased for resale), minus the purchases of goods and services for resale, plus capitalised production, plus other operating income (excluding subsidies). Capitalised gross output includes the own-account production of all goods that are retained by their producers as investment. The latter includes the gross output of fixed tangible assets (buildings, etc.) as well as intangible assets (development of software, etc.). Capitalised gross output is unsold gross output and is valued at production cost. It should be noted that these capital goods are also to be included in investment" (*Definition of Economic Variables*, Code 12120, Eurostat).

249. Special considerations arise in defining gross output in service industries. As noted in Chapter 4 of the MSITS, "Service activities do not involve stocks of finished goods, and changes in work-in-progress will usually be impossible to measure. In practice, therefore, measured output will be identical to sales for most service activities. For wholesale and retail distribution, although the sales are of goods, the output is defined as a service, equal not to the total value of sales but to the trade margins realised on goods purchased for resale. For financial intermediaries, output is equal to service charges actually levied, plus *financial intermediation services indirectly measured*, the values of which are estimated from the difference between the property incomes received by financial intermediaries from the investment of borrowed funds, and the interest they themselves pay on such funds. For insurance, output is measured not by total premiums earned, but by a service charge that takes into account income on technical reserves and also the actual or expected value of claims. In all these cases, output will generally be considerably lower than sales because it, unlike sales, excludes the amounts – which may constitute a large portion of total operating revenues – that pass through the enterprise without being considered a part of its intermediate consumption" (MSITS Chapter 4, §4.49).

Sales (turnover)

250. "Sales and turnover are used here interchangeably to mean the same thing. Following the 1993 SNA (which may be consulted for additional details and examples), *gross output* differs from sales because it includes changes in stocks of finished goods and work-in-progress and because of differences in measurement applicable to activities involving trade or financial intermediation. Gross output is a superior and more refined measure of activity for most purposes and is recommended as the preferred variable for compilation. However, turnover/sales data are easier to collect and may present more options for disaggregation. Thus, there may be a continuing role for both measures in statistics on foreign-controlled enterprises" (MSITS, Chapter 4, §4.48).

251. "Turnover comprises the totals invoiced by the unit of observation during the reference period, and this corresponds to market sales of goods or services. Turnover includes all duties and taxes on the goods or services invoiced by the unit with the exception of the value added tax invoiced by the unit *vis-à-vis* its customer and other similar deductible taxes directly linked to turnover. It also includes all other charges (transport, packaging, etc.) passed on to the customer, even if these charges are listed separately in the invoice. Reduction in prices, rebated as well as the value of returned packing must be deducted. Income classified as other operating income, financial income and extra-ordinary income in enterprise accounts is excluded from turnover. Operating subsidies received from public authorities are also excluded" (*Definition of Economic Variables*, Code 11210, Eurostat).

252. "Sales measure gross operating revenues, less rebates, discounts and returns. Sales should be measured exclusive of consumption and sales taxes. Although lacking the duplication-free quality of value added, the sales variable generally presents fewer collection difficulties and thus is likely to be more widely available than value added. Also, unlike value added, sales indicate the extent to which foreign affiliates are used to deliver outputs to customers, irrespective of the extent to which the output originated in the affiliates themselves or in other firms. Further, sales are more comparable than value added with regard to such variables as exports and imports, which are themselves measures of sales" (MSITS, Chapter 4, §4.50).

253. "In addition to disaggregation by industry and by country (following the principles of attribution discussed later), other breakdowns of sales may be useful for particular purposes. One such breakdown for inward investment would be to distinguish among: *a)* sales within the host country (local sales), *b)* sales to the country of the parent company (immediate investor) and *c)* sales to third countries[3]. All three types of sales result from a commercial presence by the home country in the host country. However, only the local sales represent the delivery of output within host economies and thus relate directly to the commitments made under the GATS Mode 3[4] by those economies. In addition, elimination of the sales to the country of the parent company (which would already be included as imports in that country's balance of payments accounts) may be desired in an analysis of variables on the activity of multinational enterprises in conjunction with data on the parent company country's trade with non-residents to avoid duplication" (MSITS, Chapter 4, §4.51).

254. Sales of services would include both sales of services by enterprises that produce services as a primary activity and sales of services by enterprises that produce goods as a primary activity but have secondary operations in services. It should be observed that sales made by units included in the trade sector mainly reflect sales of goods. However, for other indicators such as output employment, these units are classified among services (see below).

Gross fixed capital formation

255. Gross fixed capital formation is measured by the total value of a producer's acquisitions, less disposals, of fixed assets during the accounting period plus certain additions to the value of non-produced assets realised by the productive activity of institutional units. Fixed assets are tangible or intangible assets produced as outputs from processes of production, that are themselves used repeatedly or continuously in other processes of production for more than one year. There is substantial diversity in different types of gross fixed capital formation that may take place. The following main types may be distinguished:

i) Acquisitions less disposals of new or existing tangible fixed assets subdivided by type of asset into:
- Dwellings.
- Other buildings and structures.
- Machinery and equipment.
- Cultivated assets that are used to produce products.

ii) Acquisitions less disposals of new and existing intangible fixed assets, subdivided by type of asset into:
- Mineral exploration.
- Computer software.
- Entertainment, literary or artistic originals.
- Other intangible fixed assets.

iii) Major improvements to tangible non-produced assets, including land.

iv) Costs associated with the transfers of ownership of non-produced assets. (SNA 1993, §10.33-10.34)

256. "All these investments are valued gross, *i.e.* prior to all adjustments of book value and before deduction of sales. The assets purchased are valued at purchase cost, *i.e.* including transport and installation costs, duties and fees, and property transfer costs. Own-account produced tangible assets are valued at product cost. When investments are large-scale and spread over more than one reference period, each instalment of expenditure must be booked as an investment made during the reference period to which that instalment relates. Assets acquired through mergers are not counted. Purchases of minor non-fixed assets count as current expenditure. This category of investment also includes additions, alterations, improvements and repairs to extend the normal useful life or increase the productivity of existing fixed assets. It excludes current expenditure on capital equipment used under lease or lease with option of purchase. It also excludes investment in intangible fixed assets and in financial assets" (*Definition of Economic Variables*, Code 15110, Eurostat).

Number of people in employment

257. "The number of persons employed is defined as the total number of persons working in the unit observed (including owner operators, associates performing a regular activity in the unit and unpaid family helpers). Included in this category are workers on short leave but not workers absent for an unlimited period. Also included are part-time workers considered as such under the national legislation and figuring on the unit's list of employees, together with seasonal workers, apprentices and family workers figuring on that list. Excluded from this category are workers loaned to the unit by other enterprises, persons performing repairs and maintenance in the unit on account of other enterprises, and draftees" (*Definition of Economic Variables*, Code 16110, Eurostat).

258. "In the context of statistics on the activity of multinational enterprises, employment would normally be measured as the number of persons on the payrolls of foreign affiliates. Employment data are sometimes converted to a 'full-time equivalent' (FTE) basis, in which part-time workers are counted according to the time worked (*e.g.* two workers on half-time schedules count the same as one full-time worker). Although FTE employment may provide a better measure of labour input, this measure is not as widely available as numbers of employees and may be difficult to implement consistently in the context of internationally varied employment practices. For these reasons, the recommendation of this *Handbook* is that the employment variable be the number of persons employed. The number should be representative of the period covered, but in the absence of strong seasonal or other fluctuations in employment, it may be measured as of a point in time, such as the end of the year, following national practices" (MSITS, Chapter 4, §4.55).

259. "Data on employment by affiliates can be used in several ways in a system to establish statistics on the activity of foreign-controlled enterprises. They can be used in determining the share of foreign-controlled enterprises in host country employment, or in attempts to determine the extent to which employment by foreign affiliates complement or substitute for domestic (home country) employment by parent companies or other domestic enterprises. An industry breakdown of affiliates' employment can yield further insights into the impact of foreign-owned enterprises on specific parts of the economy. Used in conjunction with data on compensation of employees, the employment variable may be used in examining compensation practices of foreign affiliates relative to those of domestically owned enterprises" (MSITS, Chapter 4, §4.56).

Employee compensation

260. "Employee compensation is defined as the total remuneration, in cash or in kind, payable by an enterprise to an employee in return for work done by the latter during the accounting period. Compensation of employees has two main components:

i) Wages and salaries payable in cash or in kind.

ii) The value of the social contributions payable by employers; these may be actual social contributions payable by employers to social security schemes or to privately funded social insurance schemes to secure social benefits for their employees; or imputed social contributions by employers providing unfunded social benefits." (SNA 1993, §7.21 and 7.31)

261. "Social security costs for the employer include the employer's social security contributions to schemes for retirement pensions, sickness, maternity, disability, unemployment, occupational accidents and diseases, and family allowances as well other schemes. Optional social benefits are also a cost for the employer" (*Definition of Economic Variables*, Code 13330, Eurostat).

Number of establishments or enterprises

262. "The number of enterprises (or establishments, where that is the statistical unit) meeting the criteria for coverage by statistics on foreign-CAs is a basic indicator of the prevalence of majority ownership by foreigners in the host economy. This number may be compared with the total number of enterprises (or establishments) in the economy. It may also be assessed in relation to the other variables because it allows the computation of ratios – such as value added or number of employees per enterprise – that may be compared with the same ratios for national enterprises, thus giving an indication of the behaviour of foreign affiliates" (MSITS, Chapter 4, §4.64).

263. It should be made clear that the enterprises to be taken into account in these statistics are those with a genuine economic activity. Firms which have no activity, but simply set up an office in a country for the purpose of transferring funds or taking advantage of certain tax breaks, should be excluded from this category of data.

264. "It should be recognised that the number of enterprises alone may not give an accurate picture of the overall importance of foreign-owned enterprises, because of differences in size between these enterprises and those that are domestically owned. If the foreign-owned enterprises tend to be larger, for example, then their share in the total number of enterprises would be smaller than their share in the various measures of operations and would thus tend to understate the role and importance of these enterprises in host country economies" (MSITS, Chapter 4, §4.65).

265. As a rule, the statistics currently gathered in a majority of OECD countries show that the ratio of the number of foreign-controlled enterprises to the total number of host country enterprises is between one-third and one-fifth as great as the same ratio in respect of turnover or output.

266. "Typically, information on numbers of enterprises will be a natural by-product of collection of data on other variables, rather than a separate object of the data collection effort. As such, the number is likely to be affected, often significantly, by the level of enterprise consolidation and by thresholds for reporting on surveys. To assist users in

interpreting counts of enterprises (or establishments), countries are encouraged to indicate in explanatory notes how the numbers were derived" (MSITS, Chapter 4, §4.66).

Number of consolidated enterprises

267. The threshholds adopted for surveys of foreign CAs and on the degree of consolidation are the two most significant sources of distorsion that can affect comparisons with other variables – even inside the same country. The fact is that some enterprises present consolidated accounts and have the appearance of being a single enterprise, while others present separate, non-consolidated accounts. In such cases, it is in fact impossible to make comparisons between the number of foreign-controlled enterprises and the number of resident-controlled enterprises, so national authorities ought ideally to collect data on the number of enterprises on the basis of both concepts: in non-consolidated and consolidated form. Recording the number of CAs in consolidated form will also have the advantage of providing data that are more comparable with parent company data which are systematically requested in consolidated form. The result is that both types of firm will be more comparable within a given compiling country.

Gross operating surplus

268. Gross operating surplus is the balancing item. In the generation of income account, it is defined as:

- Gross value added:

  minus: compensation of employees payable;

  minus: taxes on production payable;

  plus: subsidies receivable (SNA 1993, §7.80).

269. It will be remembered that employee compensation includes: *a)* wages and salaries; and *b)* employer's social security contributions.

Taxes on income

270. "These consist of corporate income taxes, corporate profit taxes, corporate surtaxes, etc., as well as taxes that accrue to owners of incorporated enterprises as a result of the income of those enterprises. Taxes on income include only taxes in the host country of the affiliate and not any taxes paid by the parent in the home country as a result of income earned or distributed by the affiliate. Taxes on income are usually assessed on the total income of corporations from all sources and not simply on profits generated by production" (MSITS, Chapter 4, §4.68).

R&D expenditures

271. R&D expenditures cover all expenditures for activities undertaken for the purpose of discovering or developing new products (goods and services) including improved versions of existing products or discovering or developing new or more efficient processes of products. These expenditures in the framework of this *Handbook* concern exclusively the enterprise sector, in which are included "all firms, organisations and institutions whose primary activity is the market production of goods or services for sale to the general public at an economically significant price ..." (*Frascati Manual*, §163).

272. Three types of R&D may be distinguished:

- *Basic research*, which is experimental or theoretical work undertaken primarily to acquire new knowledge of the underlying foundations of phenomena and observable facts, without any particular application or use in view.
- *Applied research*, which is also original investigation undertaken in order to acquire new knowledge. It is, however, directed primarily towards a specific practical aim or objective.
- *Experimental development*, which is a systematic work, drawing on knowledge gained from research and practical experience that is directed to producing new materials, products and devices; to installing new processes, systems and services; or to improving substantially those already produced or installed (*Frascati Manual*, §240, 245, 249).

273. R&D expenditure comprises: *current costs* and *capital expenditure*. Current costs are composed of: labour costs, which are the largest component of current costs and other current costs which comprise non-capital purchases of materials, supplies and equipment to support R&D in a given year. Capital expenditure is the annual gross expenditure on fixed assets used in the R&D programmes. It should be reported in full for the period when it took place and should not be registered as an element of depreciation (*Frascati Manual*, §358, 360, 374.) Capital expenditure is composed of expenditure on:

- Land and building.
- Investment and equipment.
- Computer software.

274. The role of R&D in the activity of multinationals (parent companies and their affiliates), the main reference indicators and all the associated variables are presented in Chapter 4 of the *Handbook*, entitled "Internationalisation of Technology".

Number of researchers

275. According the *Frascati Manual* definitions, "researchers are professionals engaged in the conception or creation of new knowledge, products, processes, methods and systems and also in the management of the projects concerned" (*Frascati Manual*, 2002 edition, §301). "Managers and administrators engaged in the planning and management of the scientific and technical aspects of a researcher's work also fall into this category" (§303). "Postgraduate students at the PhD level engaged in R&D should be considered as researchers" (§305). As for the other categories of data on the number of persons in employment, the number of researchers should be calculated in "full-time equivalents".

Technology payments and receipts

276. What is involved here is measuring the outward and inward financial flows deriving from a compiling country's multinational firms' sales and purchases of technologies in the form of transfers of patents, non-patented inventions, the granting of franchises linked to patents, the communication of know-how, transfers of designs, brands or models, and technical and R&D services of an industrial nature. For more detailed information, see also Chapter 4, Section 4.4.

Total exports and imports of goods and services

277. Exports and imports of goods and services is another relevant indicator for the activity of multinational firms. "Both balance of payments data and data provided by

parent enterprises and affiliates in separate questionnaires may be appropriate sources for such information ..." "Although linkages with balance of payments data may thus provide useful information, it often will be difficult or impossible to separately identify the transactions of foreign-owned firms in those data. Thus it may be possible to develop the data on exports and imports only through the use of separate questionnaires. In that event, those same breakdowns would be useful, but it is unlikely that a large number of countries would be able to collect the necessary data with the same frequency or the same detail as provided by balance of payments data" (MSITS, Chapter 4, §463).

Intra-firm exports and imports

278. In the context of a compiling country, intra-firm exports and imports consist: *a)* of the exports and imports of foreign-CAs of the parent company abroad – to the group in the case of exports and from the group in the case of imports; and *b)* of the exports and imports of parent companies in the compiling country to and from their foreign-CAs. For more details, see also Chapter 5, Section 5.3.2.

3.3. Conceptual and methodological considerations

3.3.1. *Defining target populations*

279. This section describes briefly the target population for compiling AMNE so as to improve international comparability while meeting national requirements. It first discusses target populations for measuring AMNE within the compiling country that meet national requirements for analysis and produce internationally comparable and additive data. Second, the target populations measuring AMNE abroad are discussed. Recommendations are made so as to demonstrate how countries could provide internationally comparable data without prejudice to these national requirements.

3.3.1.1. *Target populations for AMNE data in compiling country*

280. Policy makers and analysts interested in the activities of MNE in their country are concerned with:

- The impact of foreign-CAs on their economy and how they compare to other enterprises in their economy. Are they more profitable or productive, are they more concentrated in certain industries, do they pay higher or lower wages, etc.?
- The impact of MNE's based in their country (parent companies) on their economy. Do their foreign investments have a positive or negative impact on domestic employment and trade?
- The impact of MNE on their economy (both controlled by residents and foreigners). What is the MNE share in domestic economic activities (employment, investment, value added, trade, etc.)?

281. The first issue requires that economic variables for foreign-CAs (*e.g.* employment, value added, gross output, GFCF, etc.) be separately identifiable in national totals.

282. The second issue requires that the same economic variables be broken down by enterprises in the compiling country with CAs abroad.

283. The third issue requires that the same domestic economic variables be broken down between MNE and other categories of enterprise. Unfortunately, population estimates concerning these two categories of enterprise can not be derived from data on foreign-CAs

and parent companies. In fact, one major drawback of these two target populations (foreign-CAs and parent companies) is that they could overlap. Foreign-CAs can also control affiliates abroad and are therefore included in both the foreign-CA and parent target populations (*e.g.* Chrysler affiliates in Canada). This overlap creates double-counting when estimating total AMNE in a country and across countries, as adding up foreign-CAs' and parent companies' activities would double-count the activities related to foreign-CAs with CAs abroad. However, from the point of view of the compiling country, the overlap between foreign-CAs and parent companies is not a big deal; if data are available on both groups of enterprises, compilers will undoubtedly be able to identify enterprises that are both parents and foreign-controlled, and should be able to separately tabulate data for them. The confidentiality issues are really the main constraint on making such detail public.

284. There are two ways to estimate total AMNE in the compiling country. To better understand these two options, the following presents a mutually exclusive classification of enterprises that satisfies the three issued mentioned above:

i) Foreign-CAs without CA abroad.

ii) Parent companies under foreign control (foreign CAs with CAs abroad).

iii) Parent companies controlled by residents of the compiling country.

iv) Enterprises controlled by residents of the compiling country and without CAs abroad (non-MNEs).

285. With this classification, foreign-CA based analysis would sum up the first two classes; parent based analysis would aggregate classes 2 and 3; total MNE activities could be derived as the sum of classes 1, 2, and 3 or as the residual between the total and the non-MNE population.

286. This classification can be very useful to analysts and researchers. First, it provides mutually exclusive population classes to compare performance among firms or group of firms. For example, to find out if foreign-controlled MNEs do better than MNEs controlled by residents, analysts need to compare macro or micro economic data that can split domestic enterprises into these two groups. The foreign-CA and parent company's data would not provide them with such a distinction, as both include some foreign-controlled MNEs (foreign-CAs controlling affiliates abroad). If this type of firm is important in one country, statistical inference using a classification based on foreign-CAs and parent companies would be problematic, as the assumption of independence between the two populations would be violated. Second, the foreign-CAs with affiliates abroad is an interesting population to study, especially if it is important in a country. Is this type of firm increasing? Are there any advantages to use particular countries to indirectly control affiliates abroad rather than controlling them directly? Does their performance differ from other foreign-CAs and other parent companies? These questions can only be answered with statistics on these different populations. Third, international studies require national statistics that can be compared with some analytical validity. Comparing parent companies' statistics from different countries could be misleading if the foreign-controlled MNE portion of this population varies significantly among countries under study.

287. Analysts and statistical agencies would benefit from a breakdown of domestic activities into these four target populations. At present, countries do not have the same practices regarding parent companies. Some countries count jointly as parent companies both resident-controlled and foreign-controlled companies, while others consider only companies controlled solely by residents as parent companies. The present *Handbook* encourages countries that do not yet distinguish between the two categories of parent

company to do so, even at an aggregated level. Countries which do not identify foreign-controlled parent companies should also endeavour to do so at an aggregated level.

288. Note that if one of these first three target populations is known as well as the totals for all foreign-CAs and all parent companies, then the other populations can be derived. For example, if employment in foreign-CAs with CAs abroad is known, then the employment in foreign-CAs without CA abroad can be derived as a residual from the total foreign-CAs' employment. The employment in parent companies under foreign control should be equal to employment in foreign-CAs with CA abroad. Thus, the employment in parent companies controlled by residents of the compiling country can be derived residually. The employment in the non-MNEs (enterprises controlled by residents in the compiling country and without CA abroad is the residual between total and MNE employment (the sum for the other three populations).[5]

289. Countries developing their AMNE statistics programme should use the four target populations to compile data. It is important to remember that confidentiality issues are very important when publishing data. For example, if the number of foreign-CAs with CAs abroad is very small, it might be impossible to disseminate data for this population by industry and country of control. In this case, it is recommended that countries publish the most relevant population estimates to meet national requirements and provide estimates that would show how important the overlap is (for example, total employment for class 2 with no breakdown by industry or country of control).

Box 3.3. **Recommendations for target populations in compiling country**

Countries which start producing AMNE data for their economic territory are invited to classify enterprises into the following four categories:

Under foreign control

1. Foreign-controlled affiliates (CAs) without CA abroad.
2. Foreign-controlled affiliates (CAs) with CAs abroad (parent companies under foreign control).

Controlled by residents of compiling countries

3. Parent companies with CAs abroad.
4. Non-MNEs (no CAs abroad).

If member countries are not able to distinguish between parent companies controlled by residents and parents under foreign control at the sectoral level owing to the confidentiality of data, they are invited to make this distinction at least at the most aggregated level (grand total) for each variable.

3.3.1.2. *Target populations for AMNE abroad*

290. Policy makers and analysts interested in the activities of MNE abroad are mostly concerned with:

- The impact of the activities of CAs abroad on their domestic economy (trade, employment, etc.).
- The impact of CAs abroad on the economic activity of other countries.

291. For AMNE abroad two target populations have to be determined:

i) The population of the parents controlled by residents of the compiling country and those under foreign control.

ii) The population of the CAs abroad should include affiliates under direct (and, if possible, indirect) control.

292. Analysts are mostly interested in the world-wide impact of MNEs investing abroad (all parent companies and all their affiliates). Some countries that have developed surveys trying to measure AMNE abroad have used this approach. This leads however to double counting at the international level, as the direct and indirect impact of the parent companies under foreign control are included in both the country of immediate and ultimate control.

293. Two options can be considered to resolve this double-counting problem:

- The *immediate control approach* where the target population includes all parents but only measures the CAs abroad under the direct or immediate control of parent companies residing in the compiling country. In this approach only the relationship between firms residing in two countries are considered. This approach is recommended to measure FDI flows (see Chapter 2). This avoids duplications resulting when aggregating flows across countries.
- The *ultimate control approach,* where the target population includes only enterprises under the ultimate control of residents of the compiling country with CAs abroad controlled directly and indirectly.

294. Given that AMNE data analysis is concerned primarily with who controls what and where rather than what the direct impact of the control is, the second approach is the most appropriate for international comparison. This is of course very different than for FDI flows, which is concerned with who invests where. But, given that available data on the activity of multinationals abroad generally include all CAs abroad of all parent companies and that this approach is recommended by MSITS for collecting this type of data, this

Box 3.4. **Recommendations for the target population of AMNE abroad**

First priority

It is recommended that countries provide data on CAs' activity abroad under direct control of all the parent companies in the compiling country. These data should be broken down by industry and by CAs' country of location. In order to enhance the analytical value of these data, it is advisable to split them into parent companies under the ultimate control of *a)* residents and *b)* non-residents.

Second priority

Member countries are invited to provide data separately on the activity of CAs abroad controlled directly and indirectly (see definitions, Section 3.3.3.2) by all parent companies in the compiling country.

Third priority

Member countries providing data based on the second priority are also invited to provide data consistent with the "ultimate control approach" on the activity of CAs abroad controlled directly and indirectly by parent companies under the ultimate control of residents of the compiling country.

Handbook recommends that this approach be adopted by OECD countries. It is recognized, however, that some countries are not able to collect data on the activity abroad of all their affiliates, especially those controlled by their own affiliates (indirect control). This is why it is suggested that the first priority be to identify the activity of CAs abroad controlled directly by the parent companies in compiling countries (whether they be resident-controlled or foreign-controlled). As a second priority, however, countries are strongly recommended also to provide data on the activity of their indirectly controlled CAs abroad (without necessarily separating the data for directly and indirectly controlled affiliates). Moreover a number of countries receive consolidated data on the activity of their CAs abroad and are unable to distinguish between the activities of directly and indirectly controlled affiliates. Lastly, countries able to do so are also invited to identify separately the activity of CAs (direct and indirect) of parent companies controlled exclusively by residents of the country in question.

3.3.2. *Identifying foreign control of an enterprise*

295. Recommendations for identifying foreign control of an enterprise are summarised in Box 3.5 and discussed below. These recommendations and the following discussion which supports them are primarily oriented towards inward investment. The focus is on majority control and no attempt is made to specifically address the issues of minority control or influence. (Annex 3.1 contains a series of "special cases" that compilers may face such as the issue of foreign influence but no attempt is made to provide methodological recommendations.)

296. Because the overriding criterion in AMNE data is that of control, not all direct investment companies are included. By definition, enterprises under foreign control are in principle a sub-population of direct investment enterprises. In Figure 2.1, foreign-CA statistics would cover companies A, B, H, K and L (subsidiary or branches) but would exclude the other direct investment enterprises, *i.e.* companies C, D, E, F, G, J, P and Q (associates). Companies A, H and K are controlled by enterprise N directly, and companies B and L indirectly.

3.3.2.1. *The notion of "control" of an enterprise*

297. It was indicated in Chapter 2, in talking about FDI data, that the basic criterion used to determine whether an investment is a direct investment is its capacity to exert "influence" on company management. The notion of influence is reflected, in statistical terms, in the holding of more than 10% of the ordinary shares or voting rights, while any investment below 10% is considered to be portfolio investment. Concerning data on the activities of multinational enterprises, the notion of influence is not sufficient to allow data to be collected in a coherent and operational manner, whence the need to resort to the notion of "control".

298. The notion of control implies the ability to appoint a majority of administrators empowered to direct an enterprise, to guide its activities and determine its strategy. In most cases, this ability can be exercised by a single investor holding a majority (more than 50%) of the shares with voting rights.

299. The notion of control allows all of a company's activities to be attributed to the controlling investor. This means that variables such as a company's turnover, staff or exports are all attributed to the controlling investor and the country from which he comes.

300. Switching from the notion of "influence" to the notion of "control", used mainly for data on the activity of multinational enterprises, reflects two different rationales. Where

OECD HANDBOOK ON ECONOMIC GLOBALISATION INDICATORS – ISBN 92-64-10808-4 – © OECD 2005

influence is concerned, production, value added, the number of employees or other variables are attributed according to the shareholders' percentage stake in the enterprise, and in this way it is the "financial" aspect that predominates, whereas in the case of control it is the "power to take decisions" and "decide corporate strategy" that comes first.

301. When, in the case of control, all of an enterprise's economic variables are attributed to a single majority shareholder, it does not of course mean that the latter appropriates all the enterprise's output or profits, but that it determines all the strategic choices. Where firms' activity is concerned, however, there are other reasons for taking a control-based approach. When there are numerous minority shareholders and when the chain of indirectly controlled companies is also included, the process of attributing the variables according to the principles of ownership becomes much more complicated, and that difficulty is compounded when the investors' countries of residence have to be attributed to these variables. The notion of control is not really new, having already been defined in SNA 1993 and then in MSITS (§4.17).

302. SNA 1993 (§4.27) cites majority ownership by an organised group of shareholders acting in concert as clear evidence of control. In their definition of a direct investor, IMF *MBP5* and OECD *Benchmark Definition* also consider the shares held by members of a group of associates as equivalent to shares held by a single investor. However, the question that arises in this case is how to know whether the foreign investors are linked and have a concerted strategy.

303. NA 1993, IMF *MBP5* and OECD *Benchmark Definition* do not specify the criteria that should be applied in order to identify an associated group of investors. Only the MSITS (§4.20, footnote 62) gives some examples – themselves extracted from the *Benchmark survey of foreign direct investment in the United States* – that may be taken into account. It states that an associated group consists of "two or more persons who, by the appearance of their actions, by agreement, or by an understanding, exercise or appear to exercise their voting privileges in a concerted manner to influence the management of a business enterprise". The following entities are considered to constitute groups of associates: members of the same family, a business enterprise and one or more of its officers or directors, members of a syndicate or joint venture, or a corporation and its domestic subsidiaries.

304. It should be specified that, in contrast with the principles adopted in the framework of the National Accounts (SNA 93), this *Handbook* does not recommend that countries identify the share of enterprises that are under minority foreign control. It is aligned rather on the recommendations in Chapter 4 of the Manual on Statistics of International Trade in Services (MSITS), which excludes from the statistics data on the activity of firms under minority control.

305. In some countries, control of a company is determined by law; in Canada, for example, it is a matter of being able to choose a company's board of directors. This means that the statistical surveys proposed by the *Handbook* will have to be combined with national choices. In any event, the recommendation is that, whenever the national authorities are not in a position to prove that a company is under foreign control, the said company should be considered to be controlled by the residents of the compiling country. For cases which do not belong to any broad categories, countries are invited to provide separate and additional statistics (examples including the control of certain companies in the developing countries, where foreign investors are prevented by law from taking a majority holding).

Box 3.5. **Recommendations for identifying companies under foreign control**

Recommended definition

To classify an enterprise within a country on the basis of the presence or absence of effective foreign control, the criterion recommended for use is whether or not a majority of ordinary shares or voting power (more than 50% of the capital) is held by a single foreign investor or by a group of foreign associated investors acting in concert, such as members of the same family or enterprises and their affiliates (see §303). Application of this criterion avoids the use of subjective concepts or case-by-case review. The advantage of this absence of subjectivity is to eliminate a potential source of bilateral asymmetry. This recommendation is consistent with MSITS.

Other accepted but not recommended cases of control

For some countries, and especially small ones, if foreign control can be demonstrated objectively in respect of an enterprise having multiple investors or where there is a minority shareholding, it is recommended that these countries follow the rules proposed in Annex 3.1 and Box 3.8. The countries including these cases in their definition of control are invited to provide additional statistics assessing the prevalence of such special cases. These statistics could be particularly useful in cases where certain countries impose restrictions on majority ownership by foreigners. Portfolio investment enterprises should be excluded.

3.3.2.1.1. *Direct and indirect control*

a) Inward perspective

306. Control may be either direct or indirect. In the framework of inward investment, determining the direct and/or indirect lines of control allows compilers to determine the country of immediate and ultimate control of foreign-CAs. For example, in Figure 3.1, enterprise X is a foreign-CA in compiling country 1 that is controlled directly by enterprise Y in country 2. Because enterprise Z in country 3 controls 60% of the voting shares of enterprise Y, enterprise Z indirectly controls enterprise X. Country 2 is the country of immediate control and country 3 is the country of ultimate control of enterprise X.

307. Determining direct and indirect lines of control also allows compilers to determine which enterprises within the compiling country are foreign-CAs. For example, in Figure 3.2, enterprise Y of country 2 directly controls enterprise X located in the compiling country 1; enterprise X in turn directly controls enterprises X_1 and X_3 while enterprise X_2 is directly controlled by enterprise X_1 and indirectly controlled by enterprise X. Since enterprise X of the compiling country A is under foreign control, enterprises X_1, X_2 and X_3 are also under foreign control because they are controlled directly or indirectly by enterprise X. Thus, country A would include as enterprises under foreign control the enterprises X, X_1, X_2 and X_3. Further, if AMNE data were collected at the level of the fully consolidated foreign-CA, a single consolidated report would be filed covering the consolidated activities of enterprises X, X_1, X_2, and X_3 and all intra-company transactions among those enterprises would be eliminated in consolidation.

Example of indirect control

Figure 3.1. **Indirect control in inward perspective: case 1**

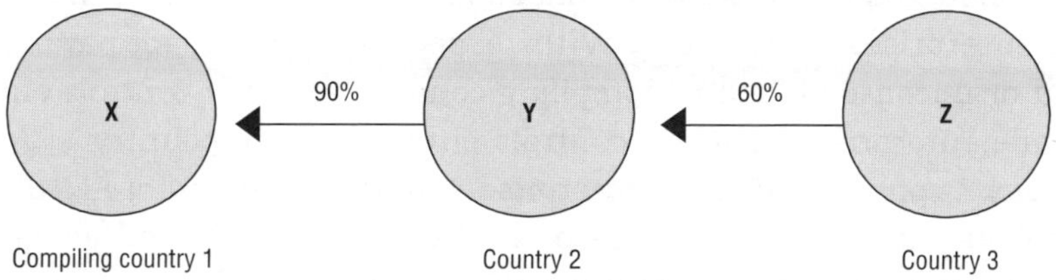

Figure 3.2. **Indirect control in inward perspective: case 2**

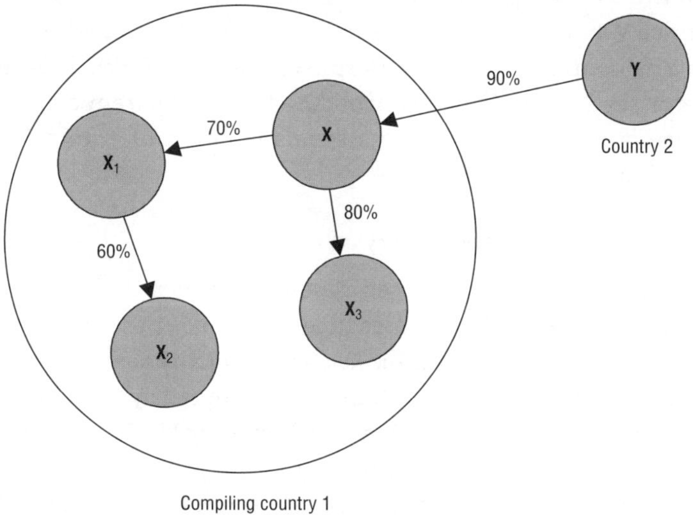

Figure 3.3. **Indirect control in outward perspective**

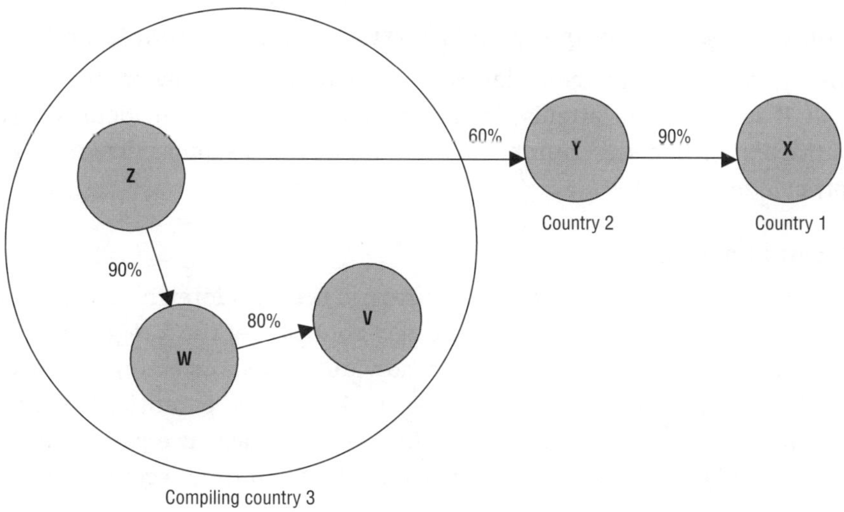

b) Outward perspective

308. In the framework of outward investments, determining direct and indirect lines of control allows compilers to identify the fully consolidated parent company in the compiling country, and to identify the country of location of each CA abroad. For example,

in Figure 3.3 in compiling country 3, enterprise Z controls directly enterprise W and controls indirectly enterprise V. Thus, if AMNE data for parent companies were compiled on a fully consolidated basis, a single consolidated report would be filed covering the activities of enterprises Z, W, and V. With respect to CAs abroad, parent company Z (consolidated or unconsolidated) in compiling country 3 directly controls enterprise Y in country 2 while enterprise Y directly controls enterprise X in country 1. Consequently, parent company Z controls indirectly enterprise X. In the collection of AMNE data for CAs abroad, variables associated with enterprise Y would be classified geographically in country 2, its country of operation, and variables associated with enterprise X would be classified in country 1, its country of operation.

309. However, in the compiling country 3, enterprise Z controls directly enterprise W and indirectly enterprise V. In other words, enterprises Z, W and V constitute a set (group) and then, enterprise Y is controlled by the enterprise group (Z, W, V). This involves that the accounts of enterprises Z, W and V are consolidated and the parent company of enterprise Y is the enterprise group (Z, W, V). Account consolidation of enterprise groups will be discussed later in this chapter.

3.3.2.1.2. Special cases based on supplementary criteria

310. Although one of the primary purposes of collecting such data is to be able to classify each country's enterprises according to presence or absence of foreign control, it has been seen earlier that the criterion applied is *the holding of majority voting power by one investor or a group of investors acting in concert*. This criterion was adopted by a Eurostat expert group on trade of foreign affiliates in the mid-1990s and adopted by MSITS. Special cases of control could nevertheless be considered in the absence of a single majority investor or a group of investors acting in concert. Although these cases are rather exceptional, they could have potential importance especially to small countries. Annexes 3.1 and 3.2 provide examples of an approach that can be used in order to determine the presence of effective control.

3.3.3. Defining the parent company and investor or unit of ultimate control

311. In theory, a firm could consider that its parent company is the firm directly controlling it. If, however, the latter is also controlled by another firm, identifying the *parent company* of the first firm raises a number of different questions, in particular that of finding the *company of ultimate control*.

3.3.3.1. Inward investment

312. The *parent* of a foreign-CA in a host country is the first foreign investor outside the borders of the country exercising direct or indirect control over the foreign subsidiary. If the parent is an individual investor or a group of individual investors acting in concert, then it is also the ultimate controller. If it is an enterprise, then the parent can be the ultimate controller or be part of an enterprise group. In this latter case, the *parent enterprise group abroad* comprises all enterprises that are controlled by the ultimate controller.

313. Thus, the parent group abroad plus its foreign-CAs in the compiling country constitute the whole enterprise group [see Box 3.7*iii)*].

Box 3.6. **Identifying the populations of direct investment companies and those relating to the activity of multinational firms**

The question is whether the population of enterprises concerned by the data on activity is a sub-population of direct investment companies.

The answer to that question depends on:

- Whether just one compiling country is being referred to, or the whole world.
- How the population of FDI enterprises is defined.
- The way in which national surveys are organised.

i) Case of a compiling country:

a) Inward investment

In principle, given that the firms concerned by the data on activity are those whose shareholders control more than 50% of the voting shares, these enterprises constitute a *sub-population* of direct investment companies.

When foreign affiliates in a compiling country set up their own affiliates in that country, these new affiliates are in principle enterprises in direct investment relations in a consolidated accounting system but in practice in some countries they are excluded from the direct investment statistics. On the other hand, they are included among the foreign-controlled companies. In this case, the population of these latter companies is a sur-population of direct investment companies. In France, for example, foreign-controlled employment is twice as high if firms excluded from direct investment statistics are taken into account.* Also, the fact that, in the case of direct investment, the investing country is the country of the immediate investor, whereas for activity data it is the country of ultimate control, does not really affect the number of enterprises concerned inside the compiling country but only changes the attribution of the investing country.

b) Outward investment

The same problems are encountered in the case of outward investment. The enterprises concerned by activity data are in large part a *sur-population* of direct investment companies, inasmuch as the compiling country's parent companies that invest abroad are included in the statistics on activity as a group (consolidated form: see the definition of parent companies in this chapter). This may not be the case in the direct investment statistics.

Also, the population of a compiling country's affiliates abroad in direct investment statistics corresponds to those affiliates in which the compiling country's parent companies invest directly, whereas statistics on activity ought in principle also to take account of indirectly controlled affiliates abroad which are often located in different countries (second priority in Box 3.4).

The population of firms in the data on activity is at the same time a *sub-population* of direct investment enterprises in the sense that the latter category also includes firms whose investors have minority holdings and do not exercise control.

It needs to be emphasized that, where inward and outward investment are concerned, the population of firms concerning activity data excludes all portfolio investment companies even if, in some extreme and clearly identified cases, a foreign investor may control a company with fewer than 10% of ordinary shares or voting power (see also Annex 3.1).

Box 3.6. **Identifying the populations of direct investment companies and those relating to the activity of multinational firms** *(cont.)*

ii) Case of the whole world

When all the countries in the world are considered at the same time, a large proportion of indirectly controlled firms excluded from a compiling country's direct investment statistics are recorded by other countries as direct investment companies. In this case, the two populations of firms come closer together, but care will have to be taken to avoid double counting (see also Section 3.3.8 on international comparability).

iii) Organisation of surveys

Another cause of differences between the population of direct investment firms and that of activity data is the way in which surveys are organised. When surveys focussing on activity data are derived from balance-of-payments and direct investment surveys, the two populations of firm are closer together. When, on the other hand, the surveys are organised separately and the data stem from company statistics (ledgers), the two populations differ quite substantially.

* The way in which the population of direct investment firms should be defined is a subject of debate and the European Central Bank set up a Task Force in 2003 to consider this matter.

Box 3.7. **Parent company and unit of ultimate control**

i) Parent company

Inward investment

The parent company of a foreign-CA in a compiling country is the first foreign investor outside the borders of the country exercising direct or indirect control over the foreign affiliate.

Outward investment

From the point of view of a compiling country, the parent company of an affiliate controlled by residents of this country and located abroad is the consolidated enterprise (enterprise group) comprising the domestic UBO controlling the firm investing abroad and the domestic firms which the preceding firm controls directly or indirectly.

ii) Unit of ultimate control

An investor (company or individual) is considered to be the *investor of ultimate control* of an investment if it is at the head of a chain of companies and directly or indirectly controls all the enterprises in the chain without itself being controlled by any other company or individual.

It might be thought that a firm's parent ought to be the company of ultimate control. While this might seem obvious in theory, it can in practice not be the case because of the difficulty of obtaining all the necessary information. In fact, it is just a question of identifying the ultimate controller and the country it belongs to, which does not pose any serious problems for the national authorities of the compiling country. It is not, on the other hand, a matter of asking for other information about the activity of the ultimate controller (*e.g.* the number of employees, value added, R&D expenditure, exports, etc.), such information being difficult to obtain when the company of ultimate control is located in a foreign country.

OECD HANDBOOK ON ECONOMIC GLOBALISATION INDICATORS – ISBN 92-64-10808-4 – © OECD 2005

Box 3.7. **Parent company and unit of ultimate control** *(cont.)*

In many cases, therefore, the parent can be a company other than the unit of ultimate control, and also have different characteristics as regards inward and outward investment.

The Ultimate Beneficial Owner (UBO) concept used in certain manuals, and especially in the MSITS, is closer to the concept of ownership than to that of control. If the foreign parent is now owned more than 50% by another person, the foreign parent and the UBO are the same. Note that a UBO, unlike a foreign parent, may be a person. Where this *Handbook* is concerned, the term "ultimate beneficiary" has been replaced by the term "unit of ultimate control".

iii) Foreign parent group

When considering the whole of a group abroad, it needs to be defined as a foreign parent group. This comprises: 1) the foreign parent; 2) any foreign person, proceeding up the foreign parent's ownership chain, that owns more than 50% of the person below it, up to and including the affiliate's ultimate controller; and 3) any person proceeding down the ownership chain that owns more than 50% of the person above it.

Figure 3.4. **Inward investment: identifying the parent company and the parent group abroad**

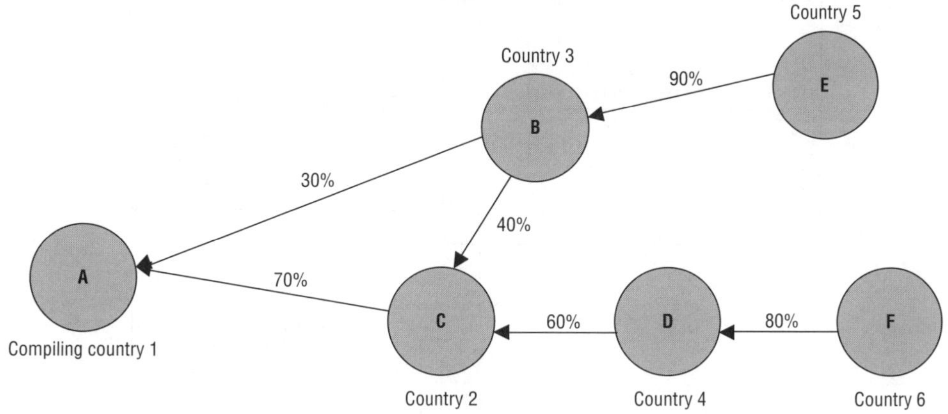

314. Figure 3.4 provides a better illustration of the definition of a first foreign parent and a parent enterprise group abroad.

315. In the example in Figure 3.4, company A in compiling country 1 is directly controlled (70%) by company C located in country 2. The remainder of its capital (30%) is owned by company B in country 3 which also owns 40% of the capital of company C. Company C is directly controlled by company D and company D by company F which are located, respectively, in countries 4 and 6. Similarly, company B has a 40% holding in company C, while the former is 90% controlled by company E which is located in country 5. Companies E and F are not controlled by any other investor.

316. In this example, company A's parent is company C which is located in country 2. Also, the ultimate controller of company A is company F and not company E, even though company E directly and indirectly holds 52.2% = [(40% × 70% = 28%) + 30%] × 90% of the capital of A, while company F owns only 33.6% = [(70% ×60%) ×80%] of the capital of A. However, company F exercises clear control over company A, which is not the case of company E. It thus transpires that company A's parent is not the same as its ultimate controller.

317. Also, company A's parent enterprise group abroad is made up of companies A, C, D and F.

3.3.3.2. *Outward investment*

318. Where outward investment is concerned, the parent company is in principle located in the compiling country. There are two possible situations: *a)* when the parent company is located in the compiling country and is controlled by the residents of the compiling country and, *b)* when the parent company, located in the compiling country, is under foreign control.

a) Parent company controlled by residents of the compiling country

319. Figure 3.5 will help to clarify this situation.

Figure 3.5. **Outward investment: identifying the parent company of compiling country 1**

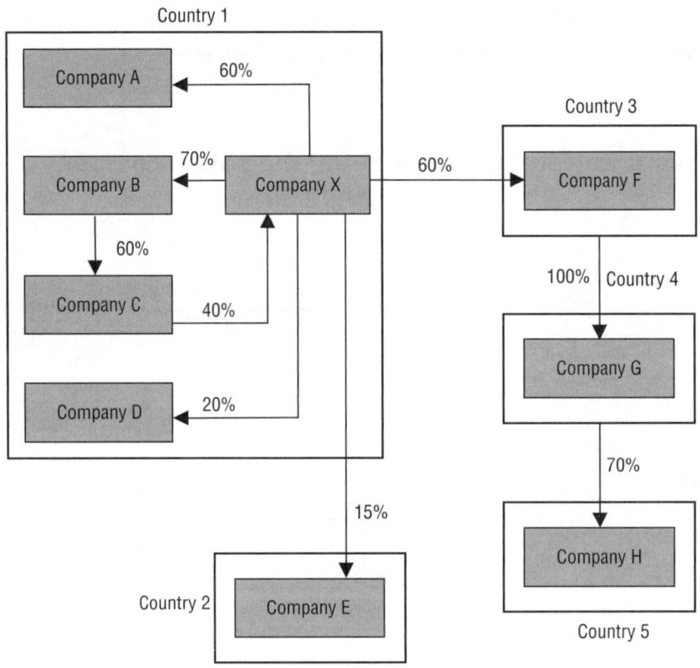

320. Companies X, A, B, C and D are located in country 1 or compiling country, while companies E, F, G and H are located in countries 2,3,4 and 5, respectively.

321. Company X owns 60% of the voting power of companies A and F, 70% of company B, 20% of company D and 15% of company E.

- Company B owns 60% of the voting power of company C.
- Company C owns 40% of the voting power of company X.
- Company F owns 100% of the voting power of company G.
- Company G owns 70% of the voting power of company H.

322. Company X directly controls companies A and B through a majority share in their capital, and has a minority share in firm D, all four being located in country 1. Similarly, company X has a minority share in company E in country 2 and directly controls company F in country 3. Company X indirectly controls company G through company F and company H through companies F and G.

323. The parent of company F in country 3 is company X in country 1. The parent of company G in country 4 is company F in country 3, while the parent of company H in country 5 is company G in country 4.

324. From the point of view of a compiling country, the parent company of its CAs abroad is the consolidated enterprise comprising: *i)* the domestic UBO controlling the firm investing abroad; and *ii)* all domestic firms in which the preceding firm or person control directly or indirectly.

325. In the context of a compiling country, *parent company* is used in this *Handbook* to refer to the *parent consolidated enterprise* or *parent enterprise group in the compiling country*. This is done to simplify terminology. In other words, there should not be any confusion because the parent company in the compiling country has to be fully consolidated for collecting data on AMNE. For example, in Figure 3.5, collecting information only on company X – which could only be an investment holding company – could greatly underestimate the activities of this MNE controlled by residents.

326. Under these circumstances, the parent company of company F is the consolidated group in country 1 made up of companies X, A, B and C. Company D is excluded from the parent company in that company X has only a minority holding in this company which could be either an independent company or belong to another group.

327. Company G's parent company is company F, while company H's parent company is company G.

328. However, the ultimate controller of companies F, G and H is the consolidated group of companies X, A, B and C.

329. The parent company in country 1 which controls the MNE consists of companies X, A, B, C, F, G and H.

b) Parent company under foreign control

330. It is possible for a company located in a compiling country, and which is under foreign control, to have CAs abroad.

Figure 3.6. **Parent company under foreign control**

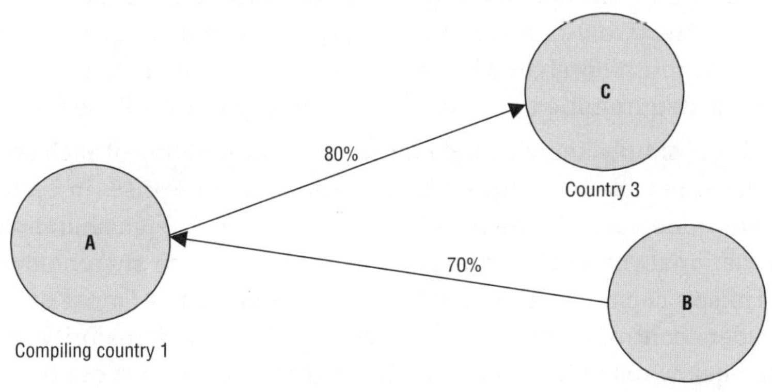

331. In the example in Figure 3.6, company A in compiling country 1 is controlled by company B in country 2, whereas company A controls company C in country 3. In this case, company A is the parent company of company C, while company B is the parent company of company A and the ultimate controller of companies A and C.

3.3.4. Classification by country of control and location

332. This *Handbook* recommends that data on the economic activity of multinational enterprises are broken down both by country of ultimate control (inward) and country of location (outward). It is therefore necessary to identify the control and location country of these enterprises in each of the two cases. In principle, an MNE investor country is that of the parent that controls it. However, it has to be established whether the majority stockholder is the immediate investor (foreign parent company) or the final investor (ultimate controller). For foreign direct investment flows, IMF *BPM5* and the OECD *Benchmark Definition* recommend attribution to the immediate investor. For stocks of direct investment, IMF *BPM5* proposes that these likewise be attributed to the immediate investor, while OECD *Benchmark Definition* proposes that they also be booked to the ultimate host (outward) or controlling country (inward). (See Chapter 2, Box 2.17 for further information.)

333. A team of Eurostat experts[6] meeting in the mid-1990s to establish statistical standards for collecting data on service activities of foreign affiliates, considered that "ultimate institutional controller" or ultimate parent was a more relevant basis. However, recognising that this principle might raise difficulties for some countries, the experts recommended a procedure in two stages: first, collection of data based on the country of the first foreign parent, to be followed later by data classified by the country of ultimate control. The data collected subsequently through the OECD/Eurostat joint surveys revealed that more than half of the reporting countries were able to provide data classified by the country of ultimate control. Consequently, the present *Handbook* recommends data collection on this basis (Box 3.7).

3.3.4.1. Foreign-CAs (inward investment)

334. In the case of inward investment, the country of control of a foreign-CA should match the country of the unit with ultimate direct or indirect control over the affiliate (see also Figure 3.4). From the example given in Figures 3.4 and 3.5, it can be seen that, on a practical level, the parent and the ultimate unit of control of a foreign-CA may be different entities.

3.3.4.2. Country of ultimate control in the absence of a single majority investor

335. The general rule recommended is to attribute to the enterprise the country of the shareholder that effectively controls the enterprise (see description in the previous section). However, if control is shared between two or three major shareholders resident in different countries, determining the country of ultimate control will be more difficult.

336. As noted above, simply knowing the percentage shareholding of each enterprise is not always sufficient to be able to deduce who controls the enterprise. In certain cases it is necessary to determine not only the possible links between foreign shareholders, but also those between national shareholders in cases where the foreign shareholders do not own all of the enterprise's capital. In the final analysis, the enterprise must be able to specify which shareholders control it, even if no one shareholder has a majority ownership. The cases illustrated below make it possible to shed light on some of these difficulties and to propose guidelines for the treatment of joint ventures and holdings.

Joint ventures

337. Two enterprises, usually from different countries, may decide to create a third enterprise in one of the countries in which they are located, or in a third country, with each

Box 3.8. **Recommendations for identifying the country of a foreign-CA in a compiling country (inward investment)**

In view of problems in identifying the country of control of foreign-CAs, it is recommended that the following rules be adopted for data collection:

- The country of control of foreign-CAs should be that of the country of residence of the ultimate controller. (See Box 3.7 for the definition of ultimate unit of control.)
- If there is ***no single majority investor***, as in the case of a joint venture, efforts should be made to avoid creating a separate category and to find some basis on which to attribute country of control to just one country. That basis, proposed in the Manual on Statistics of International Trade in Services (MSITS), could take into consideration:
  - The presence of a dominant investor;
  - The presence of investors acting in concert and between themselves holding a majority of shares (see recommendation concerning forms of control);
  - Preference should be given to an investor exercising direct control rather than to one exercising indirect control.
  - If one of two equal investors is a public entity, it should be considered as the dominant investor.
  - Given a choice between two equal investors, preference should be given to the one that is not based in a tax haven and that does not constitute a portfolio enterprise.

of them providing 50% of the assets of the new enterprise. In some cases, the assets may be split unequally. The independent status of such enterprises has certain advantages for the enterprises involved in that they can allocate quite specific tasks to it. Also, these enterprises are found in certain non-OECD countries whose legislation does not allow foreign enterprises to acquire the majority of the capital of enterprises controlled by residents.

Example

338. The most usual case occurs when two enterprises, X and Y, located in Countries 1 and 2, create a joint venture Z, in which each enterprise has a 50% interest, and which is located in Country 3.

Figure 3.7. **Example of joint venture**

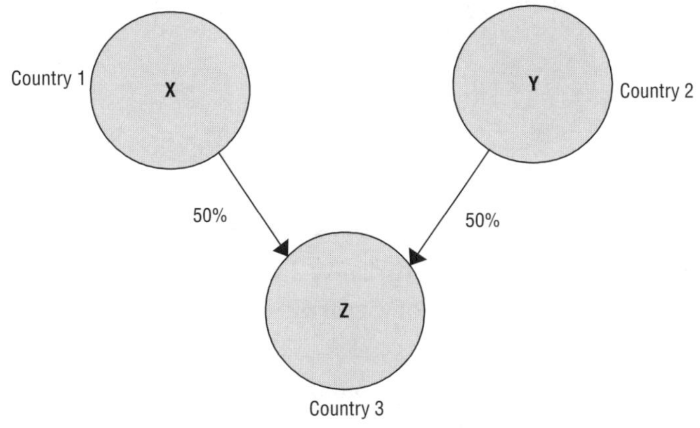

339. In the absence of any other information, the joint venture Z will have dual ownership countries, but it is important to identify one of them which could have the ultimate control.

340. In practice, as it is proposed in Box 3.8, it would be important to look at:

- Whether either of the two firms, X or Y, is the dominant investor, even if it does not hold more shares than the other. If so, the country of that dominant investor could be attributed to the joint venture Z.
- Other cases can also be examined so as to be able to attribute the totality of the variables to a single country. For example, if one investor's interests in the affiliate are held directly and the other's interests are held indirectly (see example 2), the affiliate could be classified in the country of the investor whose interests are held directly.
- In another case it can be ascertained whether one of the foreign parent is a public entity, in which case the country of that entity could be deemed to be the country of the ultimate controller.
- Lastly, if one of the owners is an investment company or a company located in a tax haven, the country of the other owner would probably be considered dominant.

Multiple ownership

Example 1

341. Enterprises X and Y in countries 1 and 2 respectively each own 50% of enterprise Z, which is located in country C. However, enterprise Y is 100% owned by enterprise W in country D.

342. In this example, the ultimate controllers of enterprise Z are enterprises X and W, but enterprise X exercises direct control while enterprise W's control is exercised indirectly.

Figure 3.8. **Example of multiple ownership with indirect control**

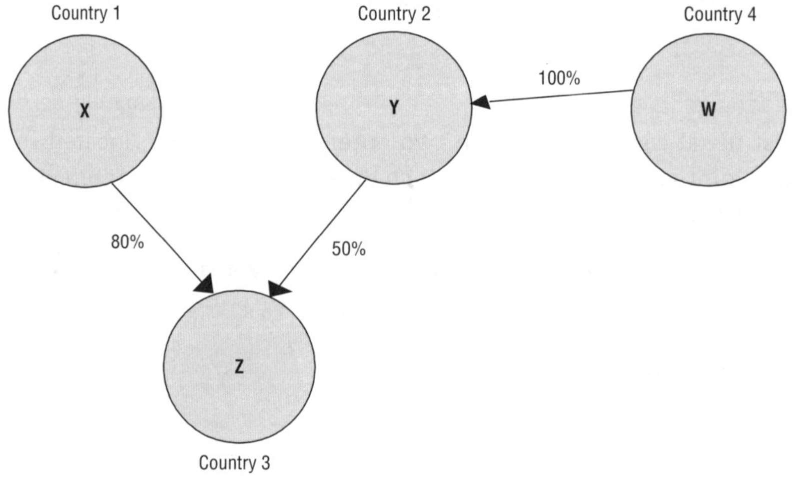

343. In this example, it will be necessary to look at whether:

- The indirect control exerted by enterprise W is weaker than that of enterprise X, in which case enterprise Z's country of control would be that of enterprise X (*i.e.* of country 1), or;
- the control exerted by enterprise W is not weaker than that of enterprise X or Y, in which case the situation is the same as in the example of joint ventures.

Example 2

344. In this example, companies X, Y and Z, located in countries 1, 2 and 3 respectively own 49%, 21% and 30% of the voting power in enterprise W, which is based in country 4. Enterprises X and Y decide to exercise joint control over enterprise W.

Figure 3.9. **Example of multiple ownership with three immediate owners**

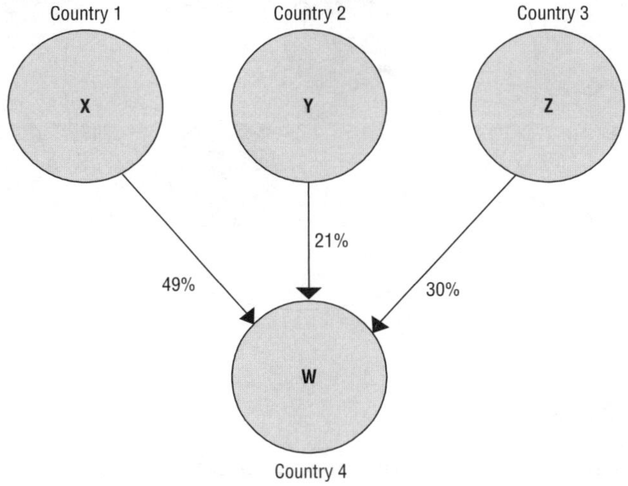

345. In this example, the capital of enterprise W is under foreign ownership and is very probably controlled by enterprise X. In practice, it will however be necessary to:

- Check whether enterprise X really controls W, and in particular whether links exist between enterprises X and Y.
- And, if the links between enterprises X and Y do prove to exist, to consider that enterprise X (country 1) controls enterprise W inasmuch as enterprise X is the dominant investor.

Holding companies

346. Holding companies are CAs abroad whose primary activity is holding the securities or financial assets of other CAs abroad located in the same or in different countries as the holding company. Use of holding companies affects the country classification of AMNE data for CAs abroad. A holding company may, or may not, have secondary activities in production or services in the country in which it is located.

347. In the case of data on economic activity, the ultimate controller will be the institutional unit(s) controlling the holding; the immediate controller would be the holding enterprise itself for investment outside the country in which it is located.

348. In the event that the holding enterprise H has no activity but finances the activities of CAs in countries 3 and 4 other than country 2 where the holding enterprise is located, it is necessary to identify the ultimate controller of enterprises Y and Z (in countries 3 and 4) which is the enterprise P of country 1 controlling the holding H. The case of holdings owned by individuals is discussed in the paragraphs that follow.

Figure 3.10. **Example of multiple owners: with holding companies**

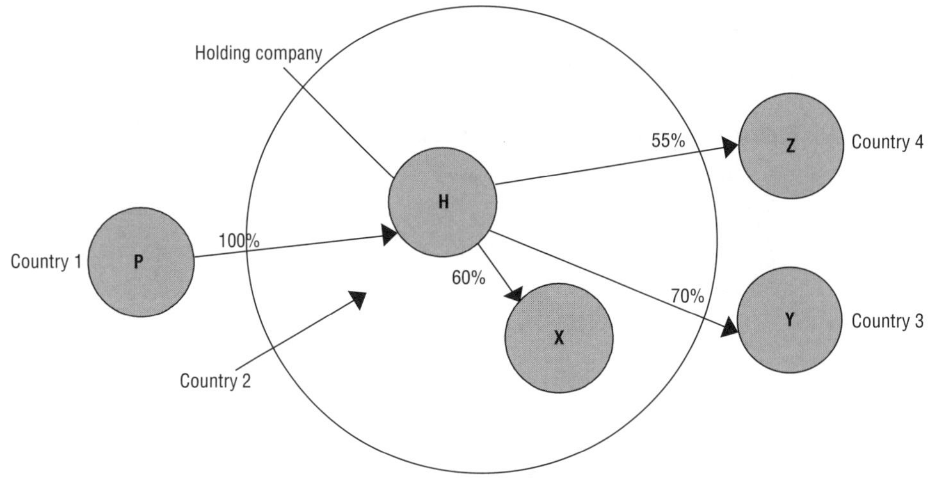

Control by a individual investor

349. Individual investors can create two more specific issues related to accounting for holding companies:

- The individual investor establishes a holding enterprise abroad for tax reasons and the holding enterprise in turn controls an enterprise in the country of residence of this individual.
- The individual investor establishes a holding enterprise in a foreign country which controls an enterprise in the country of residence of this individual, while this investor lives in the foreign country of which he becomes a resident.

350. In the first case, both the ultimate and immediate country of control must be the country of the controlling investor. In the second case it is the foreign country in which the investor lives and becomes resident which will be both the immediate and the ultimate country of control.

3.3.4.3. *Country of location of CAs abroad*

351. For outward investment, unlike the case with inward investment, identifying the country of location of CAs abroad does not pose any difficulties. The location of a CA abroad is the country where it resides.

3.3.5. Classification by industry and product

352. Data on AMNE are classified by sector according to the main industrial activity of the enterprises involved and are usually based on one key variable (generally employment or sales). For some variables, however, such as sales or output and for exports and imports in particular, data classified by product, in respect of both manufacturing and services would be very valuable. In contrast, other variables, such as value added and employment, do not lend themselves to classification by product.

353. In light of the above considerations, the collection of activity data by industrial sector is recommended as the first priority for statistics on affiliates under foreign control, in

respect of manufacturing and services alike. Nevertheless, countries are encouraged to adopt a long-term objective of establishing statistics by type of product for variables that can be classified on that basis (Box 3.9).

354. The recording period is also an important factor to take into account. The results for activity data ought in principle to correspond to the situation of the company at the end of the calendar year, but this is not systematically the case and some countries may instead adopt the financial year. This distorts international comparability, which is why the countries in question are invited to indicate their choice of period for indicating data and say what differences there are between the calendar and financial years.

Box 3.9. **Recommendations on collecting data on activity by industry and product**

- While the usefulness of simultaneous classification by industrial sector and by product is acknowledged, the collection of data on activity by industrial sector is considered the top priority. For the requirements of international organisations, the chosen sector-based classification is ISIC, Rev. 3 (NACE Revision 1 or NACE, Rev. 1).

Data by industrial sector

- The industry classification of a CA abroad (outward investment) should be based, as a first priority, on its own main industrial activity and not that of its parent company in its compiling country. However, since compilers have AMNE data on parents before they have AMNE data on CAs abroad, then information on the industry of the parent is likely to be available. Therefore as a *second priority* data on CAs abroad could be provided *both* by industry of affiliate and by industry of parent, particularly for some variables such as R&D or employment.

Data by product

- The collection of data by product will be a long-term objective. The classification system proposed for goods is that of the Harmonised System or the United Nations' Central Product Classification (CPC, Version. 1.0), while the system for services will be the Extended Balance of Payments Services (EBOPS) Classification. If countries cannot collect data at this level of aggregation, they are invited to break down sales between *goods and services* as a first step towards classification by product.

Recording period

- Activity variables for goods and services (flows) should be recorded on the basis of current-year accounting. They should correspond to the end of the reference year. Moreover, countries are invited to indicate whether calendar or fiscal years are used, as well as the differences between them.

3.3.5.1. *Data by industry*

355. To facilitate cross-country comparability, it is recommended that AMNE data be classified by industrial sector according to the International Standard Industrial Classification scheme (ISIC, Rev. 3) of the United Nations. A presentation of the level of aggregation concerning manufacturing and the service sector (FATS)[7] can be found in Tables 3.1 and 3.2. It must be emphasised that under the industrial sector approach,

Table 3.1. **ISIC categories requested for the collection of AMNE data in the manufacturing sector**

ISIC headings	ISIC code, Rev. 3
1. Mining and quarrying	10 to 14
2. Manufacturing	15 to 37
3. Food, beverages and tobacco	15 to 16
3.1. Manufacture of food products and beverages	15
3.2. Manufacture of tobacco products	16
4. Textiles, wearing apparel, leather, footwear	17 to 19
4.1. Manufacture of textiles	17
4.2. Manufacture of wearing apparel; dressing and dyeing of fur	18
4.3. Tanning and dressing of leather; manufacture of luggage, handbags, saddlery, harness and footwear	19
5. Wood and paper products, publishing, printing	20 to 22
5.1. Manufacture of wood and of products of wood and cork, except furniture; manufacture of articles of straw and plaiting materials	20
5.2. Paper and products, printing and publishing	21, 22
5.2.1. Manufacture of paper and paper products	21
5.2.2. Publishing, printing and reproduction of recorded media	22
6. All chemical products	23 to 25
6.1. Manufacture of coke, refined petroleum products and nuclear fuel	23
6.2. Chemicals, rubber and plastics products	24, 25
6.2.1. Manufacture of chemicals and chemical products	24
Of which: Manufacture of pharmaceuticals, medicinal chemicals and botanical products	2 423
6.2.2. Manufacture of rubber and plastics products	25
7. Manufacture of other non-metallic mineral products	26
7.1. Manufacture of glass and glass products	261
7.2. Manufacture of non-metallic mineral products n.e.c.	269
8. Basic and fabricated metal products	27 to 28
8.1. Manufacture of basic metals	27
8.1.1. Manufacture of basic iron and steel	271
8.1.2. Manufacture of basic precious and non-ferrous metals	272
8.1.3. Casting of metals	273
8.2. Manufacture of fabricated metal products, except machinery and equipment	28
8.2.1. Manufacture of structural metal products, tanks, reservoirs and steam generators	281
8.2.2. Manufacture of other fabricated metal products; metal working service activities	282
9. Total machinery and equipment	29 to 32
9.1. Non-electrical machinery and equipment	29, 30
9.1.1. Manufacture of machinery and equipment n.e.c.	29
9.1.2. Manufacture office, accounting and computing machinery	30
9.2. Electrical machinery and electronic equipment	31, 32
9.2.1. Manufacture of electrical machinery and apparatus n.e.c.	31
9.2.2. Manufacture of radio, television and communication equipment and apparatus	32
10. Manufacture of medical, precision and optical instruments, watches and clocks	33
10.1. Manufacture of medical appliances and instruments and appliances for measuring, checking, testing, navigating and other purposes, except optical instruments	331
10.2. Manufacture of optical instruments and photographic equipment	332
10.3. Manufacture of watches and clocks	333
11. Transport equipment	34 to 35
11.1. Manufacture of motor vehicles, trailers and semi-trailers	34
11.2. Manufacture of other transport equipment	35
11.2.1. Building and repairing of ships and boats	351
11.2.2. Manufacture of railway and tramway locomotives and rolling stock	352
11.2.3. Manufacture of aircraft and spacecraft	353
11.2.4. Manufacture of transport equipment n.e.c.	359

Table 3.1. **ISIC categories requested for the collection of AMNE data in the manufacturing sector** *(cont.)*

ISIC headings	ISIC code, Rev. 3
12. Furniture, recycling and manufacturing n.e.c.	36 to 37
12.1. Furniture and manufacturing n.e.c.	36
12.1.1. Manufacture of furniture	361
12.1.2. Manufacturing n.e.c	369
12.2. Recycling	37
13. Electricity, gas and water supply, construction	40 to 45
13.1. Electricity, gas and water supply	40, 41
13.2. Construction	45
14. Total services	50 to 99

certain secondary manufacturing activities are included in the service category, and, conversely, certain secondary service activities are put in the category of manufacturing. Some differences could exist between the proposed ISIC Rev. 3 or NACE Rev. 1 classifications and the national ones (*i.e.* US NAICS). It is important to identify these differences and establish conversion keys in order to respond to the needs of international organisations.

356. Regarding data on the industrial sector of CAs abroad, it is recommended that the industry attributed to such affiliates be based their own main activity and not that of their parent company in the compiling countries. In the case of certain variables such as R&D expenditure, both might be collected (as in the United States).

3.3.5.2. Data by product

357. Data collection by product ought to be a long-term objective for countries. Priority should be given to variables that lend themselves best to such a classification, including sales (turnover), output, exports and imports. Product-based statistics do not give rise to problems of interpretation involving secondary activities. Statistics on services should be compatible with commitments undertaken in connection with the GATS, and with the classification of trade between residents and non-residents.

358. The classification by product should, as much as possible, be compatible with the Harmonised System, in respect of goods, and with EBOPS, for trade in services, in order to facilitate comparisons concerning trade between residents and non-residents. If countries cannot attain this level of detail, they are invited to break down sales between goods and services as a first step towards classification by product. Another option for classifying goods by product would be to adopt the United Nations' CPC, Version 1.0).

3.3.6. Selecting data collection methods

359. In general there are two main approaches for collecting data on AMNE. The first is to conduct surveys asking directly foreign-CAs for information about their operations in the compiling country and parent companies for both their operations and those of their CAs abroad. The second, which would work only for MNEs operating in the compiling country (foreign-CAs and parent companies), make use of existing economic surveys including FDI statistics and business registers to estimate AMNE data. More specifically, enterprises and establishments on business registers are classified according to the AMNE target populations in the compiling country using available sources, including existing FDI databases; information on immediate and ultimate country of control also needs to be

Table 3.2. **ISIC categories requested for the collection of data on foreign affiliates (ICFA) (disaggregated service sector)**

	ISIC code, Rev. 3
1. Agriculture, hunting, forestry, and fishing	**01, 02, 05**
1.1. Agriculture, hunting, and related service activities	01
1.2. Forestry, logging, and related service activities	02
1.3. Fishing, operation of fish hatcheries and fish farms; services activities incidental to fishing	05
2. Mining and quarrying	**10, 11, 12, 13, 14**
of which: Services activities incidental to oil and gas extraction excluding surveying	112
3. Manufacturing	**15 to 37**
4. Electricity, gas, and water supply	**40, 41**
5. Construction	**45**
6. Trade and repair	**50, 51, 52**
6.1. Sale, maintenance, and repair of motor vehicles and motorcycles; retail sale of automotive fuel	50
6.2. Wholesale trade and commission trade, except of motor vehicles and motorcycles	51
6.3. Retail trade, except of motor vehicles and motorcycles; repair of personal and household goods	52
7. Hotels and restaurants	**55**
8. Transport, storage, and communications	**60, 61, 62, 63, 64**
8.1. Transport and storage	60, 61, 62, 63
8.1.1. Land transport; transport via pipelines	60
8.1.1.1. Transport via railways	601
8.1.1.2. Other land transport	602
8.1.1.3. Transport via pipelines	603
8.1.2. Water transport	61
8.1.2.1. Sea and coastal water transport	611
8.1.2.2. Inland water transport	612
8.1.3. Air transport	62
8.1.3.1. Scheduled air transport	621
8.1.3.2. Non-scheduled air transport	622
8.1.4. Supporting and auxiliary transport activities; activities of travel agencies	63
8.1.4.1. Supporting and auxiliary transport activities	6301, 6302, 6303, 6309
8.1.4.2. Activities of travel agencies and tour operators; tourist assistance activities, not elsewhere classified (n.e.c).	6 304
8.2. Post and telecommunications	64
8.2.1. Post and courier activities	641
8.2.2. Telecommunications	642
9. Financial intermediation	**65, 66, 67**
9.1. Financial intermediation, except insurance and pension funding	65
9.2. Insurance and pension funding, except compulsory social security	66
9.2.1. Life insurance	6 601
9.2.2. Pension funding	6 602
9.2.3. Non-life insurance	6 603
9.3. Activities auxiliary to financial intermediation	67
9.3.1. Activities auxiliary to financial intermediation, except insurance and pension funding	671
9.3.2. Activities auxiliary to insurance and pension funding	672
10. Real estate activities	**70**
11. Renting of machinery and equipment without operator and of personal and household goods	**71**
12. Computer and related activities	**72**
13. Research and development	**73**

Table 3.2. **ISIC categories requested for the collection of data on foreign affiliates (ICFA) (disaggregated service sector)** *(cont.)*

	ISIC code, Rev. 3
14. Other business activities	**74**
14.1. Legal, accounting, market research, and consultancy	741
14.1.1. Legal activities	7 411
14.1.2. Accounting, bookkeeping, and auditing activities; tax consultancy	7 412
14.1.3. Market research and public opinion polling	7 413
14.1.4. Business and management consultancy activities	7 414
14.2. Architectural, engineering, and other technical activities	742
14.3. Advertising	743
14.4. Business activities, n.e.c.	749
15. Education	**80**
16. Health and social work	**85**
17. Sewage and refuse disposal, sanitation, and similar activities	**90**
18. Activities of membership organisations, n.e.c.	**91**
19. Recreational, cultural, and sporting activities	**92**
19.1. Motion picture, radio, television, and other entertainment activities	921
19.1.1. Motion picture and video production and distribution; motion picture projection	9211, 9212
19.1.2. Radio and television activities	9 213
19.1.3. Other arts and entertainment activities	9214, 9219
19.2. News agency activities	922
19.3. Library, archives, museums, and other cultural activities	923
19.4. Sporting and other recreational activities	924
20. Other service activities	**93**

Note: The following ISIC categories have been excluded from ICFA because they are not relevant for foreign direct investment or for FATS: *i)* public administration and defence; compulsory social security (ISIC division 75), *ii)* private households with employed persons (division 95), and *iii)* extraterritorial organisations and bodies (division 99). All other ISIC categories are included.

updated or added to business registers. Establishment and enterprise data from existing surveys or administrative records are then linked to the business registers to get the target population identifiers and country of control information. Finally, these micro-data are aggregated to produce the required AMNE data. Recommendations on data collection methods are summarised in Box 3.10 and discussed below.

360. Whichever approach is adopted, it is necessary to identify the target populations. The population of direct investment enterprises can provide one solution to identifying foreign-CAs. Some countries also have specific program to identify the control structure of

Box 3.10. **Recommendations on data collection methods**

The two main approaches – conducting special surveys and using available data – necessitate identifying the target populations using existing FDI data or other data sources. While each country is free to choose its own approach, a combination of the two may represent an ideal: namely, to use available data with target population identifiers and country of control information derived from FDI or other data sources for activity data related to foreign-CAs and parent companies in the compiling country, and to conduct separate surveys for data on CAs abroad. An important consideration is the need to adopt the same concepts and definitions for both approaches in order to avoid asymmetry and problems of international comparability.

enterprises controlled by residents. This information can be used to identify the structure of enterprise groups within the country and the country of (immediate and/or ultimate) control. But it might not be possible to use it to identify parent companies; in fact, outward FDI statistics are the only known source that can be used to identify parent companies.

361. If AMNE data are collected in conjunction with FDI surveys, there are three drawbacks: *a)* it may entail annualising the data, which could make calculations more ponderous; *b)* it would provide a relatively high level of sectoral aggregation; and *c)* it would have to be limited to a handful of key variables such as turnover and employment. It does, however, make it possible to identify investors' geographical origins. But separate surveys would enable a more detailed level of sectoral aggregation and include a larger number of variables, in respect of both inward and outward investment as well as parent companies. Such surveys would, however, demand more resources and increase the response burden on enterprises. To minimise costs, full use should be made of already existing data sources (*e.g.* business registers) before starting a separate data collection exercise.

362. One advantage of gathering data from available data along with business registers is that they usually provide more detailed disaggregations by industry sector, and may provide some detail by product, mainly for sales and turnover. Another is that information about parent companies is easier to collect. Until recently, only a few OECD countries were able to compile data on parent companies operating in their home countries through regular investment surveys.

363. In any event, care must be taken to ensure that the data on multinational enterprises are comparable to national statistics.

364. In conclusion, it would seem that the best solution is in fact a combination of both approaches. Available data along with business registers could be a more appropriate source for compiling data on the activity of foreign-CAs and parent companies, whereas separate surveys would be better suited to data collection on CAs abroad. One of the main challenges for this new statistical domain stems from the fact that the collection and definition of statistics on AMNE may draw on expertise and responsibilities that are scattered among multiple institutions, such as central banks, national statistical offices and various ministries. Thus, as the statistics are developed, there will be a need for close co-operation among the different institutions involved.

3.3.7. Selecting the statistical unit

365. In principle, the problem of the statistical unit is relevant to all activity or industry data, but it takes on very special significance in the case of data on AMNE. If comparisons are to be made between the activity of foreign-CAs in a particular industrial sector and aggregate activity of all enterprises (the national total) in the same sector, it is crucial that the two aggregates be expressed in the same statistical unit. Problem of comparability is important, but it is secondary to the point that certain variables are available *only* at the establishment level, and certain others *only* at the enterprise level. (See MSITS, §4.27.) Recommendations on the choice of statistical unit are given in Box 3.11 and discussed below.

3.3.7.1. *Defining the statistical units*

366. The statistical units correspond essentially to three levels of production:

- The ***establishment***, as defined in the System of National Accounts (SNA 1993), is an enterprise, or part of an enterprise, that is situated in a single location and has the most

Box 3.11. **Recommendations on statistical units**

Statistical units include: 1) establishment, 2) enterprise, or 3) enterprise group. No statistical unit in particular is recommended. Data on AMNE must be developed within the framework of existing statistics. However, these units must be specified clearly, and the member countries are invited to ensure comparability between AMNE data and national totals.

Regarding enterprise groups:

i) ll OECD countries are invited to collect consolidated data (enterprise groups) on parent companies in the framework of outward investment.

ii) They are also invited to specify the methods they use to consolidate accounts.

iii) As regards transactions within MNE (intra-firm trade, technology payments and receipts, etc.), national authorities are invited to specify the rules applied in order to determine whether or not an enterprise belongs to the group at the world level.

homogeneous production, or whose principal productive activity accounts for most of the value added. In the European System of Accounts, this entity is also called a "local kind-of-activity unit" (local KAU)[8]. The establishment theoretically has no legal autonomy, but this is not necessarily true as there are many single establishment firms that have legal autonomy while its accounts contain a great deal of information such as employment, gross value of production and intermediate consumption, apart from overheads, which are reported in the enterprise's accounts.

- The ***enterprise*** (as defined by Council Regulation EEC No. 696/93 of 15 March 1993) is "the smallest combination of legal units that is an organisational unit producing goods or services, which benefits from a certain degree of autonomy in decision-making, especially for the allocation of its current resources. An enterprise carries out one or more activities at one or more locations. An enterprise may be a sole legal unit.
- This definition is more precise than the one provided by SNA 1993, where an **enterprise** is defined as "an institutional unit engaged in production. An enterprise may be a corporation (a quasi-corporate enterprise being treated as if it were a corporation in the System), a non-profit institution, or an unincorporated enterprise" (SNA 1993, §5.1).
- These two definitions leave some room for interpretation about the degree of consolidation and control of an enterprise. Does an enterprise include all the resident entities under the same controlling entity? For the purpose of this *Handbook*, the term enterprise is used in the broad SNA sense and qualifiers will be used to specify its meaning when required (*e.g.* consolidated enterprise). When referring to statistical units, an enterprise is an institutional unit that regroups one or more establishments under its control.
- The ***enterprise group*** (again according to Council Regulation EEC No. 696/93) is an "association of enterprises bound together by legal and/or financial links. A group of enterprises can have more than one decision-making centre, especially for policy on production, sales and profits. It may centralise certain aspects of financial management and taxation". Its activities may be in the industrial, service or banking sectors, and sometimes concurrently in two or all three (conglomerates). It may be located within a

country (in which case it is a domestic group) or, as is more commonly the case, in several countries (multinational group).

367. There are two types of enterprise group to be considered associated with outward investments:

a) The first is an association of enterprises or establishments directly or indirectly majority-controlled by a parent. All the enterprises and their parent are located in the same country and represent one enterprise with consolidated accounts. This corresponds to what has been defined above as "parent company" in the home country. By reference to Figure 3.11, we are dealing with the consolidated accounts of parent company X covering companies X, A, B and C located in country 1.

b) The second is a group comprising parents and directly or indirectly controlled affiliates located in different countries or MNE.

3.3.7.2. Identifying enterprise members of an MNE

368. Figure 3.11 shows the structure of an enterprise group with operations located in three countries (MNE). The example in Figure 3.11 is intended to illustrate the rules to identify the member enterprises of an MNE. It shows which enterprises belong to an international enterprise group and which do not. It is essential for the enterprises of these groups to be able to provide data on certain variables such as intra-firm trade or technology transfers between parent companies and their CAs or between CAs of the same group (see Chapters 4 and 5). For example, said, foreign-CAs in reporting countries ought to be in a position to provide data on their trade with parent companies and other enterprises in the same MNE. In doing so, they should apply the rules proposed in Figure 3.11.

Figure 3.11. **Example of an MNE**

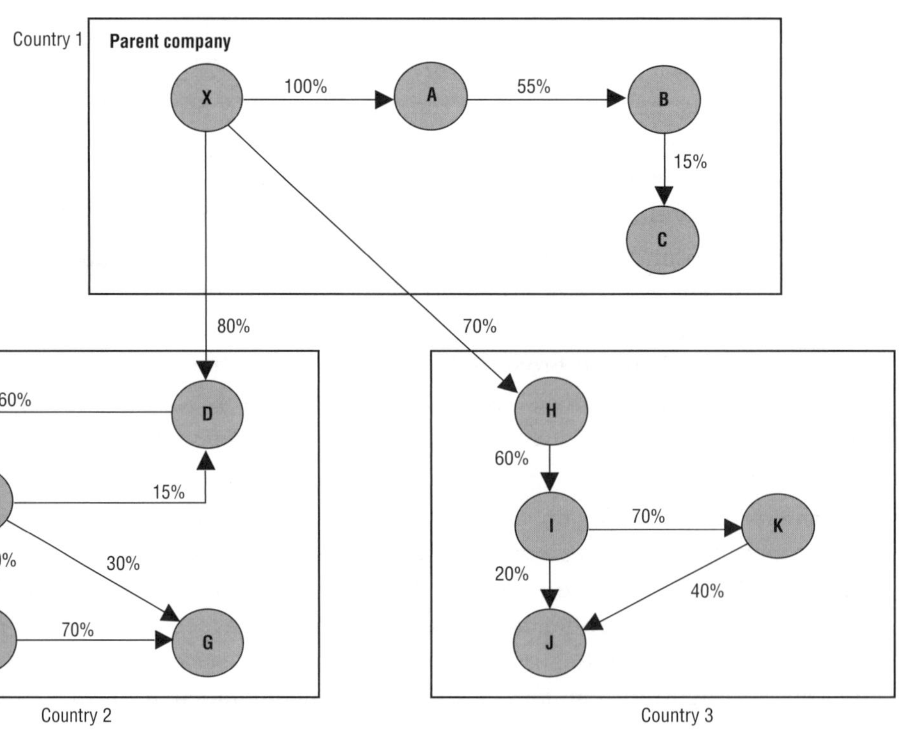

369. For the purpose of surveys on parent companies, the data requested are the figures for the consolidated accounts of the group in compiling country 1. From this point of view, the parent company in country 1 corresponds to the consolidated accounts of the companies X, A and B but not C. The accounts of the group at world level are not required, although many parent companies in home countries have these accounts. What is important for the surveys organised by member countries is that parent companies in home countries should be able to collect data on commerce and technology trade within these groups at world level (*e.g.* intra-firm trade, technology revenue and payments). Consequently, it is necessary to know which companies are part of the global group.

370. Let us assume that an enterprise X located in country 1 is the parent company of a group of enterprises located in countries 1, 2 and 3.

Country 1		
A :	Is a subsidiary of X 100% controlled by X	(100% of X)
B :	Is a subsidiary of A which owns 55% of B	(55% of X)
C :	Is an associate of B which owns 15% of C	(8.2% of X)
Country 2		
D :	Is a subsidiary of X which owns 80% of D and an associate of E which owns 15% of D	(80% of X)
E :	Is a subsidiary of D which owns 60% of E	(48% of X)
F :	Is an associate of E which owns 20% of F	(9.6% of X)
G:	Is a subsidiary of F which owns 70% of G and an associate of E which owns 30% of G	(24% of X)
Country 3		
H :	Is a subsidiary of X which owns 70% of H	(70% of X)
I :	Is a subsidiary of H which owns 60% of I	(42% of X)
K :	Is a subsidiary of I which owns 70% of K	(29.4% of X)
J :	Is an associate of K which owns 40% of J and an associate of I which owns 20% of J	

371. If the IMF/OECD "Fully Consolidated System" (see Chapter 2, Section 2.5.1.1., §136-137) as it applies not to the concept of "ownership" but to that of direct or indirect "control", is transposed into this structure, the result is as follows:

- In Country 1: Only enterprises X, A and B belong to the group insofar as enterprise A is directly controlled by X and enterprise B is indirectly controlled by X (through enterprise B). Enterprise C has been excluded as it may be controlled by another group.
- In Country 2: Only enterprises D and E belong to the group insofar as D is a direct subsidiary of X and E is an indirect subsidiary of X. In contrast, F and G are associates of X and are therefore excluded from the group.
- In Country 3: All of the enterprises, *i.e.* H, I, K and J, belong to the group insofar as they are controlled directly (> 50% of the shares) or indirectly by X. Enterprise J also belongs to the group since 60% of its shares are held by enterprises I and K which are themselves indirect subsidiaries of enterprise X.
- On an international level, then, the enterprises belonging to the group or MNE are: X, A, B, D, E, H, I, K and J.

3.3.7.3. *Considerations in selecting statistical units*

372. With respect to the selection of statistical units, it is important to underline that the most relevant unit may vary depending on the variable in question, the industry or the analytical context, but all three types are likely to be necessary at various times. At the establishment level, the production process does not vary to any great extent and tends to

focus on individual industries, which in respect of certain variables such as employment, output, turnover or value added makes it possible to convey a more accurate image of the true weight of these activities in the national economy. If these same variables are compiled at enterprise level, the resulting statistics will incorporate many secondary activities which can alter the results. The more vertical integration there is in the industrial structure, the more these results will be distorted.

373. In contrast, other categories of variables, notably gross operating surplus (but also R&D or technology receipts and payments – see Chapter 4), should be collected at enterprise level only. Lastly, as was made mention earlier, some variables, such as intra-firm exports or imports (see Chapter 5), can be collected only at enterprise group level. A direct consequence of this situation for surveys of AMNE is that the surveys are organised at three different levels of statistical units, depending on the variables being compiled. This can raise practical difficulties in establishing samples, but it also poses problems of comparability between sectors corresponding to the various variables. For example, if gross output statistics are compiled at establishment level and R&D at enterprise level, the ratio of R&D to gross output for a given sector would be meaningless. The consequence for national authorities of this situation is the need to organise at regular periods surveys for all enterprises either at establishment level or enterprise level (*i.e.* the US organise surveys in the framework of benchmarking at establishment level for CAs).

374. The vast majority of countries have chosen the enterprise as the statistical unit for collecting data on AMNE, with only a minority choosing the establishment. With establishments, there is greater uniformity of sector activities, whereas with enterprises more importance is given to the autonomy of decision centres. In both cases, an essential concern is to be able to compare data on foreign-CAs and parent companies with other national data. This means that these categories of data must be expressed using the same statistical unit. Table 3.3 shows the differences observed in certain sectors, depending on whether they are assessed at the establishment or enterprise level, along with the various ratios obtained when the statistical units are not the same for affiliates under foreign control as for the national total.

375. In order to be able to make more reliable comparisons of variables collected at the establishment level and those collected at the enterprise level (the latter being the case of affiliates under foreign control), most countries collect at least some variables at both

Table 3.3. **Example of classification of sectors by enterprise and by establishment: the case of Germany, 1995**

Sectors	Total national employment* at:		Foreign-controlled employment[1] (%)	
	Establishment level	Enterprise level	Enterprise/enterprise[2]	Enterprise/establishment[3]
Textiles, clothing	117.2	287.2	3.1	7.7
Chemicals	330.5	552.8	12.7	21.2
Pharmaceuticals	137.2	106.5	–	–
Computers	36.2	66.5	19.5	35.9
Electric machinery	210.4	538.9	5.2	13.3
Electronics	360.7	165.5	23.6	10.8

* Thousands of persons.
1. Share of foreign-CAs in the national total.
2. Identical statistical units: ratios correct.
3. Different statistical units: ratios incorrect.

Source: AFA database, OECD.

 OECD HANDBOOK ON ECONOMIC GLOBALISATION INDICATORS – ISBN 92-64-10808-4 – © OECD 2005

levels: enterprise and establishment. Some variables, such as intra-enterprise trade, can be collected only at the level of enterprise groups. Other variables could be collected at this level as well, which would be a great advantage in understanding and better analysing the role of enterprise groups having considerable weight and importance in the global economy. While it is desirable to compile variables other than intra-firm trade at enterprise group level, it would still be necessary to collect the same information at establishment or enterprise level as well, to ensure comparability with each country's aggregate industrial activities, by sector in particular.

3.3.7.4. Consolidation issues

376. The level of accounts consolidation within an enterprise group can have serious implications for certain variables. Sales, gross output, assets and number of enterprises are the most affected variables. Sales and gross output can vary substantially with the level of account consolidation because consolidation excludes sales between enterprises and establishments of the same group. Assets are also affected by consolidation as enterprises within a group can loan financial assets to each others. Finally, the count of enterprises could vary substantially depending on whether or not establishments or enterprises within a group are counted or the enterprise groups only. Other variables such as employment and value added should not be affected by the level of consolidation, as they are additive across members of the same enterprise group.

377. It is therefore important to ensure that national totals correspond to the consolidation level used in the target populations. If the number of foreign-CAs is based on the count of enterprise groups under foreign control, then it should be compared to the number of enterprise groups in the compiling country.

378. Consistency within a country does not however ensure international consistency as the level of consolidation often depends on national statistical system prerogatives.[9]

3.3.8. International comparability

379. A major difficulty involves data comparability, where numerous problems subsist. An initial step towards international harmonisation of basic concepts and definitions was taken via MSITS.[10] These concepts have been accepted internationally, but they need to be supplemented and extended to all of the activities of multinational enterprises. Listed below are the factors which most frequently affect the international comparability of data and also, sometimes, comparability between data from different national sources. It is unlikely that all of these problems will be resolved in the short term making it essential that data be complemented by informative meta-data that clearly outlines the methodological characteristics of the data. In the longer term the goal will be to strive towards greater international harmonisation of techniques while maintaining national flexibility.

3.3.8.1. Distortions due to non-compliance with international standards

Definitions of variables

380. International comparisons can be distorted by the fact that national authorities assign different definitions to variables. For example, an investing country may attribute certain expenses of its affiliates to R&D, while a host country may attribute those expenditures to another item such as outlays for innovation (if the criteria of the *Frascati Manual* are not followed). The definitions of concepts can also differ within the same

country between statistical departments belonging to different ministries or institutions. One statistical department may take both direct and indirect financial links between enterprises into account when computing foreign-controlled production or employment, while other statistical departments may use direct ties only.

Industry classification

381. Industry can be reported differently depending on whether it is done by the country whose investors exercise control or the host country. This may be due to differences in national classification, but also to the fact that some countries prefer to classify their CAs abroad to the industry of their parent companies in the compiling countries. Very few countries are in a position to classify their CAs abroad according to both the CA's own industrial activity and the industrial activity of the parent company.

Statistical units

382. Countries may use different statistical units, *e.g.* establishment, enterprise or enterprise group. This makes it hard to compare variables relating to the domestic economy as a whole with those relating to data on affiliates under foreign control. International comparisons may also be affected by derived indicators such as the percentage of output or employment under foreign control.

Data recording periods

383. It is important that the activity data collected by countries should correspond to the end of the calendar year. International comparisons may be affected if some countries collect data at the beginning or end of the financial year.

Inward and outward investment

384. Conceptions of activity data for inward and outward investment may differ creating distortions not only in the international comparability of data, but also in national data put out by one country. For example, activity data for outward investment may cover majority-controlled affiliates only, whereas activity data for inward investment may also encompass affiliates under minority control. Or outward investment activity may be limited to a country's largest multinationals.

Trade data for foreign affiliates and enterprises controlled by residents

385. International trade by foreign affiliates raises two problems which hamper national and international comparisons: 1) the use of two categories of data (by product or reclassified by industry, and data on foreign-CAs collected by industry from the outset) which are not strictly comparable; and 2) the tracing intra-firm trade by multinational groups. Other problems arising from international trade data involving MNEs will be examined in Chapter 5, in particular the possibility of double counting between parent companies controlled by residents and those under foreign control, on the one hand, and data on CAs as a whole, on the other.

Definition of control

386. One of the major distortions in international comparability stems from the different approaches to the "control" of an enterprise. The authorities in each country do not treat

all cases in the same way, hence the need for harmonised rules. At present, the same enterprise can be classified "by some countries" as being "under domestic control" and "under foreign control" by others.

Country of control

387. Divergences are found when the country of an enterprise's ultimate unit of control is to be determined, if there is no single majority shareholder. Experience has shown that, in the absence of explicit guidelines, national authorities can attribute different countries of control to the same enterprise.

Immediate and ultimate unit of control

388. Many OECD countries still have problems identifying the ultimate unit of control. As a result, the geographical distribution of foreign-CAs within the same country can differ widely, depending on whether the criterion applied is that of the immediate controller or that of the ultimate controller. Limited knowledge of the capital structure of the group to which each affiliate belongs leads to mistaken applications regarding the identification of the country of control, when the latter has to correspond to that of the ultimate controller.

Degree and methods of consolidating accounts

389. Depending on the degree to which multinational firms' accounts are consolidated, some comparisons will pose no problems and others will prove impossible. If, for example, a country collects some data on the number of CAs in a consolidated manner and others in a non-consolidated manner, the variable in question will not be comparable. With respect, likewise, to the activity of foreign affiliates, in a lot of countries these variables are consolidated and no distinction is made between direct and indirect control. Other countries only collect data relating to direct control, while there can also be differences with regard to the method of consolidation used (see also Chapter 2, Section 2.5.1.1.).

Measuring affiliates abroad controlled by geographical areas (set of countries)

390. Indirect control may pose some double accounting problems if a number of countries are taken into account as a whole as is done with regional groupings such as the EU, NAFTA, APEC, etc. To take the example shown in Figure 3.12 if it is assumed that countries 1 and 2 are members of the European Union and country 3 is not, company X controls company Z (indirectly) and company Y controls company Z (directly). If it is sought to aggregate the companies abroad under European control, there is a risk that company Z will be counted twice over. This double-counting can be avoided if, in such case, only the country of direct control is counted. Thus only company Y can declare that it controls company Z. That company will declare that it is directly controlled by company Y and indirectly controlled by company X. It is seen from the definition of "parent company" that company Z will have detailed activity data only for company Y which controls it directly and could be considered its parent company.

Parent companies and affiliates under foreign control

391. An affiliate under foreign control in a country that has its own CAs abroad may be counted both as a foreign-CA and as a parent company. There exist the potential for some duplication between AMNE data concerning foreign-CAs and parent companies. This

Figure 3.12. **The accounting problems of indirect control**

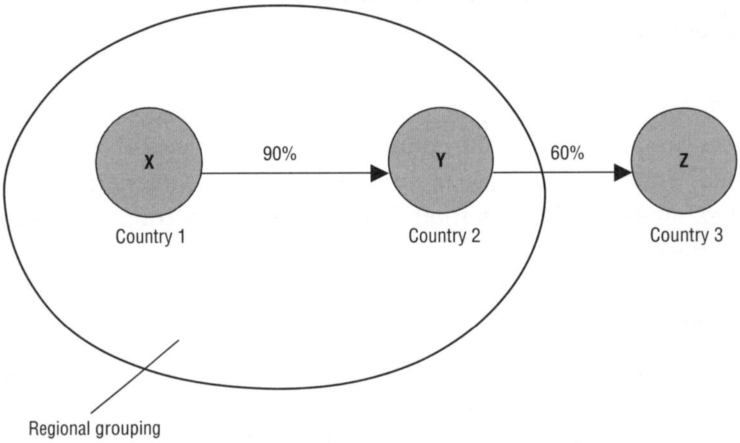

phenomenon might very in magnitude from country to country. In order to avoid duplication, it is suggested a distinction be made between data for parent companies controlled by residents of the compiling countries and data for parent companies under foreign control.

3.3.8.2. Other categories of distortion (where the recommendations in the Handbook do not apply)

Organisation of surveys

392. Some distortions in international comparability may derive from the way national surveys are organised. The enterprises concerned may differ according to whether the survey on the activity of multinationals is conducted within the balance-of-payments framework or by means of independent surveys. In which case, the populations of enterprises concerned may be fairly different.

Size-of-enterprise thresholds

393. Depending on the country or national agency in charge of the survey, enterprises below a certain size (*e.g.* with fewer than 20 or 50 employees) may be excluded from the sample. If these thresholds are not the same everywhere, the samples will not be comparable across countries.

Conversion of national classifications to international classifications

394. In some countries, converting the national classification to the international classification can pose problems when it is not performed directly by the national authorities, who have access to all the detailed data, but on the basis of more aggregated published data. When, for example, the components of certain items of the NAICS (North America Industry Classification System) adopted by the United States and Canada are not broken down separately, converting them to an international classification is very difficult, particularly as some items come under manufacturing and others under services (*e.g.* the information industry).

Notes

1. A glossary at the end of this *Handbook* more fully explains these terms. For example, the term "foreign-controlled affiliate in the compiling country" ("foreign-CA") refers to an affiliate of unique or associated foreign investors in the compiling country (the country which collects the statistics) that is more than 50% foreign-owned.
2. See "The performance of foreign affiliates in OECD countries", Table A.1.5, OECD, 1994.
3. In some cases, it might be possible to derive a close proxy for this breakdown by examining data on total sales in conjunction with data on exports. Export data may indicate sales to the country of the parent separately from sales to third countries, and local sales may be derived by subtracting these export sales from total sales.
4. See MSITS.
5. This derived population estimates assume consistent population units (*e.g.* enterprises above a threshold). If this is not the case, adjustments would have to be made to derive the most appropriate and consistent estimates for each of the four target populations.
6. FATS task force report (Eurostat Directorate B, Unit B5, January 1997).
7. The acronym FATS, devised by the Eurostat Group of Experts, originally stood for Foreign Affiliates Trade in Services. More recently, however, Eurostat has used it to designate all the activities of affiliates with the exception of trade, including manufacturing. Thus FATS now stands for Foreign Affiliates Trade Statistics.
8. See also Regulation (EC) No. 696/93 of 15 March 1993 on the statistical units for the observation and analysis of the production system in the Community.
9. Not all countries that collect these data on groups apply the same rules of consolidation, which can affect international comparability. For example, the American and French approaches to consolidation are different. With the American approach, enterprises are required to file reports according to the rules of the US system of full consolidation under which an enterprise is considered to be under indirect control only if the parent company or the enterprise that controls it indirectly holds more than 50% of the voting shares. In the French approach, however, there is an external reconstitution of the group using these enterprises and their accounts and making no use of consolidated data. This choice is necessary in France because so few enterprises publish consolidated data.
10. The main recommendations formulated in MSITS are reproduced in Annex 3.2.

ANNEX 3.A1

Approaches to be Adopted in the Absence of a Single Majority Investor

395. First it should be remembered that in the great majority of cases effective control of an enterprise is exercised by a single majority shareholder or a group of investors acting in concert. The approaches proposed below concern only countries (generally small ones) that are able to examine enterprises on a case-by-case basis according to qualitative criteria as well. It is important for such data to be collected separately (as least for the totality of each variable) so as to be able to gauge their weight relative to the total number of enterprises under foreign control. The various scenarios for multiple resident or foreign owners with majority shareholdings are summarised in Box 1.

396. If the foreign owner* is not a single individual or entity, it must be ascertained whether the multiple foreign owners together own an absolute majority of the voting power or not.

397. If the foreign owners have the majority of shares, it must be ascertained whether there are direct links between them, *i.e.* whether they belong to the same group or alliance, or if they have no links.

398. If they are linked, then the enterprise will be classified in the "foreign-controlled" category.

399. If they are not linked, and they do not control all the capital, it must be simultaneously ascertained how the capital is split between resident shareholders.

- If there is a dominant but minority resident shareholder, with more shares than each of the nonresident shareholders, it is highly likely that this national shareholder will have effective control. This is a strong presumption, which would need to be verified, of the existence of a joint venture. If it proves to be founded, then the enterprise can be classified in the "resident-controlled" category.
- If the resident shareholders are dispersed and if none of them has a significant stake, the enterprise can be classified as being "under foreign control", if the foreign investors are direct investors, *i.e.* who hold at least 10% of the voting power, and not portfolio investors.

* The same reasoning applies to resident owners in the compiling country.

- If the resident shareholders have links with one another, and if their aggregate share of the capital is significantly larger than that of any of the foreign shareholders, then the enterprise can be classified as being "under resident control".

400. If the foreign owners do not have a majority shareholding, this means that the majority is held by multiple residents of the compiling country shareholders. If this is so, the same reasoning can be applied as for foreign owners with a majority shareholding.

Box 3.A1.1. **Approaches for multiple shareholders (implications for enterprise control)**

Shareholders	Links	Situation	Classification
Non-resident (foreign) Multiple minority shareholders	Associated		*Foreign-controlled*
	Not associated	There is a main resident shareholder	Domestically *controlled* (to be verified)
		Associated resident shareholder	Domestically *controlled* (to be verified)
		Dispersed resident shareholder	*Foreign-controlled* (to be verified)
Resident (domestic) Multiple minority shareholders	Associated		Domestically *controlled* (to be verified)
	Not associated	There is a single large foreign shareholder	*Foreign-controlled* (to be verified)
		Associated foreign shareholders	*Foreign-controlled* (to be verified)
		Dispersed foreign shareholders	Domestically *controlled* (to be verified)

401. The cases which have been described show that, when the majority of an enterprise's equity is held by multiple residents of the compiling country or foreign owners, the fact that together they have a majority of shares does not necessarily mean that the enterprise can be classified as being "foreign-controlled" or "domestically controlled". Before that can be done, it is necessary to examine the nature of the links between the shareholders, including residents of the compiling country shareholders.

402. For the sake of consistency with the data on direct investment enterprises, it will be necessary not to apply the qualitative criteria (even on a voluntary basis) to enterprises where the principal shareholder could in exceptional cases control the enterprise while holding less than 10% of the voting power. The case just mentioned is comparatively marginal, but if it were taken into account there would be a danger of classifying as foreign-controlled certain enterprises in the category of portfolio investment as opposed to direct investment. This also shows the difficulty of reconciling an unavoidable statistical convention with economic reality.

403. It is acknowledged that in some countries, for example small ones, the authorities have information about individual enterprises that enable them to make determinations regarding effective control, even if a majority of voting shares are not held by a sole foreign investor. In such countries, the use of additional information about individual enterprises (case by case) can be important, because to place a large enterprise in the wrong category (under foreign control or control by residents) could distort the results of the entire sector concerned. For countries finding themselves in that situation, the following cases could be taken into consideration: minority control, ownership shared among two or more stockholders, and control in non-financial forms. Some examples of these special cases follow.

Minority control

404. Minority control means having the effective control of an enterprise without having the majority of voting power. It does not include indirect control via a majority-controlled subsidiary. In the case in question, we are talking about a minority but large shareholder and a scattering of small shareholders, none of whom owns a significant part of the capital. The minority shareholder can thus exercise effective control insofar as no majority of shareholders is really able to oppose it. However, it is possible in some cases that the small shareholders join forces in order to have more influence over the enterprise's strategic decisions.

405. In most countries, the rights of minority shareholders are regulated in order to protect them against abuses by majority or main shareholders. In principle, portfolio investors do not influence an enterprise's management but they can sometimes have a decisive impact on policy.

406. In practice, the Board of Directors cannot disregard demands from institutional investors (*e.g.* pension funds) that the enterprise show a profit unless it can replace the said investors without adverse consequences for the share price and the other shareholders. In many cases, therefore, there are certain limits to the main shareholder's control and sometimes it is not easy to show how it is distributed or shared. Both the rules on *corporate governance* in each country and also national legislation on the definition of control can shed more light on this question.

Shared ownership

407. In many cases the ownership and management of an enterprise is divided between two or more main shareholders. The most common scenario, which was described in Section 3.3.4.2, is a "*joint venture*" in which each of the two shareholders holds half of the equity. Sometimes, several joint subsidiaries are set up by a limited number of enterprises, each of which has a significant number of shares. In the case of mergers between two or three enterprises, the ownership and management of the new enterprise can be shared, though it not easy without further investigation to say which of the enterprises has more power of control than the others.

Control in non-financial forms

408. In the foregoing examples, the criterion for determining control of an enterprise is control of its capital. But other forms of control exist, in particular via technology and knowledge flows. In the 1980s, a European enterprise concluded co-operation agreements with a non-European enterprise on which it became increasingly dependent for technology. Although the non-European enterprise had only a minority stake in the European enterprise, objectively it controlled the enterprise's strategy. Several years later, the non-European enterprise took over the European one outright. This case is fairly typical of the complex power relationships between multinationals, which are not based solely on financial aspects and ownership of the capital.

ANNEX 3.A2

MSITS Main Recommendations Concerning FATS Statistics (FATS: "Foreign Affiliates' Trade in Services")

409. FATS statistics should cover those affiliates in which the direct investor (or an associated group of investors acting in concert) holds a majority of the ordinary shares or voting power. However, countries are encouraged to provide supplemental statistics, covering cases in which foreign control may be deemed to be present, even though no single foreign direct investor holds a majority stake.

410. FATS variables should be compiled for all foreign affiliates, not only those affiliates in services. However, the activity classification to be used for reporting to international organisations provides more detail for services than for goods.

411. For statistics on foreign-owned affiliates *in* the compiling economy (inward FATS), the first priority for geographical attribution should be the country of ultimate beneficial owner. However, to facilitate linkages with FDI data, countries are encouraged also to provide some data in which attribution is based on the country of the first foreign parent. Statistics for foreign affiliates *of* the compiling economy (outward FATS) should be attributed based on the country of location of the affiliate whose operations are being described.

412. Because it is the basis required for some variables as well as the basis on which data probably are, at present, most widely available, an activity basis is recommended as the initial priority for FATS statistics. However, data on a product basis are recognized as a longer-term goal and countries are encouraged to work towards providing product detail for those variables that lend themselves to this basis of attribution (namely, sales (turnover) and/or output, exports and imports).

413. For reporting to international organisations, FATS variables should be disaggregated according to the ISIC Categories for Foreign Affiliates. Any product detail that is developed should be disaggregated on a basis compatible with EBOPS.

414. The *Handbook* recommends that the FATS variables to be collected include at least the following basic measures of foreign affiliate activity: *i)* sales (turnover) and/or output, *ii)* employment, *iii)* value added, *iv)* exports and imports of goods and services, and *v)* number of enterprises. Additional measures are suggested for countries wishing to expand FATS data collection beyond this basic set.

415. The *Handbook* envisages that a variety of sources and methods be used to collect and compile FATS statistics. Separate surveys may be conducted or links may be made with domestic enterprise statistics that are already collected. In either case, there are likely to be links with existing data on foreign direct investment.

ISBN 92-64-10808-4
OECD Handbook on Economic Globalisation Indicators

Chapter 4

The Internationalisation of Technology

4.1. Introduction

416. Chapter 1 called attention to the important role played by technology and information and communication technologies in particular in the globalisation of the economy. The forms that the internationalisation of technology can take are extremely varied, but this *Handbook* will limit its examination of them to the following three:

i) The internationalisation of industrial research and development (R&D).

ii) Technology receipts and payments.

iii) Trade in high-technology products.

417. Not included in the present version of this chapter are other important forms of internationalisation of technology, such as government R&D, international filing of patents, strategic technology alliances between firms, co-operation agreements between public institutions and also the migration of highly skilled individuals. Such forms of internationalisation of technology, some of which have gained in importance over the past twenty years, still require extensive methodological work and could be incorporated in a subsequent revision of the *Handbook*.

418. This chapter is in two parts. The first describes the proposed indicators for measuring the degree of globalisation of technology. As in the other chapters, the indicators are presented in the form of reference indicators which are of a priority nature and are in principle available to the majority of OECD countries. These are followed by a set of supplemental relevant indicators which are of secondary importance and are available in fewer countries. Finally, a third category of experimental indicators is proposed for those OECD countries that want to take their research further. Some countries are already collecting this latter category of indicators, but the *Handbook* does not consider them to have priority. The second part of the chapter deals more specifically with certain conceptual and methodological questions raised by the construction of the indicators proposed in each of the three areas discussed in this chapter.

4.2. The proposed indicators

419. As mentioned in the introduction, this chapter deals with three important forms of internationalisation of technology: that of industrial R&D, intangible trade in technology (technology balance of payments) and trade in high-technology products (technology embodied in the goods). These three forms of internationalisation of technology are interdependent, but also take place upstream and downstream from the process of technological development and internationalisation.

420. Industrial R&D is the main technological input that can be developed by a firm or parent company in a particular country, or else under the control of the latter it could be developed in various countries via a network of affiliates and R&D centres. Trade in non-embodied technology in the form of patents, licences, know-how, technical studies or R&D usually represents the results of this research. So the technology used by multinational

 OECD HANDBOOK ON ECONOMIC GLOBALISATION INDICATORS – ISBN 92-64-10808-4 – © OECD 2005

firms' affiliates abroad could either originate from R&D developed locally by these affiliates, or be the result of a transfer by the parent company of technology it has developed or purchased from other firms. Whether the parent company chooses to have the technology produced locally by its affiliates abroad (in R&D laboratories) or to transfer it, more often than not in the form of licences and know-how, depends on numerous factors which will be more amply explained in the second part of the chapter.

421. The third form of internationalisation of technology via trade in technology-intensive products (high-technology products) is located downstream from the process of technological development. It would be interesting, whenever a country becomes an exporter of high-technology products, to seek the origin of the technology used: is it R&D developed by the exporting country itself or a technology imported in licence form? This check could concern not just foreign-controlled affiliates, but all the firms in the country in question.

4.2.1. Describing the proposed indicators

4.2.1.1. Main questions to which the proposed reference indicators for compiling countries relate

- What is the share of R&D expenditure and of researchers in foreign-controlled affiliates in the country's overall industry?
- What share of a country's industrial R&D is financed from abroad?
- What share of turnover, value added and employment is accounted for by foreign-controlled affiliates whose main activity is R&D?
- What is the share of R&D expenditure by parent companies and what is the proportion of researchers?
- What is the share of R&D expenditure and of researchers in multinational firms (parent companies and foreign CAs) in a given country?
- What share of GDP is accounted for by overall technology receipts and payments?
- What is the proportion of technology receipts and payments in total R&D expenditure?
- What share of manufacturing output is accounted for by high-technology exports and imports of manufactures?
- What is the share of high-technology exports and imports of manufactures by foreign-controlled affiliates and parent companies in total high-technology exports and imports?

4.2.2. Developing and interpreting the proposed indicators

422. As in the other chapters, the proposed indicators are divided into three categories: reference indicators, supplemental indicators and experimental indicators. Reference indicators are those to which the *Handbook* attaches the highest priority because they are relevant, and also because they are available in a large number of OECD countries.

423. Supplemental indicators, which are of lesser priority, are often of equal analytical interest but are frequently only available in fewer countries. As for experimental indicators, while of analytical interest, they are available in only one or two countries and sometimes no countries, and the *Handbook* attaches no priority to them. Reference indicators cover the activities of foreign-controlled affiliates and parent companies' activities, or else international technology (embedded or non-embedded) transactions by

Box 4.1. **Proposed reference indicators for measuring the degree of globalisation of technology**

Reference indicators

Degree of internationalisation of the R&D of multinational firms in the compiling country

- Share of R&D expenditure by foreign-controlled affiliates.
- Share of the number of researchers in foreign-controlled affiliates.
- Share of industrial R&D expenditure financed from abroad.
- Share of value added attributable to foreign-controlled affiliates whose main activity is R&D.
- Share of turnover attributable to foreign-controlled affiliates whose main activity is R&D.
- Share of employment attributable to foreign-controlled affiliates whose main activity is R&D.
- Share of parent companies in R&D expenditure.
- Share of the number of parent company researchers.
- Share of R&D expenditure and researchers in multinational firms (parent companies and foreign CAs)?

Degree of internationalisation of the diffusion of technology in the compiling country (total and by industry)

- Technology payments as a percentage of GDP.
- Technology payments as a percentage of R&D expenditure.
- Technology receipts as a percentage of GDP.
- Technology receipts as a percentage of R&D expenditure.

Degree of internationalisation of trade in technology-intensive products in compiling countries (total and by industry)

- Share of foreign-controlled affiliates' high-technology manufacturing exports in high-technology manufacturing output.
- Share of foreign-controlled affiliates' and parent companies' high-technology manufacturing exports and imports in total high-technology exports and imports.

all firms in compiling countries. These categories of data make up the first priority recommended by the *Handbook*. Supplemental indicators relate above all to the activities of compiling countries' affiliates abroad and to certain aspects of technology transactions. As in the other chapters, the share of foreign-controlled affiliates and of parent companies in compiling countries' aggregate activity emphasizes the degree of intensity of globalisation of a country's domestic market. Specifically, it indicates its exposure to technological activities of foreign origin and the intensity of activity of its own multinationals (parent companies), while increased diversity as to the geographic origin of foreign-controlled affiliates reflects greater interdependence between countries. All the reference indicators can be constructed, in the majority of OECD countries, on the basis of data collected in the framework of national surveys or data supplied to the OECD by the same authorities.

Box 4.2. **Supplemental indicators for measuring the degree of globalisation of technology**

Degree of internationalisation of R&D in compiling countries (total and by industry)

Inward investment

- Share of R&D expenditure performed for foreign-controlled affiliates in total R&D expenditure.
- Share of R&D expenditure performed for all parent companies and resident-controlled companies in total R&D expenditure.
- Share of value added attributable to the parent companies performing R&D.
- Share of the parent companies performing R&D in sales or turnover.
- Share in employment of parent companies performing R&D.
- Share of parent companies whose main activity is R&D in value added.
- Share of parent companies whose main activity is R&D in sales or turnover.
- Share in employment of parent companies whose main activity is R&D.

Outward investment

- R&D expenditure by affiliates abroad as a percentage of domestic R&D expenditure.
- R&D expenditure by affiliates abroad compared with expenditure by their parent companies in the compiling country.
- Number of researchers in affiliates abroad compared with the number of researchers in the compiling country.
- Number of researchers in affiliates abroad compared with the number of researchers in their parent companies in the compiling country.

Degree of internationalisation of technology diffusion in compiling countries

- Technology payments between parent companies and affiliates compared with the compiling country's overall technology payments.
- Technology receipts between parent companies and affiliates compared with the compiling country's overall technology receipts.

Degree of internationalisation of trade in technology-intensive products in compiling countries

- Share of intra-firm high-technology manufacturing exports in total high-technology manufacturing exports (total and by industry).
- Share of intra-firm high-technology manufacturing imports in total high-technology manufacturing imports (total and by industry).

4.2.2.1. *Reference indicators*

Degree of internationalisation concerning multinational firms in compiling countries

- Share of R&D expenditure performed by foreign-controlled affiliates and of the number of researchers in the said affiliates in the business sector total in the compiling country

  This indicator shows the share of industrial R&D which is under foreign control and that which is controlled by the residents of the compiling countries. In the majority of countries, the ratio is between 18% and 30%. In some countries, it is in excess of 70%

Box 4.3. Proposed experimental indicators for measuring the degree of globalisation

Degree of internationalisation of R&D in compiling countries

- Share of value added attributable to foreign-controlled affiliates performing R&D.
- Share of sales or turnover attributable to foreign-controlled affiliates performing R&D.
- Share of employment attributable to foreign-controlled affiliates performing R&D.
- Number of foreign-controlled affiliates performing R&D as a proportion of the total number of firms.
- R&D expenditure by affiliates abroad aimed at adapting products to the local market, by comparison with their parent companies' R&D expenditure in the compiling country.
- R&D expenditure by affiliates abroad aimed at developing new technologies for world markets, by comparison with their parent companies' R&D expenditure in the compiling country.

Degree of internationalisation of technology diffusion in the compiling country

- Share of gross output produced under foreign licence (total and by industry).

when the firms controlled by residents do little research and there are large numbers of foreign affiliates. The higher the ratios, the more a country's domestic market is internationalised and reflects its interdependence with other countries. The same could be said with regard to the number of researchers. It is very important that the definitions applied to these indicators should be those in the *Frascati Manual*, as outlined in Chapter 3 of this *Handbook*.

- Share of industrial R&D funded from abroad

  The object of these indicators is to determine whether a country finances its own R&D investment or if a certain proportion is funded from abroad. It needs to be made clear that funding from abroad in this context implies funds that cross borders and does not refer to local financing from foreign-controlled affiliates located inside a country. At present, data collected through national surveys and, above all, communicated to the OECD, differentiate between R&D financing by publicly-funded companies, private financing (partly from equity capital) and financing from abroad. This distinction, which is also made at sectoral level, makes no reference either to lenders or to categories of recipient firm. In the second part of the chapter, a few elementary distinctions will be proposed on an experimental basis.

- Share of the value added, turnover and employment of foreign-controlled affiliates whose main activity is R&D in the compiling country's total for these variables

  Amongst service enterprises, there is one category in which firms' main activity is R&D. The research performed by these companies, which are legally independent, could be intended to meet either the needs of their own group of companies (see Chapter 3), or those of other non-affiliated companies that are controlled by compiling country residents or are under foreign control. In the latter two cases, what is involved are services offered to firms in the form of R&D studies (case of R&D sub-contracting). The object, via these indicators, is to gauge the importance of these firms' value added, turnover and employment compared with the same aggregates for all compiling country firms.

- Share of R&D expenditure performed by parent companies in the R&D expenditure of the compiling country.

  Bearing in mind the way a parent company is defined in Chapter 3, this indicator measures within a given country, the share of total business R&D expenditure accounted for by that country's own multinationals (resident-controlled and foreign-controlled parent companies). For all R&D expenditure by parent companies (whatever their origin) to be taken into account, R&D expenditure by parent companies has to be added to the numerator of the ratio in question. It will be seen in the second part of this chapter, however, that not all the R&D performed by these two categories of firm is automatically designed to meet the needs of the compiling country and does not directly enhance its innovative capacity.

- Share of the number of parent company researchers in the total number of business sector researchers

  The comments concerning parent company R&D expenditure could also be made about the number of researchers. As in the case of expenditure, it goes without saying that the number of parent company researchers has to be defined in the same way as it is for all companies if the two aggregates are to be really comparable.

- Share of R&D expenditure and researchers of multinational firms (parent companies and foreign CAs) in the total for the business sector

  This ratio makes it possible to determine what share of a country's industrial R&D is performed by multinational firms and what is the share of these firms' researchers. It is assumed that the definitions of these categories of firms, as contained in Chapter 3, are correctly applied. It needs to be remembered, however, that to avoid double counting, foreign-controlled parent companies should be counted just once – either as parent companies or as foreign CAs.

Degree of internationalisation of technology diffusion in the compiling country (total and by industry)

- Technology payments and receipts as a percentage of GDP

  These ratios give a more accurate idea, for all of a country's firms, of the value of trade (sales and purchases) in patents, licences, know-how, designs, technical assistance and R&D studies in GDP. The reference to GDP makes the sums involved more comparable between countries, bearing in mind that their volume depends on the size of the countries involved and their technology effort. Interpreting the indicators does, however, pose certain problems which will be discussed in the second part of this chapter. When technology payments very significantly outstrip receipts, it does not necessarily mean that a country's technology position has worsened, given that purchasing foreign technologies can contribute a great deal to innovation.

- Technology payments and receipts as a percentage of R&D expenditure

  The comparison between trade in technology (non-embodied) and R&D expenditure is of interest in that it makes it to some extent possible to calculate whether trade in technology is substantial or on a small scale. More specifically, when the ratio of technology receipts to R&D expenditure is high, it could mean that the R&D effort is contributing to substantial technology-exporting capacity. In other words, a country is unlikely to be in a position to export technologies without making a considerable R&D effort. When the ratio in question is low, however, it could be either that the R&D results are not sufficiently significant, or that they are not exportable.

When the ratio of technology payments to R&D expenditure is high (in some extreme cases, it can exceed 1), it implies a development strategy based on imports of foreign technology rather than the use of native technology. This sort of situation occurs in countries whose industrial research is not sufficiently developed, but in which there are a great many foreign multinationals buying the technology that they use abroad (from their parent companies or from other non-affiliated firms abroad)

When the technology payments/R&D expenditure ratio is low, it could mean that the domestic R&D effort to a large extent satisfies a country's technology requirements. Conversely, when the domestic R&D expenditure of the country in question is similarly very low and the country imports little foreign technology, it could mean that the country is finding it difficult to absorb the said technologies. This latter situation is mainly encountered in developing countries.

Generally speaking, the above indicators reflect the scale of the technological internationalisation of the economies concerned, first because they relate to international transactions, but also because trade in technology is very closely correlated with the presence of multinational firms (see also supplemental indicators and the second part of the chapter).

Degree of internationalisation of trade in technology-intensive products in compiling countries

- Share of high-technology manufacturing exports in high-technology manufacturing output (total and by industry)

  This indicator reflects a country's propensity to export high-technology products. The more a country exports a large share of its high-technology output and directs it towards a large number of partner countries, the more internationalised it is from the point of view of trade. Exports of embodied technologies compared with R&D expenditure and technology payments may indicate whether the technology used for such exports is native or is largely imported.

- Share of high-technology manufacturing exports and imports by foreign-controlled affiliates and their parent companies in the compiling country's high-technology manufacturing exports and imports

  In other words, the object is to measure the share of high-technology exports and imports attributed to foreign-controlled affiliates and parent companies. Identifying the role of multinationals in this type of trade is of particular interest in that these firms play a decisive role in high-technology production and exports, and also because it is of interest to know whether or not a large proportion of the high-technology products imported by a given country comes from its own affiliates abroad. These questions will be considered in more detail in Chapter 5 on trade issues.

4.2.2.2. Supplemental indicators

Degree of internationalisation of R&D in compiling countries

Inward investment

424. In the case of R&D activities within the territory of a compiling country, three categories of indicator are proposed:

i) The share of R&D performed *for* foreign-controlled affiliates and not *by* the said affiliates, compared with total domestic R&D expenditure by the business sector. Thanks to this distinction it is possible to identify, at sectoral level, the research targeted at foreign-controlled affiliates, given that these affiliates perform R&D partly or totally on behalf of others.

ii) The share of business sector value added, turnover and employment attributable to parent companies. In other words, the purpose of these indicators is to measure the contribution that parent companies make to a country's economic growth. Since it is often the case that virtually all of a country's parent companies are controlled by the residents of that country, it is the same thing as measuring the economic weight within the country of its own R&D-performing multinationals.

iii) The share of business sector value added, turnover and employment attributable to parent companies whose main activity is R&D. This is in fact a sub-category of the previous indicators. Within the framework of surveys on services, a particular category relates to firms whose main activity is R&D. These are the main variables relating to the parent companies of these firms that are concerned by these indicators.

Outward investment

425. In the case of outward investment, and for R&D activities, two types of indicator are proposed:

i) The share of R&D expenditure and the number of researchers in affiliates abroad compared to total R&D expenditure and the total number of researchers for the business sector in the compiling country.

ii) The share of R&D expenditure and the number of researchers in affiliates abroad compared to R&D expenditure and numbers of researchers in parent companies in the compiling country.

426. These indicators are some of the most significant for illustrating the scale of the internationalisation of R&D. For a compiling country, the R&D expenditure and number of researchers in its affiliates abroad can in some cases exceed R&D expenditure and numbers of researchers within the country (*e.g.* Switzerland). It is also interesting to know what share of R&D (expenditure and personnel) parent companies perform abroad via their affiliates. The higher the preceding ratios, the more these countries' R&D is internationalised, especially since the geographical distribution of R&D expenditure abroad will not be highly concentrated.

Degree of internationalisation of technology diffusion in compiling countries

427. As an addition to the reference indicators, the object here is to measure the share of technology receipts and payments deriving from transactions between parent companies and their affiliates compared to the aggregate transactions by all the firms in a country. In fact, the data available show that the bulk of technology receipts and payments relate to

transactions between parent companies and their affiliates. These indicators, combined with R&D indicators, reveal the origin of the technology used by foreign-controlled affiliates (native or imported) and also which country is the owner of the said technology (see also the second part of the chapter).

4.2.2.3. *Experimental indicators*

428. The information about R&D that is being sought via the proposed experimental indicators is:

i) The economic profile of the affiliates performing the R&D.

ii) The market targeted by these affiliates' research.

429. The economic profile (value added, turnover, employment, etc.) would show whether foreign-controlled affiliates that perform R&D create more value added and employment than other R&D-performing firms that are controlled by residents of the compiling country.

430. The target market for R&D by foreign-controlled affiliates is also an important piece of information. R&D can concern either the local market, when R&D is confined to adapting products to that market, or else world markets when it sets out to develop new technologies. These indicators afford a better understanding of the technological choices made by these affiliates and their parent companies, and also make it easier to gauge the attractiveness of the compiling country as a host country for foreign R&D laboratories.

431. The experimental indicator of technology transfers measures the extent of foreign technology in local production. Gauging this technology cannot be confined to technology payments alone, since these are phased out over long periods (royalties) and can sometimes be very modest. In many countries, the share of production under a foreign licence can be over 50% in some sectors.

4.3. Methodological and conceptual aspects

4.3.1. *The internationalisation of industrial R&D*

432. The decentralisation of R&D by multinational enterprises, *i.e.* the establishment of laboratories outside the parent company's home country, or the acquisition by foreign firms of R&D laboratories belonging to firms which were controlled by residents, are clearly not new phenomena inasmuch as decentralised R&D had in some cases already been underpinning and accompanying the shift to relocate production.

433. While the growth of this phenomenon is recognized, there is a need to assess the significance of that growth and its impact on different countries' technological and innovative capacity. The indicators proposed in the first part of the chapter provide a basis for that assessment.

434. The intention in this part is to look at the main forms that the internationalisation of R&D can take, the information that is collected by national authorities, the nature of the data forwarded to international organisations and certain methodological and conceptual problems concerning the basic data.

4.3.1.1. *Main forms of internationalisation of R&D*

435. The internationalisation of industrial R&D can take various forms. In what follows, a distinction will be made between the aspects that concern the implementation of R&D and those relating to its financing. Implementation falls into two categories: on one hand, the

OECD HANDBOOK ON ECONOMIC GLOBALISATION INDICATORS – ISBN 92-64-10808-4 – © OECD 2005

establishing of R&D activities by foreign-controlled affiliates in the host country and, on the other, the setting up (or relocation) of R&D laboratories abroad. With respect to financing, there are all those firms (foreign-controlled or otherwise) whose R&D funding comes partially from abroad, and then there are firms located within the compiling country but which finance research that is performed abroad.

4.3.1.1.1. *Aspects linked to R&D implementation*

1) *Establishment of R&D activities in the host country by foreign-controlled affiliates (inward investment)*

a) As a rule, the establishment of R&D activities in a host country follows the setting up of the production units. Laboratories can either be created out of nothing, like greenfield investments, or they can be obtained through the acquisition by foreign investors of existing firms' R&D laboratories.

b) Corresponding to a sub-category of the above firms are foreign-controlled affiliates whose main activity is R&D. Such affiliates, whose legal status is that of an independent company, can perform R&D for other firms controlled by the residents of the compiling (host) country, or for the foreign group to which they belong, or again for other foreign-controlled affiliates. To a large extent, it is these firms which perform the R&D of firms controlled by residents. The latter can either perform R&D and subcontract the part deemed less strategic, or for which they do not have the requisite in-house skills, or else they may be firms which do not themselves perform R&D but subcontract their entire R&D requirements.

2) *Setting up R&D activities abroad (outward investment)*

As in the case of inward investment, the setting up of R&D activities abroad can concern either R&D laboratories created out of nothing (greenfields), existing laboratories bought up as a result of a merger/acquisition, or laboratories transferred abroad (relocation) as part of the restructuring of the R&D activities of a group of companies.

4.3.1.1.2. *Aspects relating to R&D financing*

i) Financing of R&D from abroad

This category comprises all of a compiling country's companies whose R&D funds come partly from abroad. In some countries, more and more R&D – as much as 20 to 30% of total expenditure – is financed from abroad. These funds can be either public, as in the case of government contracts or aid from international institutions such as the European Commission, or they can be private, as when parent companies finance the R&D of their affiliates abroad or when other firms abroad commission R&D work from compiling country firms.

ii) Financing of R&D destined for abroad

This is R&D which is funded by companies located in the compiling country, but performed abroad.

iii) Financing of the R&D of foreign-controlled affiliates either from abroad or destined for abroad.

While the previous two categories relate to all the firms in a given compiling country, the final category concerns foreign-controlled affiliates. It relates mainly to funds from abroad that finance the R&D of these affiliates in the compiling country.

4.3.1.2. *What the Frascati Manual proposes*

436. Without going back to the basic definitions repeated in Chapter 3, the latest 2002 revision of the *Frascati Manual* takes much more account of globalisation-linked data and indicators than do earlier versions. To examine trends in the internationalisation of industry, the *Frascati Manual* recommends in §179 that the following classification by type of institution be used if possible:

- Private enterprises
  - Enterprise not belonging to any group.
  - Enterprise belonging to a national group.
  - Enterprise belonging to a foreign multinational group.
- Public enterprises
  - Enterprise not belonging to any group.
  - Enterprise belonging to a national group.

437. The internationalisation of R&D in industry is gauged mainly on the basis of the difference between intramural funding (BERD = firms' domestic expenditure on R&D) and extramural funding (NBERD = national R&D expenditure). For a given country, these two aggregates are defined as follows:

BERD: Total intramural business expenditure on R&D performed on the national territory during a given period. It includes R&D performed within this country and funded from abroad but excludes payments made abroad for R&D.

NBERD: National business expenditure on R&D. It comprises business sector R&D expenditure financed by the institutions of the country during a given period. It includes domestic funding of business sector enterprise R&D performed abroad but excludes business sector enterprise R&D performed within the country and funded from abroad.

Therefore: NBERD = BERD + funding of R&D conducted abroad – funding of R&D received from abroad.

438. The experimental table X5, which corresponds to the questionnaire in the OECD Secretariat surveys based on the recommendations in the *Frascati Manual*, asks for a breakdown of the business enterprise sector by type of funding and by researcher nationality. Table 4.1 summarises what is proposed in the OECD Secretariat's questionnaire.

Table 4.1. **Source of funds and nationality of researchers in the business enterprise sector**

Source of funds, business enterprise sector	Nationality of researchers
1. Subtotal coming from foreign companies:	Nationality of compiling country
1.1. Enterprise belonging to the same group	Foreign nationality, of which:
1.2. Other enterprises	• European Union
2. Other governments	• United States
3. Higher education	• Other OECD countries
4. Non-profit bodies	• OECD non-member countries
5. European Commission	• Unknown
6. Other international organisations	
7. Not included elsewhere	
Sub-total, foreign funds	Total number of researchers

439. For further information, the *Frascati Manual* recommends in §181 referring to the *OECD Handbook on Economic Globalisation Indicators*.

4.3.1.3. Proposals in this Handbook

440. Whereas the *Frascati Manual* covers the internationalisation of R&D by placing the emphasis on questions to do with the origin of R&D financing in the business enterprise sector and the nationality of researchers, the present *Handbook* on Economic Globalisation Indicators insists rather on the implementation of R&D in compiling countries, taking into account:

First and foremost:

- Foreign-controlled affiliates, singling out those whose main activity is R&D.
- Parent companies in compiling countries.

Secondly:

- Affiliates performing R&D abroad.
- The economic profile of foreign-controlled affiliates performing R&D (in the compiling country).
- The economic profile of parent companies performing R&D (in the compiling country).

441. The basic R&D data that constitute the first priority, together with some of those that make up the second priority, are collected by the OECD as part of its globalisation surveys concerning the activity of multinational firms. It has to be stressed, however, that national authorities also have supplemental information which is not systematically passed on to the OECD Secretariat. All of this information, which is supplementary to that requested in the overall R&D surveys in the *Frascati Manual* framework, is collected by national authorities either via overall R&D surveys or via specific surveys concerning multinational firms.

4.3.1.3.1. Priority data and indicators

442. Expenditure on R&D performance and the number of researchers, which are variables of prime importance, are also the basic data for building up the reference indicators. To ensure that these indicators are really comparable, it is important to abide by the *Frascati Manual* definitions which are reiterated in Chapter 3. Also, if the data on foreign-controlled affiliates are to be comparable with data for other compiling country firms, they must be expressed in the same statistical unit. This is also very important for calculating R&D intensities, as will be seen further on.

443. The data on R&D activity in services, which more especially concern firms whose main activity is R&D, do not single out expenditure intended solely for R&D, notably when the said firms also have other secondary activities not directly linked to R&D. As a result, neither these firms' turnover nor their value added (variables collected under the heading of FATS surveys[1]) can be likened to R&D expenditure inasmuch, for example, as turnover includes business services, whereas value added excludes intermediate consumption even when the firms in question have no other secondary activity apart from R&D. It will be recalled in this connection that, according to the *Frascati Manual*, intermediate consumption should not be excluded from R&D expenditure.

444. Data on funding from abroad which, as stated above, are collected as part of the OECD's international R&D surveys, concern all firms and make no distinction between backers and

recipient firms. If the new *Frascati Manual* recommendations are taken into account, the experimental tables in the present questionnaires could be filled in and submitted in the following form:

Table 4.2. **R&D funds from abroad intended for a compiling country's industry**

Sector	Total funding	Affiliated firms (including parent companies)	Non-affiliated firms	International organisations (including the European Commission
Sector 1				
All firms				
Foreign-controlled firms				
Firms controlled by residents				
Sector 2				
All firms				
Foreign-controlled firms				
Firms controlled by residents				
Total, industry				
All firms				
Foreign-controlled firms				
Firms controlled by residents				

445. Concerning the data on parent companies, it should be remembered that they relate not to a single firm, but to a group of firms controlled by the company that constitutes the head office (see also Chapter 3). As was already pointed out in Chapter 3, parent companies are made up of parent companies controlled by compiling country residents and foreign-controlled parent companies. Member country authorities are encouraged to collect separate data for each of the two categories of parent company, as long as confidentiality problems permit.

446. Parent company R&D data offer two possibilities. First, they could be used to gauge the R&D impact of the headquarters of multinational firms in each country and in the OECD area as a whole. Second, for each country, they would offer a sample of nationally-controlled firms that would be more comparable to foreign affiliates, comparisons being less relevant if the population of nationally-controlled firms includes small and medium-sized enterprises whose structures and performances are very different from those of foreign affiliates.

4.3.1.3.2. Supplemental data and indicators (second priority)

447. Despite being relevant, the supplemental indicators proposed are of lower priority in that they relate to data that only a limited number of countries possess. The data corresponding to these indicators may be divided into four major categories:

- The activity of compiling countries' affiliates abroad.
- The economic activity of foreign-controlled affiliates performing R&D in a compiling country.
- The economic activity of parent companies performing R&D in the compiling countries.
- R&D expenditure *for* foreign-controlled affiliates (and not just *by* these affiliates) in a compiling country.

Box 4.4. Recommendations concerning priority data

- R&D data deemed of prime importance are those which relate to the R&D activity of firms located within the national territory of each compiling country. The firms concerned are:
  - ❖ Foreign-controlled affiliates, including those whose main activity is R&D
  - ❖ Parent companies in compiling countries (both nationally and foreign-controlled).
- The variables requested for these firms are *R&D expenditure* and the *number of researchers*, the two aggregates being defined according to the *Frascati Manual*. For foreign-controlled affiliates whose main activity is R&D, the information more especially requested concerns *value added, turnover, employment and exports and imports*, but other variables could also be added in the future.
- It is essential that these data be comparable with total national R&D data (same basic definitions and same statistical units). From this point of view, care must be taken not to liken an innovation centre (see *Oslo Manual*)[1] to a research centre (Frascati).[2]
- Indicators of expenditure and the number of researchers should be broken down by industrial sector according to ISIC Rev. 3 and by country of origin, opting first for the country of the ultimate controler (see Chapter 3).
- The sector activity of foreign-controlled affiliates with R&D activities measured by expenditure should correspond first of all to their own principal activity. The activity of their parent companies in the countries of origin may also be selected as a second-ranking priority.
- With regard to R&D funding from abroad, national authorities are encouraged to collect the data set out in Table 4.2. However, only the data in the first column of the table (total funding) and the first row of each sector (total firms) are considered to be of prime importance.

1. Oslo Manual: Guidelines proposed by the OECD for collecting and interpreting data on technological innovation, OECD, Paris, 1992.
2. *Frascati Manual*: Standard method proposed for surveys of experimental research and development, OECD, Paris, 2002.

448. The first category relates to the R&D activities of outward investment. For a compiling country, it is a matter of collecting data on expenditure by affiliates abroad and the number of their researchers. Like most other data on the activity of multinational firms abroad, these data are only available in a certain number of countries. Apart from making it possible to compare the R&D activity of nationally controlled firms with R&D activity within the country in question, the said data also make it possible to measure the share of R&D performed by all multinational firms $(R - D)_{mult}$ within a reference area such as the OECD, compared with the area's total industrial R&D:

$$\sum_i RD_i$$

- Share of R&D performed by multinational firms within the OECD area, compared with the area's aggregate industrial R&D:

i.e.: $(R + D)_{mult} / \sum_i RD_i$

where: $(R+D)_{mult} = \sum_i ARD_i + \sum_i PC_i$

and R-D	= the R&D expenditure of all multinational firms belonging to the OECD and non-OECD countries located in the OECD area.
$\sum_i ARD_i$	= R&D expenditure by all foreign-controlled affiliates in i countries of the OECD, in whatever country they are situated.
PC_i	= R&D expenditure by the parent companies of these same affiliates in counties i.

449. To avoid any double counting, in particular between foreign-controlled affiliates and foreign-controlled parent companies situated in the same country, it would be better if foreign-controlled parent companies could be excluded from the parent company total. Another solution would be to keep the two parent company categories (*i.e.* nationally-controlled and foreign-controlled), but to exclude foreign-controlled parent companies from the total number of affiliates under foreign control inasmuch as foreign-controlled parent companies are also foreign-controlled affiliates.

- Share of nationally-controlled R&D expenditure, either worldwide or in a particular geographical area.

450. Reference and supplemental indicators also make it possible to calculate other aggregates of political interest. Some countries' authorities may be interested to know what proportion of R&D is performed in the OECD area or in the world by firms that are controlled by the residents of the country in question. This means identifying, for country i, the R&D expenditure of firms under domestic control, firms under foreign control and affiliates of firms controlled by the residents of country i that are situated abroad. The aggregate in question, $DNRDE_i$, could then be defined as follows:

$$DNRDE_i = RD^i - \sum_j RD^j_{in,\,i} + \sum_j RD^i_{out,\,j}$$

where $DNRDE_i$	= Aggregate R&D expenditure by all enterprises in country i and abroad controlled by the residents of country i.
RD^i	= R&D expenditure of firms controlled by the residents of country i within country i.
$\sum_j RD^j_{in,\,i}$	= Total R&D expenditure by foreign-controlled affiliates from countries j performed in country i (where $i \neq j$); and
$\sum_j RD^i_{out,\,j}$	= The sum of R&D expenditure by affiliates controlled by residents of country i located in countries *j*.

451. Similar indicators could also be constructed for the number of researchers, assuming the information is available.

- Indicators relating to the economic activity of foreign-controlled affiliates with R&D activities

452. In national surveys of R&D activity, it is usually only data linked directly to R&D that are asked for. In the majority of OECD countries, moreover, no systematic connection has so far been made with company registers or other sources of information which could be used to identify the economic variables corresponding to R&D-performing firms.

453. This situation concerns not only the R&D surveys involving all the firms in a particular country, but also the surveys of foreign-controlled affiliates. The lack of economic data for firms performing R&D (whether nationally or foreign-controlled) presents two major drawbacks:

- It is not possible to measure the performance solely of firms that perform R&D by comparing it to the performance of firms that do no R&D.
- It is more difficult to interpret R&D intensity, *i.e.* the share of turnover, gross output or value added devoted to R&D.

454. In order better to illustrate this latter problem with respect to foreign-controlled affiliates in particular, it may be assumed that, in a compiling country:

RD_{in}: is the R&D expenditure of foreign-controlled affiliates.

P_{in}^{RD}: is the gross output of foreign-controlled affiliates performing R&D.

P_{in}: is the gross output of all foreign-controlled firms.

455. At present, the only ratio that can be calculated for measuring the R&D intensity of foreign-controlled affiliates is RD_{in}/P_{in}, and not RD_{in}/P_{in}^{RD} because P_{in}^{RD} is not available. When the first ratio is calculated for a given sector, what it means is that if, in that sector, there are a lot of small and medium-sized firms not performing R&D, the ratio will be lower than in another more concentrated sector in which, compared to the first sector, firms performing R&D devote a relatively smaller share of their production to R&D.

456. In other words, when using the data available, sector intensities depend very much on the breakdown of firms which do not perform R&D and not enough on the breakdown of firms that do perform R&D. Collecting economic data through company registers or separate surveys would make possible performance evaluations that currently cannot be carried out.

457. The above comments concern not just foreign-controlled affiliates, but also parent companies, including those controlled by compiling country nationals. It would be useful if this information could also be collected for nationally-controlled firms that perform R&D without being parent companies.

458. A final improvement that would greatly help the analysis would be to collect R&D expenditure *for* an affiliate instead of just *by* an affiliate, which is the approach adopted up to now in the *Frascati Manual*.

(Frascati Definition) : R&D performed *by* an affiliate.

= R&D performed by itself on its own behalf.

+ R&D performed by the affiliate on behalf of others.

(New definition) : R&D performed *for* an affiliate.

= R&D performed by itself on its own behalf.

+ R&D performed by others on the affiliate's behalf.

459. R&D performed by other countries on behalf of affiliates corresponds to contracts to purchase R&D entered into by affiliates on their own behalf.

460. Such indicators are regularly collected by certain countries, such as the United States.

461. For this information to be collected as part of national surveys, firms (foreign affiliates or parent companies) need to be asked what portion of R&D expenditure goes on their own account and what portion on behalf of others.

Box 4.5. Recommendations concerning the collection of data of lesser priority

- As a second priority, countries are invited to collect data on the activity of compiling countries' affiliates abroad concerning:
  - These affiliates' R&D.
  - The number of researchers.
- These data will be broken down by sector of implementation and country of location. It will be remembered that the sectors should first of all be those of the affiliates and, second, those of the parent companies.
- As regards parent companies in compiling countries that perform R&D (including those whose main activity is R&D), the national authorities ought as their first priority to collect data on turnover, gross output and the number of employees.
- The *Handbook* also recommends questioning foreign-controlled affiliates in compiling countries, as well as these countries' affiliates abroad, to determine what share of their R&D expenditure is *on their own behalf* and what share *on behalf of others*.

4.3.1.3.3. Experimental indicators

462. The indicators proposed above as experimental indicators are very important analytically, but since they are not available and in view of the cost of developing them and, above all, the methodological problems still to be solved, the *Handbook* invites countries which have the necessary resources and want to develop them to do their best to do so. In so doing, they will gain extremely valuable experience and will be better able to identify the practical difficulties involved in developing such indicators. Depending on the outcome, some of the proposed indicators could be classified in the second category (supplemental indicators) in a forthcoming revision of this *Handbook*.

4.3.2. Reminder of the main distortions in international comparisons

463. Most of the distortions affecting the international comparability of R&D indicators stem from inappropriate definitions concerning foreign affiliates, their geographical origins or their sectors of activity. Some distortions, however, are due to the R&D data themselves. The rules necessary for proper international comparability are therefore reiterated below.

464. *Defining foreign-controlled affiliates*. It should be borne in mind that an affiliate is deemed to be under foreign control if a majority of voting rights is held by a foreign investor. Accordingly, a distinction must be made between this type of data and data pertaining to firms in which non-residents have a minority participation (between 10% and 50%). Many cases not fitting into the general category are examined in Chapter 3. The proposed solutions for these cases, if applied by all countries, could significantly improve international comparisons.

465. *Identifying the investor country*. The main difficulty in determining the investor country stems from the intricate web of control relationships between firms. If the search is not limited to the immediate controller, but an attempt is made to identify the ultimate controller of an investment, it is necessary to be able to go to the end of the chain – to the point at which a firm is no longer subject to any outside control.

466. *Determining the sector of activity.* As emphasised above, the sector of activity is defined on the basis of the main activity of the affiliate, not of the parent company. The sectors must also correspond to international standard classification systems (ISIC Revision 3 or NACE Revision 1). In some cases there may be a lack of symmetry between declaring countries (home countries and host countries) if they do not adopt the same criteria for determining the main activity of each affiliate.

467. *Defining R&D activity according to Frascati Manual criteria.* In some cases, investor countries and host countries do not adopt the same criteria (those of the *Frascati Manual*) in determining whether an activity is an R&D activity. In some cases, innovation centres are considered research laboratories by the investing country but not by the host country.

468. *Differences between inward and outward R&D investment.* In some cases, the level of aggregation, sectors of activity or majority control criteria are not applied in the same way to R&D data on foreign CAs and affiliates abroad of resident-controlled firms – in respect of either one and the same country or from one declaring country to another.

469. Other distortions may stem from the fact that definitions stray from the Frascati rules on the intramural R&D expenditure of affiliates or assessment of the number of researchers (failure to adhere to the method for computing "full-time R&D equivalent"), or from the fact that foreign funding has not been associated with its geographical origin (Frascati), but with criteria involving ownership.

470. The distortions mentioned in this section are not exhaustive, but they do reflect the cases encountered most frequently in surveys and analytical work.

4.4. The international diffusion of technology (technology balance of payments: TBP)

471. International trade in technology as represented by patenting, licenses, know-how, technical assistance and the provision of R&D services constitutes another form of internationalisation of technology in which the authorities play an important role in collecting basic data and constructing indicators.

472. The accelerating pace of globalisation has facilitated and at the same time spurred an increase in inter-company trade in technology. The keen competition that characterises globalisation has prompted more and more firms to refocus on core competencies in which they enjoy competitive advantages. Because of that strategy, businesses are compelled to purchase the technologies which are essential to them but which they do not have the means to develop themselves, in many cases acquiring them abroad. Sharp growth in direct investment has also contributed to an acceleration of technology transfers from parent companies to their affiliates abroad.

473. The importance of technology balance of payments indicators is frequently underestimated, for two main reasons. First, there are the problems involved in collecting data consistent with international definitions. Second, there are the difficulties of interpreting the indicators, the appraisal of which involves comparison with a number of other indicators and some sometimes rather complex analyses. Adding, no doubt, to the failure to appreciate the importance of these indicators in analysing the international diffusion of technology is the fact that technology receipts and payments (royalties) are often relatively modest by comparison with R&D expenditure, are spread out over a long period of time, sometimes show large annual fluctuations and occur to a large degree within firms, making them susceptible to issues associated with transfer pricing.

474. Technology receipts are usually dependent on a country's R&D effort and correspond to foreign sales of the marketable results of that effort. Firms sell the technologies either to their affiliates abroad or to unaffiliated firms. The available data show that the bulk (over 60%) of such technology transfers in the majority of countries are between parent companies and affiliates, so the role of direct investment in these transfers is vital. Technology payments, on the other hand, correspond to knowledge that is immediately useable by countries' productive systems. In contrast with receipts, payments constitute a technology input which can supplement or take the place of a country's R&D effort.

475. Some technologies needed for countries' development are produced by just a few firms in the world, which protect their technologies by means of patents. Countries and firms that do not have these technologies have to buy them abroad, unless they themselves have the capacity to develop equivalent technologies rapidly via their own R&D. Technology balance of payments indicators tell us about a country's degree of independence with respect to non-embedded technology, the origin of the technology used in the productive system or in exports (notably high tech exports), the links between a country's R&D effort and its technology receipts, and about the technologies it is able to develop itself and those that come from abroad or that have to be developed in co-operation with other countries.

4.4.1. Main categories of TBP operations

476. In 1990, to cover the methodological aspects of the balance of payments, the OECD prepared a manual entitled "Proposed Standard Method of Compiling and Interpreting Technology Balance of Payments Data (TBP Manual)".

477. The Manual distinguishes four types of transaction:

i) Technology transfers, which can be subdivided into transfers of:

- Patents.
- Unpatented inventions.
- Licences (linked to know-how).
- Know-how.

ii) Transfers of designs (sales, licences, franchises), trademarks and patterns.

iii) Provision of technical services, comprising:

- Technical and engineering studies (project design and implementation).
- Technical assistance.

iv) Provision of industrial R&D (performed abroad or financed from abroad).

4.4.2. Definitions of the different transactions

Purchase/sale of patents

478. A patent is a right in law conferred by an official agency, national or regional. It gives the patentee a monopoly of the invention and its industrial or commercial exploitation, for a limited time (ranging from fifteen to twenty years) and within a given territory. As an item of property, a patent can be assigned or transferred under licence. Against payment, a patent may accordingly be bought or sold either in whole or in part; in the latter case, the sale may cover one or more applications.

Purchase/sale of unpatented inventions

479. Some inventions are deliberately not patented by the inventor, and others are not patentable on legal grounds (depending on the country, medical methods or mathematical formulae, for example). These inventions have no protection under industrial property law, but they may be protected by non-disclosure (or secrecy). As with patents, inventions may be bought or sold, against payment.

Award of licences linked to patents

480. Under the licensing process, the patentee (or licensor) authorises the licensee to exploit all or some of the applications of the patent. The licensing agreement is likely to contain clauses on sole rights, period and territory as well, obviously, as forms of payment.

481. The latter chiefly include:

- Payment of a pre-set amount, either as a lump sum or by installments. This may include an initial payment on signature of the licensing agreement, to cover the costs of initial disclosure and transmission of the technology;
- Payment of royalties calculated on the basis of the use made of the licence or the end result (units produced, sales or profits). The term current royalties is used to describe royalties paid at periodic intervals and calculated as a percentage of the selling price or any other value agreed upon beforehand. However it may be defined, a royalty is simply a means of payment stipulated in a patent licensing agreement, and is not in itself a form of contract.

Disclosure of know-how contracts

482. Know-how is rather a loose category. Intuitively it can be grasped easily enough, but a quick and simple definition that will satisfy everyone is hard to find. The main reason is that know-how is not industrial property, so the term has no legal definition. Lawyers have made attempts to pin down know-how by analogy with patents, however, and in particular to clarify the standing of know-how agreements.

483. The main characteristics of know-how are:

- Not being divulged or being kept secret.
- Being made up of knowledge acquired and accumulated during the implementation phase of a technology.
- It may take the form of an addition to the information contained in the patent, and be manifold in its composition: concrete and well-documented data and more or less formal information not necessarily backed by any material evidence.
- The disclosure of know-how involves various different forms of teaching, workshop courses, demonstrations, and consultations which are a vital adjunct to the transmission of documentation. These various examples are often vaguely termed "technical assistance".

484. The borderline between transmission of know-how and technical assistance is not cut and dried, therefore. For clarity, however, it seems preferable here to consider only know-how and its transmission (possibly extensive), either accompanying a licensing contract or on its own. The knowledge making up know-how is intrinsically exclusive in a way that information supplied through technical assistance is not.

Transfers of designs, trademarks and patterns (sales, licences, franchises)

485. The protection afforded by patent systems is not confined to technical knowledge. It extends to trademarks and industrial designs and patterns. Rights to industrial property of that kind may be the subject of transactions in the same way as patents, *i.e.* assigned or transferred under licence.

486. The most common transactions probably involve trademarks, particularly trademark licensing. Since they do not concern technical knowledge, such transactions are not classified as international transfers of technology. But the point has often been made that a trademark licence may be accompanied by a transfer of technical knowledge, relating to a formula or the exclusive composition of a product, for instance, or to quality control. *Given that it is impossible to isolate the technology component, trademark licences cannot be omitted.* Moreover, the case for inclusion is strengthened by the current spread of franchise agreements.

487. Franchising involves a variable mix of industrial property rights (trademarks, designs, patterns), transmission of mainly commercial *know-how* and the provision of technical assistance. The purpose of the agreement is the distribution of goods or the supply of services and not, as in the case of patents, manufacturing. They are in fact complex arrangements focusing on the exploitation of an exclusive trademark.

Provision of technical services

488. This heading covers services that call for the supplier to make use of technical skills and help the user carry out a productive activity. This is not a transfer of technology in the strict sense, in that the technical skills employed are not as a rule transmitted to the purchaser, only their result. The latter, however, does help the purchaser increase or mobilise his technological potential.

489. Transactions that fall under the heading "services with a technical content" include:

- Preliminary technical studies and engineering work required for the design and preparation of industrial projects, including product definition, process and plant specification, general design and detailed drawings for the installation.
- General technical assistance for industrial operation and maintenance, including staff training, secondment of technicians, consultancy services and assistance for quality control and trouble-shooting.

490. Note that transactions relating to commercial, legal, financial, administrative, organisation and managerial assistance are excluded. Major civil engineering contracts (construction of bridges, roads, non-industrial buildings), mineral and petroleum prospecting, contract work and repair activities, occasionally included in some countries' TBPs, are also excluded.

Industrial and technological R&D

491. The final heading covers flows to finance R&D performed outside the agents' country of residence. Taking a given country A, this will be R&D financed by residents of A and performed elsewhere, as well as R&D performed in A and financed by non-residents. The work must be industrial and technological R&D.

492. The financial flows relating to the relocated R&D seem largely of two kinds:

- First, funds provided by multinational corporations to finance R&D performed by their affiliates (which may be manufacturing concerns or specialise in R&D), as well as funds which affiliates remit to their parent companies as an "entry fee" or advance payment for a subsequent transfer of technology.
- Second, financial flows between unrelated firms which have agreed to conduct joint R&D either in existing research facilities or in a subsidiary company they have set up together for that purpose.

493. There are other international flows of finance for R&D, involving official and private-sector agencies. The financing of scientific R&D (co-operation in science, contributions to intergovernmental research bodies such as CERN) is not included in the TBP, but some borderline cases have to be taken into account. Examples are flows relating to R&D performed jointly by private-sector concerns and university laboratories, whatever their status, and official financial contributions to co-operative projects on technology, such as the European Community programmes.

494. In TBP terms, these financial flows are somewhat special. Unlike all the other items in the TBP, these flows do not represent output from past R&D; they fund science and technology inputs. It can be argued that the financing is an entry fee, for the results of the R&D that is being paid for, and that it to some degree represents payment for output as well. Whether this is so or not, the twofold and possibly ambiguous nature of financing for R&D performed abroad, and outside financing for local R&D, needs to be borne in mind when TBP data are interpreted.

4.4.3. Other characteristics of the technology balance of payments

495. Four other characteristics of balance-of-payments transactions need to be mentioned. The breakdown:

- By industrial sector,
- by geographical origin,
- according to the nature of the contracts, and
- between affiliated and non-affiliated firms.

The industrial sector

496. Payments and receipts are assigned to specific sectors. As for the other variables, the sectors correspond to the firm's main activity. As a general rule, the main activity of the reporting firm is taken into account. In OECD countries, the main activity of foreign-controlled affiliates located in these countries is taken into consideration, not the main activity of their parent company abroad. Also, in the case of affiliates abroad of firms controlled by compiling country residents, the main activity of these affiliates is taken into consideration. However, the ideal solution would be to have data based both on the main activity of affiliates and on the main activity of their parent companies abroad.

Geographical origin

497. The geographical origin of transactions is an important aspect of the data. From the analytical point of view, it is interesting to know who is the ultimate controller of the transactions. If, for example, an American holding company situated in the Netherlands

sells licences to its affiliates in the European countries, it would be interesting to know that the originator of the technology is the United States and not the Netherlands. However, given that some countries have difficulty identifying the geographical origin of the ultimate controller, it is important in these surveys to indicate clearly whether it is the ultimate or immediate controller that is involved.

Nature of contracts

498. By "nature of contracts" is meant old and recent contracts. This distinction is relevant for interpreting data because in some countries the aggregate technology balance of payments may be negative for a certain period but becomes positive for recent (or new) contracts. This may indicate that the countries in question are making a considerable effort to reduce their technological dependence, or that a change in the technological strategy of foreign firms in these countries has taken place.

Transactions between affiliated and non-affiliated firms

499. The distinction between affiliate and non-affiliate is very important in the context of globalisation. The definitions of these firms are given in Chapters 2 and 3. Depending on whether payments or receipts are involved, the following categories can be distinguished:

Table 4.3. **Technology payments and receipts between affiliates and non-affiliates**

Payments	Receipts
1. Total (affiliates and non-affiliates)	1. Total (affiliates and non-affiliates)
2. Affiliates	2. Affiliates
Payments by foreign-controlled affiliates to parent companies abroad.	Receipts received by parent companies controlled by compiling country residents from their affiliates abroad.
Payments by parent companies of firms controlled by compiling country residents to their affiliates abroad.	Receipts received by foreign-controlled affiliates from their parent companies abroad.
3. Non-affiliates (difference 1-2)	3. Non-affiliates (difference 1-2)

4.4.4. Data collected in the balance-of-payments framework

500. What was presented above relates to what it is important to know about non-embodied technology trade (technology balance of payments). A large proportion of these data are collected by the national authorities of OECD countries and forwarded to the Secretariat via specialised questionnaires. Some data, however, are collected independently in the context of the balance of payments and are split between various current and capital account headings (see Box 4.6).

I) Current account

501. It can be seen from the current account (see Box 4.6) that technology transfers can take place in addition to transactions involving high-technology goods, via certain categories of services and direct investment. Trade in high-technology goods (embodied technology), which will be described in the following section, is not part of the technology balance of payments.

502. Similarly, technology transfers via direct investment, which mainly concern intangible flows and intra-firm know-how, are quite difficult to identify separately from a firm's other assets in the context of direct investment transactions, so they ought in principle to be excluded. With regard, also, to the transfer of patent ownership, licences

Box 4.6. **The balance of payments account**[1]

I. CURRENT ACCOUNT
- A. Goods and services
  - a. Goods
  - b. Services
    - 1. Transportation
    - 2. Travel
    - 3. Communications
    - 4. Construction
    - 5. Insurance
    - 6. Financial services
    - 7. Computer and information services, of which:
      - – ***Computer services*** (BPM5 §259)
    - 8. ***Royalties and licence fees*** (BPM5 §260)
    - 9. Other business services, *of which*:[2]
      - – ***Research and development*** (BPM5 §264)
      - – ***Architectural, engineering and other technical services***
    - 10. Personal, cultural, and recreational services
    - 11. Government services not included elsewhere
- B. Income
  - 1. Compensation of employees
  - 2. Investments income
    - 2.1. Direct investments
    - 2.2. Portfolio investments
    - 2.3. Other investments
- C. Current transfers

II. CAPITAL AND FINANCIAL ACCOUNT
- A. Capital account
  - 1. Capital transfers
  - 2. ***Acquisition/disposal of non-produced, non-financial assets*** (BPM5 §312 and 358)
- B. Financial account
  - 1. Direct investment
    - 1.1. Abroad
    - 1.2. In reporting economy
  - 2. Portfolio investments
    - 2.1. Assets
    - 2.2. Liabilities
  - 3. Financial derivatives
  - 4. Other investment (assets, liabilities)
  - 5. Reserve assets

1. The categories linked to technological balance of payments are shown in bold type.
2. The categories linked to the technological balance of payments are included in item 9.3: Miscellaneous business, professional and technical services.

and know-how and the transformation of non-transferred royalties into non-voting shares in the capital of the company that received the technology input, in view of their great complexity in registration procedures, it would be preferable to exclude them from the technology balance of payments. On the other hand, other service items which relate to categories 7, 8 and 9 of the current account concern flows which are directly linked to transfers of non-embodied technology, and the same holds for part of category A.2 of the capital account.

Item 7: Computer and information services (BPM5§259)

"Computer and information services cover computer data and news-related service transactions between residents and non-residents. Included are: data bases, such as development, storage, and on-line time series; data processing – including tabulation, provision of processing services on a time-share or specific (hourly) basis, and management of facilities of others on a continuing basis; hardware consultancy; software implementation – including design, maintenance and repair of computers and peripheral equipment; news agency services – including provision of news, photographs, and feature articles to the media; and direct, non-bulk subscriptions to newspapers and periodicals."

503. Comments: It is apparent that this item covers a lot of cases which are in no way technological in nature. Also, software purchases and sales make no distinction between software programmes protected by intellectual property rights (royalties) which provide entitlement solely to their utilisation, and those involving a patent, which are protected by industrial property and allow a genuine transfer of technology to take place. Only this latter category of software should be included in the technology balance of payments.

Item 8: Royalties and licence fees (BPM5§260)

*"Royalties and licence fees cover the exchange of payments and receipts between residents and non-residents for the authorized use of intangible, non-produced, non-financial assets and proprietary rights (such as patents, copyrights, trademarks, industrial processes, franchises, etc.) and with the use, through licensing agreements, of produced originals or prototypes (such as manuscripts and films). Inclusion of this item under **services**, rather than under **income**, is in accordance with the SNA treatment of such items as payments for production of services for intermediate consumption or receipts from sales of output used as intermediate inputs."*

504. Comments: This category contains a large number of items involving technology transfers. However, it also contains items such as royalties, manuscripts and films which have to be excluded from the technology balance of payments.

Item 9: Other business services (BPM5§264)

a) Research and development

"Research and development services cover those services that are transacted between residents and non-residents and associated with basic research, applied research and experimental development of new products and processes. In principle, such activities in the sciences, social sciences and humanities are covered; included is the development of operating systems that represent technological advances."

b) Architectural, engineering and other technical services

"Architectural, engineering and other technical services cover resident/non-resident transactions related to architectural design of urban and other development projects; planning and project design and supervision of dams, bridges, airports, turnkey projects, etc.; surveying, cartography, product testing and certification and technical inspection services."

505. Comments: In principle, the item concerning R&D services to business should be included in the TBP in its entirety, except for the part relating to the humanities. On the other hand, other categories of business service, such as architectural or town planning services, ought to be included if they have an undoubted engineering content.

OECD HANDBOOK ON ECONOMIC GLOBALISATION INDICATORS – ISBN 92-64-10808-4 – © OECD 2005

II) Capital and financial account

Item A2: Acquisition/disposal of non-produced, non-financial assets (BPM5§312)

> *"In concept, acquisition/disposal of non-produced, non-financial assets comprises transactions associated with tangible assets that may be used or needed for production of goods and services but have not themselves been produced (e.g. patents, copyrights, trademarks, franchises, etc. and leases or other transferable contracts). However, in the case of resident/non-resident transactions in land (including subsoil assets), all acquisition/disposal is deemed to occur between resident units, and the non-resident acquires a financial claim on a notional resident unit. The only exception concerns land purchased or sold by a foreign embassy when the purchase or sale involves a shift of the land from one economic territory to another. In such instances, a transaction in land between residents and non-residents is recorded under acquisition/disposal of non-produced, non-financial assets. The changes recorded for all of the assets described in this paragraph consist of the total values of assets acquired during the accounting period by residents of the reporting economy* **less** *the total values of the assets disposed of by residents to non-residents."*

506. Comments: As is stressed in the Balance of Payments Manual (BPM5), only purchases and sales of royalties and licence fees should be entered in the capital account and should, in principle, be included in the technology balance of payments accounts.

4.4.4.1. *General comments*

507. It is apparent that the different balance-of-payments items relating to technology transfers, with the exception of that referring to R&D, are mingled with other categories whose technology content is not obvious. The Manual on Statistics of International Trade in Services (MSITS) recommends that some of the classifications in the BPM5 be broken down further; royalties and licence fees, for example, could be split into two categories: franchises and similar rights and other royalties and licence fees. However, in this example and in the case of other business services, the MSITS does not seek to separate transactions with a technology content from other transactions as described in the BPM5. This being the case, national authorities have for many years been organising specialised surveys. In 1990 the OECD produced a manual on this subject – which now no doubt needs some revision – and also collects annual data based on an international survey. The advantage of the specialised surveys conducted by the national authorities of member countries is that they are better at singling out the technology content of international transactions, while they also collect data by sector, by geographical origin and destination and by main category of operation (see Section 4.4.3). What is more, the specialised surveys of the activity of multinational firms also enable data to be collected on trade in technology between parent companies and their affiliates abroad.

508. Some countries organise these TBP surveys in the context of R&D surveys. While no doubt limiting the cost involved, this is an option that introduces a major distortion, particularly with regard to technology payments, in that the purchase of foreign technology concerns all firms and not just those with R&D activities.

4.4.5. *Main limits to international comparability*

509. Limits to the comparability of technology balance of payments data stem from a variety of factors. Data sources may be very different, not only from one country to another, but also within a country, necessitating the harmonisation of definitions and concepts.

Box 4.7. Recommendations concerning the collection of data on the technology balance of payments

- In view of the importance of technology balance of payments indicators for understanding and analysing the international diffusion of technology, the *Handbook* recommends that priority be given to the basic data asked for in the context of the OECD Secretariat's special survey.
- The priority data concerning this survey are:
  - ❖ Technology receipts and payments for the whole of the economy and also broken down by industrial sector (ISIC Revision 3) and by country and geographical area.
  - ❖ Technology receipts and payments of foreign-controlled affiliates, broken down by manufacturing sector.
  - ❖ Technology receipts and payments for the whole economy, broken down by sector according to the main categories of transaction (see Section 4.4.2).
- Countries are also encouraged to collect data concerning the receipts and payments of foreign-controlled affiliates in services separately (sectoral breakdown).

Note: In contrast with the principles adopted in the case of balance-of-payments flows which relate to the immediate beneficiaries of the transactions, in the context of the specialised surveys of TBPs, the recommendation is to look as far as possible for the ultimate beneficiary.

510. In some countries, surveys concerning the technological balance of payments are combined with R&D surveys (same sample). So the collected data could be underestimated, especially as far as payments are concerned, since firms without any R&D of their own which import technology from abroad are not taken into account.

511. The four categories of transactions involved in technology transfers are not defined in the same way in all countries. The main difficulty lies in distinguishing the part of services that is technology-related from the part that is not. For example, in a licensing agreement it is often impossible to distinguish aspects relating to industrial property in the pure sense from technology-type property, especially if the latter is not attached to a process that is itself patented (*e.g.* some types of software, patterns, designs, etc.).

512. Generally speaking, besides differences in the definitions of basic concepts, the number and type of components of technology transfers can vary from one country to another.

513. For example, technology receipts and payments can be overstated if they include transactions involving solely industrial property – which should be excluded – such as films, audio-visual services, copyrights, etc. They may also be overstated because of the price assigned to certain services.

514. Also, other difficulties may arise in measuring transfers inasmuch as one year's receipts (or payments) reflect not only financial flows related to technology transfers in that year, but also those related to transfers in previous years.

515. TBP data can also be underestimated for two reasons.

516. First, when there is a technology transfer that does not give rise to any payment. This is the case for certain technology transfers from multinational firms to their affiliates – especially when the latter are being set up, but also after they have come on stream. Profits repatriated to the parent company may correspond at least in part to a payment by the affiliate for the use of technology. Conversely, the parent company may benefit from

technology developed by its affiliate. Payment for the acquisition of such technology assets can form part of the funds spent on acquiring the affiliate.

517. Another reason for a technology transfer to be underestimated is if payment is made through channels other than technology payments. This is more especially the case of payments in the form of profits, dividends or overcharging for capital goods supplied by the firm that made the transfer. Contracts may in fact involve disguised payments *via* forced procurement of plant and equipment or of products required to bring the production unit on line.

518. The difficulties involved in determining transfer costs are linked to problems of "transfer pricing" due to the high volume of "intra-firm" transfers, *i.e.* trade between parent companies and their affiliates.

519. Insofar as there is not necessarily a world market price for all of the elements entering into transfer costs, especially the price of technical assistance, quality controls and certain studies, the cost of these items can be determined by the parent company in connection with a global strategy that takes the host country tax system into account (see also Chapter 5).

520. The profits paid by affiliates represent the costs of transfers and the investment risk, and they also incorporate royalties, dividends, service charges and management fees. Most such transactions are confidential and secret, which makes any attempt to estimate them difficult. Box 4.8 summarises the main distortions in international comparability.

Box 4.8. **Main distortions in the international comparability of technological balance of payments data**

- Coexistence of several incompatible national sources.
- Inappropriate samples for TBP surveys (*e.g.*, samples of R&D surveys).
- Differences in the definitions of the four main categories of TBP operation.
- Absence of some components in total receipts and payments.
- Some components include transactions involving industrial property without significant technological content.
- Royalties for technological receipts and payments could correspond to contracts covering different periods.
- TBP data could be underestimated when:

  a) They do not give rise to any payment (or monetary transaction).

  b) Repatriated profits also include TBP transactions.

  c) Parent companies acquire technological assets when acquiring an affiliate and these assets are not included in TBP transactions.

  d) For fiscal reasons, the price of technological sales are extremely low (transfer pricing problems).
- Some transactions could be confidential and secret.
- Because of favourable company laws or low taxes, some TBP transactions pass through financial holdings but these transactions are destined for other countries.

4.5. Trade in high technology products

521. A complimentary concept to that of the payments and receipts for technology as represented by patenting, licenses, know-how, technical assistance and the provision of R&D services is the international reclassification by the technological sophistication of the product being traded which represents the main channel for the diffusion of *technology embodied* in goods and services.

522. Governments and business are taking a growing interest in high-technology because of the benefits they expect to accrue from it: creation of highly skilled jobs, high wages, continuous development of skills, a steep rise in trade and productivity, high profits, a large R&D effort and R&D- and innovation- related positive externalities, increased competitiveness. All these beneficial effects are conducive to the creation of virtuous circles permitting sustainable development and contribute to promoting full employment and higher living standards.

523. This issue could have been covered in Chapter 5 which deals with certain aspects of the globalisation of trade. However, it is included here in order to emphasize the aspects relating to the international diffusion of technology rather than the commercial aspects. Trade in high technology products can concern:

- Manufacturing industry sectors.
- Service sectors.
- Manufactured products.
- Service products.

524. For each of these four categories of trade, what is needed is to identify the high technology sectors and products (as the case may be). This has been done by the OECD Secretariat over the past 25 years and approved by member countries for manufacturing. Because of the problems of data availability, it has only been done for manufacturing industry and for manufactured products. Work on identifying high technology sectors in the services sectors is still underway.

4.5.1. *Defining high technology*

525. Before defining high technology, it would seem reasonable to try to define technology itself. Technology is a "stock of (physical or managerial) knowledge which makes it possible to make new products or new processes" (Mansfield), implying the constant addition of new knowledge to existing knowledge that may make the existing knowledge totally or partially obsolete.

526. At the firm level, the sources or knowledge are internal or external. Among internal sources, a distinction may be drawn between R&D which is specific to the firm, the knowledge possessed by its personnel (acquired in the past or through learning during the innovation process) and knowledge embodied in tangible and intangible goods (equipment, software, etc). Among external sources may be mentioned: knowledge incorporated in patents, licences, know-how or technical assistance, external databases (Internet), published fundamental research findings, published or purchased applied research findings, knowledge acquired through take-overs or mergers, or through co-operation with other firms or sectors.

527. All this knowledge – the foregoing list of which is not exhaustive – is heterogeneous, the common denominator being the monetary cost of its production or acquisition. The

first big difficulty is the impossibility of estimating this cost, especially at the international level. Other difficulties relate to determining the structure of the time lags and rate of obsolescence of knowledge. However, let us assume that despite these difficulties it is possible to measure in some way the stock of knowledge for a particular area. We can then ask: above what level may this knowledge be considered high technology? The answer to this question, can only be a normative one, requires choosing between various levels of reference: technology, industrial sector, firm and product.

528. Independently of the level of reference, the work done in the OECD at the start of the 1980s showed that there is consensus on two fundamental properties of high technology: *a)* firstly, that apart from being the most advanced knowledge available, it *progresses far more rapidly* than other knowledge; *b)* secondly, its *degree of complexity* requires a vigorous and sustained research effort and a solid technological base.

4.5.2. *Measurement issues*

529. In the case of high technology, two questions emerge: the distinction between high-technology *sectors* and *products*, and between high technology *production* sectors *and user or assembly sectors*.

530. In order to make these distinctions, taking into account the criteria outline above, it was decided that:

- Only the criterion of *a rigorous R&D effort* would be used since for many countries, it is the only criterion that is readily quantifiable.
- It not being possible to measure *R&D capital stocks*, flows would be measured instead.
- The levels of reference were industrial *sectors* and *products*. Each of these levels has its advantages and disadvantages, but the "product" approach was preferred for high technology trade.
- In the product approach, the emphasis is on the *supply side* (technology production) while the industrial sector approach combines *supply and demand* (technology production and use).

4.5.3. *Identifying high technology sectors and products*

4.5.3.1. *The sectoral approach*

531. The construction of a complete classification of industries according to their technology intensity involves a number of difficulties. The first concerns the criteria for identifying the technology content of an industry. The second concerns the underlying concept. What is a high-technology industry: is it one producing technology, or is it one intensively using technology? A third problem is that there is always some degree of arbitrariness in choosing the cut-off points between the technology classes.

532. The OECD Secretariat experimented with various criteria (see above) to identify the technology content of an industry, but quantification was mainly hampered by the absence of data. As a result, R&D intensity became the sole criterion.[2]

533. Overcoming the second difficulty called for a comparison of direct and indirect R&D intensity. Two direct intensity indicators were used, and one for overall R&D intensity (sum of direct and indirect intensity). The two direct indicators were constructed for each of the 21 manufacturing sectors in ten OECD countries,[3] and the OECD list was obtained by weighting each sector for its share in the production or value added of all ten countries,

taking GDP purchasing power parities as exchange rates. With the overall intensity indicator, direct intensity was calculated in the same way. For indirect intensity, account had to be taken of technology (R&D expenditure) embodied in intermediates and capital goods purchased on the domestic market or imported. Technology moves from one industry (and one country) to another when the industry performing R&D sells its products embodying that R&D to other industries which use them as manufacturing inputs. To calculate indirect intensity, the technical coefficients of manufacturing industries extracted from input-output matrices were used. On the assumption that, for a given type of input and for all groups of products, the proportions of R&D expenditure embodied in production remained constant, the input-output coefficients were multiplied by the direct R&D intensities.

534. Taking indirect intensity into account in the calculations is unlikely to affect an industry's classification in any of these groups, but it may modify its ranking. That brings out the fact that industries which devote a high proportion of their turnover or production to R&D also make use of the most advanced equipment and intermediates. For such industries there is a strong ranking between direct intensity (production of technology) and indirect intensity (use of technology).

535. The distinction between the medium-high and medium-low groups, and between the medium-low and low groups, is more clear-cut when R&D intensity is calculated in terms of production than when it is calculated in terms of value added. In both cases, however, the cut-off points provide stability over time and median stability across countries, *i.e.* industries classified in a higher category have higher median intensity than industries in a lower category.

536. The proposed list (see Annex 4.1, Table 1) was recently updated to take account of the latest data, but it is still provisional in the sense that it concerns direct R&D intensity. It was not possible to calculate indirect intensity for the recent period because the input-output database needed for the calculations could not be updated.

4.5.3.2. The product approach

537. The product approach supplements the sectoral approach and opens the way to far more detailed analysis of trade and competitiveness.

538. It differs in at least three ways from the sectoral approach.

539. While an industry may be very technology-intensive in one country and only slightly technology-intensive in another, it is inconceivable that the same product should be classified as high-tech in some countries and as medium- or low-tech in others. If that were the case, it would imply that the products were different.[4] As a result, the existence of country lists alongside the OECD list can be justified only when, at national level, the list of high-tech products is much more disaggregated.

540. Second, the product approach includes some products which are not as a rule in the sectoral list since they are manufactured by medium-technology sectors. It also makes it possible to calculate the true proportion of high technology in a given sector, in the sense that the product approach excludes all products that are not high-tech, even if they are manufactured by high-tech industries.

541. A third feature of the product approach is that it is solely concerned with products in the high-technology category. For the time being medium-high-, medium-low- and low-tech products are not identified, at least at the level of aggregation that has been selected.

542. An initial list was prepared by the OECD Secretariat in conjunction with the Fraunhofer Institute in Germany, corresponding to the three-digit SITC Rev. 3 classification of foreign trade. It was the outcome of calculations concerning R&D intensity by groups of products (R&D expenditure/total sales) covering six countries (the United States, Japan, Germany, Italy, Sweden, the Netherlands).

543. In the product approach, in contrast to the sectoral one, the number of countries covered is of no great importance since national considerations have no bearing on whether a product is classified as high-tech or not. Accordingly, for a given level of aggregation, a list of high-tech products can be drawn up on the basis of a smaller number of countries.

544. The list proposed by the OECD Secretariat in 1994 represented an important first step in this new field and served as the basis for subsequent work culminating in the list set out in Annex 4.1, Table 2. This further work was prompted by three problems raised by the 1994 list.

545. First of all, the three-digit level of aggregation, although a considerable improvement on the sectoral approach, was still rather limited. Perhaps the greatest shortcoming was the description of the four-and five-digit products from the earlier product groups. Quite clearly, at this level of aggregation many products could not justifiably be considered high-tech, and had to be excluded in subsequent work. Where doubts remained, experts on the products concerned were consulted.

546. Second, the automobile industry as a whole was classified as high-tech. In the sectoral approach, on the other hand it is considered to be medium-high and it would be hard to justify distinct overall treatment of motor vehicles under the sector approach and under the product approach. Moreover, the significant contribution which motor vehicles make to international trade would radically change the country profile. It was therefore decided that it was preferable to exclude motor vehicles from the list of high-technology products.

547. Third, despite the calculations, the technology content of some products manufactured by medium- and low-technology sectors, even at a more disaggregated level, was not confirmed by expert opinion. Given this dilemma, it was considered preferable to exclude them from the list of high-technology products.

548. As a result, the proposed list in Annex 4.1, Table 2 is relatively compatible with the sectoral lists, inasmuch as products have been classified according to the sector to which they belong.[5] It is more restrictive than the previous product list, and much more restrictive than the sectoral lists. On the other hand, it includes some products manufactured by medium-high technology industries.

549. A new product databank has thus been created for foreign trade using the list in Annex 4.1, Table 2. For the first time, a bank of this kind incorporates the unit values of individual products (value/quantity) for total exports and imports and for bilateral trade as well. Further work will provide estimates of product ranges, from the unit values. At the same time, in order to take account of the qualitative aspects of foreign trade, each country's competitiveness, for each product, will have to be thoroughly analysed. That should enable the construction of individual country lists reflecting the range of each product traded.

4.5.4. *Principal limitations of the lists proposed*

550. Without embarking again on a theoretical and conceptual discussion of the measurement of technology itself, and high technology in particular, it is worth mentioning some of the limitations directly connected with the construction of the lists proposed.

551. The first concerns the criteria employed. Only R&D intensity, whether direct or indirect, has been taken into account. Research is an extremely important characteristic of high technology, but it is not the only one. As we have seen above, other factors can also play a significant part (*e.g.* scientific and technical personnel, technology embodied in patents, licences and know-how, strategic technical co-operation between companies, the rapid obsolescence of the knowledge available, quick turnover of equipment, etc.).

552. R&D intensity measurements have two other shortcomings as well. They are biased against the sectors and periods in which turnover or production increase more rapidly than R&D expenditure on account of strong demand in growth or exceptionally vigorous marketing. The difficulty, which mainly affects results for given countries in given years, resides in the fact that calculations are based on data for flows, not stocks. In the absence of stock data, this difficulty has been largely overcome by taking the OECD average for each year and each sector.

553. In the sectoral approach more particularly, R&D intensity can also be skewed because all research in each sector is attributed to the principal activity of the firms making up the sector. Thus, a significant proportion of the aerospace industry's R&D concerns electronics, as is also true of other sectors. Accordingly, the R&D intensity of the aerospace industry will be overestimated, and that of electronics underestimated.

554. Another limitation which applies more particularly to the sectoral approach is the lack of sufficiently disaggregated data. When the sectors are classified in terms of technology intensity, it is unlikely that basically different sector groupings would be obtained, particularly in the high-tech group, even if additional selection criteria were employed.

555. The principal limitations associated with the lack of detailed data is that many products manufactured by high-technology sectors are medium- or even low-tech, while conversely some of the products made by medium- or low-technology sectors are high-tech.

556. In principle, it was to overcome this difficulty that the product approach was developed. Even so, the latter has three other limitations of its own. First, high-tech products cannot be selected exclusively by quantitative methods unless a relatively high level of aggregation is adopted. Resorting to expert opinion does make for extremely detailed lists, but the operation as a whole is relatively cumbersome and the results cannot readily be reproduced in their entirety by other panels of experts.

557. Another limitation is that the data are not comparable with other industrial data. With the exception of the new PRODCOM classification for output data, other industrial variables, in particular employment, value added, and gross fixed capital formation are available only at sector level, not by product.

4.5.5. *Knowledge-based sectors*

558. Another important concept is the knowledge economy or knowledge-intensive industries. This is a broader concept than that of high technology. What is essential where

 OECD HANDBOOK ON ECONOMIC GLOBALISATION INDICATORS – ISBN 92-64-10808-4 –

high technology is concerned is the production and use of advanced technologies, but in the case of knowledge-based industries, the most important thing is using the technologies, and hence having the skills needed to use them.

559. It was observed above that a high technology industry is as a rule a user of advanced technologies, and not just a producer, from which it follows that any high technology industry ought also to be knowledge intensive (*e.g.* the aerospace industry). On the other hand, not all knowledge-intensive industries fall into the high technology category. The oil refining industry, for example, is very capital intensive and uses sophisticated technologies and large numbers of highly skilled people (engineers), and is therefore a knowledge-intensive industry. Compared with other industries, however, it produces fewer new technologies and its R&D intensity is not very high, with the result that it is classified as an average to low technology industry.

560. The knowledge-based industry concept is more relevant in the case of services which, on the whole, are technology users, although they are increasingly becoming producers. Preliminary work by the OECD Secretariat (see OECD Scoreboard of Science, Technology and Industry: Towards a Knowledge-Based Economy, 2003) shows that knowledge-based services include: post and telecommunications (division 64 of ISIC Revision 3), financial intermediation and insurance activities (division 65-67) and business services (with the exception of real estate) (division 71-74).

Notes

1. See Chapter 3.
2. The R&D data employed come from the OECD's Analytical Business Enterprise Research and Development (ANBERD) Database. This is an estimated database constructed with the objective of creating a consistent data set that overcomes the problems of international comparability and time discontinuity associated with the official business enterprise R&D data provided to the OECD by its member countries. ANBERD contains R&D expenditures for the period 1973 to 1995, by industry, for 15 OECD countries.
3. Sectors for which complete data were to hand, and countries for which harmonized input-output tables are available: the United States, Japan, Germany, France, the United Kingdom, Italy, Canada, Australia, the Netherlands and Denmark.
4. However, it must be acknowledged that, even at product level, the classifications are not sufficiently detailed for products which have the same name, but belong to very different ranges, to be put into separate categories.
5. For this purpose we used the concordance between SITC Rev. 3 (product classification) and ISIC Rev. 2 (sectoral classification).

ANNEX 4.A1

Classification According to Technological Intensity

Table 4.A1.1. **Manufacturing industries classified according to their global technological intensity, (ISIC Revision 3)**

List updated in 2001

	ISIC Revision 3
High-technology	
1. Aerospace	353
2. Pharmaceuticals	2423
3. Computers, office equipment	30
4. Electronics-communication	32
5. Precision instruments	33
Medium-high-technology	
6. Electrical machinery	31
7. Motor vehicles	34
8. Chemicals (except pharmaceuticals)	24-2423
9. Other transport equipment	352 + 359
10. Machinery and equipment	29
Medium-low-technology	
11. Petroleum refining	23
12. Rubber and plastics	25
13. Non-metallic mineral products	26
14. Shipbuilding	351
15. Basic metals	27
16. Fabricated metal products (except machinery and equipment	28
Low-technology	
17. Other manufacturing industry	36-37
18. Wood and furniture	20
19. Paper and printing	21-22
20. Textiles, clothing, leather	17-19

Table 4.A1.2. **High technology products list – SITC Rev. 3 (period 1988-95)**

1.	Aerospace	[7921 + 7922 + 7923 + 7924 + 7925 + 79293 + (714-71489-71499) + 87411]
2.	Computers-office machines	[75113+75131 + 75132 + 75134 + (752-7529) + 75997]
3.	Electronics-telecommunications	[76381 + 76383 + (764-76493-76499) + 7722 + 77261 + 77318 + 77625 + 7763 + 7764 + 7768 + 89879]
4.	Pharmacy	[5413 + 5415 + 5416 + 5421 + 5422]
5.	Scientific instruments	[774 + 8711 + 8713 + 8714 + 8719 + 87211 + (874-87411-8742) + 88111 + 88121 + 88411 + 88419 + 89961 + 89963 + + 89967]
6.	Electrical machinery	[77862 + 77863 + 77864 + 77865 + 7787 + 77844]
7.	Chemistry	[52222 + 52223 + 52229 + 52269 + 525 + 57433 + 591]
8.	Non-electrical machinery	[71489 + 71499 + 71871 + 71877 + 72847 + 7311 + 73131 + 73135 + 73144 + 73151 + 73153 + 73161 + 73165 + 73312 + 73314 + 73316 + 73733 + 73735]
9.	Armament	[891 –]

ISBN 92-64-10808-4
OECD Handbook on Economic Globalisation Indicators

Chapter 5

Aspects of Trade Globalisation

5.1. Introduction

561. International trade in goods and services is a major component of the globalisation process. OECD countries have made a major effort to reduce barriers to trade and to make their economies more open to foreign competition, which has contributed to the international integration of their economies. Their success in doing so is attested by the fact that the volume of world merchandise trade at the end of the 1990s was 16 times that in 1950. During the same period, its weight in world GDP tripled.

562. The first part of this chapter outlines a number of trade-related indicators that need to be developed, and more specifically the reference indicators proposed in Chapter 1. These indicators reflect: *i)* the importance of the trade in national economies, and *ii)* the role played by multinational enterprises in that trade.

563. The second part of this chapter examines various methodological and conceptual problems involved in developing these indicators and, as in the other chapters, puts forward recommendations concerning the definition and collection of basic data for national authorities. The main aspects of trade addressed in this part include, essentially, intra-firm trade, trade in intermediate products, intra- and extra-regional trade and intra-industry trade.

564. The third part of the chapter looks at a number of experimental indicators, such as trade balances based on capital ownership and international sub-contracting.

5.2. Proposed indicators

5.2.1. Choice of indicators

565. A set of core reference indicators, a broader set of supplementary indicators and a few experimental indicators are proposed in Box 5.1 to examine those issues deemed of interest to analysts and policymakers that explore the following questions, including:

- How integrated or global is the domestic economy from the trade point of view?
- What share of domestic demand is met by imports?
- What is the impact of exports on domestic value added?
- What is the degree of dependence of domestic producers on foreign markets and imported inputs?
- What is the role and importance of multinational enterprises in trade?
- Do multinational enterprises trade more with their affiliates than with unaffiliated firms?
- How important are affiliates controlled abroad in delivering goods and services to international markets?
- Does the trade balance based on ownership or control provides a different picture from the conventional method of measurement?

5.2.2. Reference indicators

566. In Chapter 1 concerning trade, eight reference indicators are proposed. The first four measure the extent of trade globalisation in the compiling country, while the last four refer to the importance of foreign CAs in the compiling country's trade. These indicators are presented in Box 5.1. This box also displays the supplemental and experimental indicators proposed in this *Handbook*. The analytical interest of the indicators and certain problems posed by their use and interpretation are discussed in the second and third parts of the chapter.

567. The indicators proposed are not intended to be indicators of market openness in the sense of markets being contestable by foreign suppliers. While they reflect the existence or changes in tariffs, non-tariff border protection and other types of institutional arrangements that limit effective contestability, they also reflect factors that do not relate to trade policy, such as the country's size, geographic isolation from trading partners and transport costs. Furthermore, these indicators also reflect macroeconomic developments such as fluctuations in aggregate demand and exchange rates.

5.2.2.1. Extent of trade globalisation in the compiling country

Share of total exports in GDP

568. This is probably the most frequently used indicator of trade integration, since it provides a measure of the degree of dependence of domestic producers on foreign markets, and their trade orientation. It is based on well-established concepts and the relevant data are readily available. The share of exports in GDP can be analysed in terms of level and in terms of growth. As pointed out in Chapter 1, in the case of some countries, this indicator may not show significant growth if, during the reference period, services that are not traded internationally and that are included in GDP grow more rapidly than exports. In terms of level, this ratio may indicate the intensity of a country's trade. However, it must be interpreted in light of *i)* a country's geographical proximity to its main trading partners; and here the importance that costs, such as transport and marketing, may have for trade flows; and *ii)* size of the economy. In this regard, smaller economies are often obliged to specialise in certain activities, which may result in a relatively high share of exports in GDP. Furthermore, independently of specialisation, larger economies tend to show lower export to GDP ratios because the relative importance of foreign markets with respect to domestic demand is lower. However, Figures 5.1 and 5.2 show that the negative correlation between GDP and the share of exports in GDP is not particularly strong, suggesting that other factors influence the ratio, especially in the cases of small countries where large disparities across countries exist. This indicator includes both domestic exports and re-exports that correspond to different globalisation dynamics. Supplemental indicators based on these trade flows are discussed later in this chapter.

Average of exports and imports in GDP

569. A second indicator that is often used to measure a country's integration in the world economy is the weight of its total trade in its economy, *i.e.* the average of exports and imports in GDP. However, it should be pointed out that this indicator should not be interpreted as a measure of openness to international trade since two countries can have the same values for this ratio but enforce differing levels of restrictions and tariff and non-tariff barriers.

Box 5.1. **Proposed indicators for measuring the extent of trade globalisation**

1. Reference indicators

Extent of trade globalisation in the compiling country (total)

- Share of total exports in GDP.
- Average of exports and imports in GDP.
- Share of domestic final demand met by total imports.
- Share of GDP linked to domestic exports.

Extent of trade globalisation related to foreign-CAs in the compiling country (total)

- Foreign-CAs' share of total exports.
- Foreign-CAs' share of total imports.
- Intra-firm exports of goods by foreign-CAs in total exports of goods.
- Intra-firm imports of goods by foreign-CAs in total imports of goods.

2. Supplemental indicators

Extent of trade globalisation in the compiling country

- Propensity to export by industry.
- Penetration of imports to meet domestic final demand.
- Penetration of imports to meet, intermediate demand.
- Penetration of imports to meet total domestic demand.
- Foreign penetration ratio.

Extent of trade globalisation related to parents in the compiling country (total for all parent companies and parent companies controlled by residents)

- Parent companies' share of total compiling country exports.
- Parent companies' share of total compiling country imports.
- Intra-firm exports of goods by parent companies in total exports of goods.
- Intra-firm imports of goods by parent companies in total imports of goods.

Extent of trade globalisation related to MNEs in the compiling country (total)

- MNEs' share of total compiling country exports.
- MNEs' share of total compiling country imports.
- Intra-firm exports of goods by MNEs in the total exports of goods.
- Intra-firm imports of goods by MNEs in the total imports of goods.

Extent of international integration of production and distribution processes

- Import content of compiling country production.
- Import content of compiling country exports.
- Share of re-exports in compiling country GDP.
- Share of intermediate goods in compiling country merchandise exports.
- Share of intermediate goods in compiling country merchandise imports.
- Share of intra- and extra-regional exports and imports.

Degree of geographic diversification (globalisation) of trade in the compiling country

- Herfindahl index of total exports.
- Herfindahl index of total imports.

OECD HANDBOOK ON ECONOMIC GLOBALISATION INDICATORS – ISBN 92-64-10808-4 – © OECD 2005

Box 5.1. Proposed indicators for measuring the extent of trade globalisation *(cont.)*

3. Experimental indicators

- Trade balances based on capital ownership.
- New forms of trade relationships.

Figure 5.1. **Links between GDP and exports/GDP**

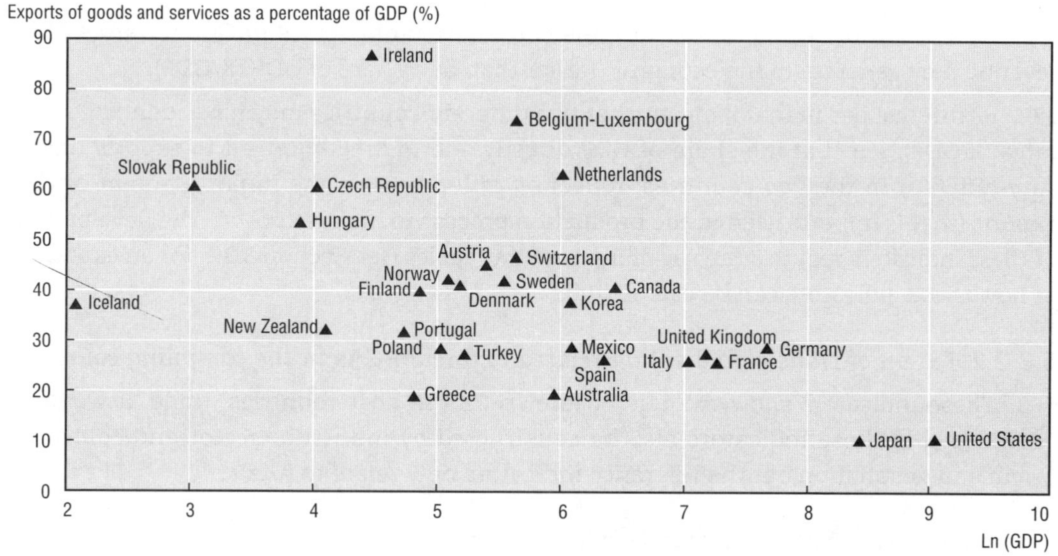

Source: IMF balance of payments statistics, *OECD Annual National Accounts*, January 2003.

Figure 5.2. **Links between population and exports/GDP**

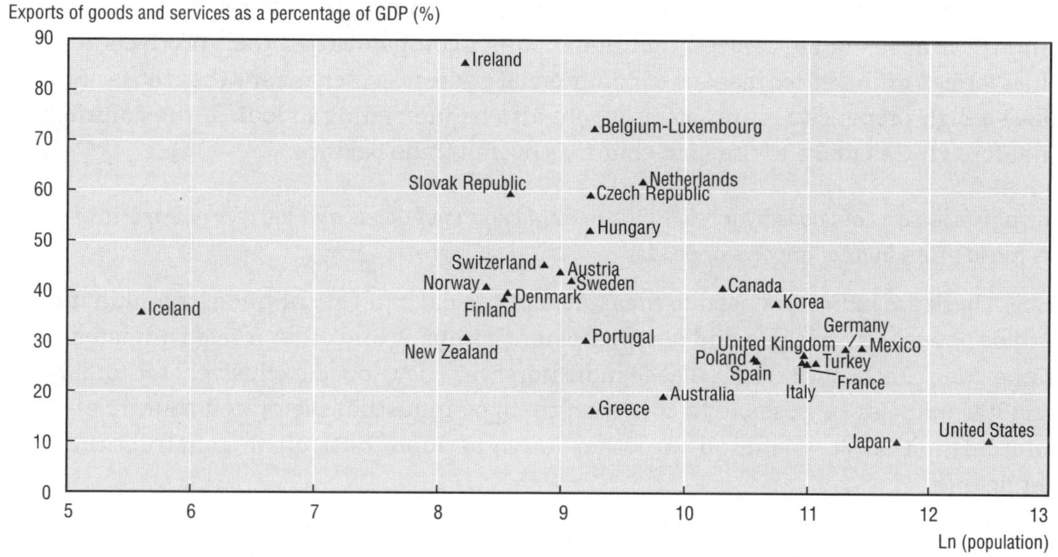

Source: IMF balance of payments statistics, *OECD Annual National Accounts*, January 2003.

Share of domestic final demand met by total imports

570. A third way of evaluating a country's integration in the world economy is to measure the share of total domestic final demand which is met by imports. As was the case with the share of total exports to GDP ratio some care should be made in interpretation. For example, small economies or those rich in mineral resources may tend to specialise in their production, and so import higher proportions of goods to meet total domestic final demand than would be the case in relatively large economies. Other factors are likely to affect the relationship too, for example the relative size of the service sector.

Share of GDP linked to domestic exports

571. This indicator serves to measure the contribution of exports to GDP in terms of the revenue they generate to the economy, rather than as a share of GDP (X/GDP).

572. Its interest lies in that it shows that two different countries may have identical export rates (X/GDP), but that the share of GDP directly and indirectly linked to exports may be very different in the two countries; reflecting differences in the import content of their exports (that is imports used in the production process to make exports). The development of these indicators requires the use of input-output tables (see Section 5.3.1. for an exposition of how these indicators can be calculated).

5.2.2.2. *Extent of trade globalisation related to foreign-CAs in the compiling country*

573. These indicators show the role of foreign-CAs in host countries' trade. It would be desirable that these indicators also be constructed by industrial sector and country of origin and destination but the reference indicators only relate to totals.

Foreign-CAs' share of total exports and of total imports

574. These two indicators measure the importance of foreign-CAs in total exports and imports of the compiling country. In many countries, foreign-CAs have a propensity to export (exports/gross production) that is higher than the national average, and a propensity to import (imports/gross production) that is also higher than the national average.

575. With regard to the importance of foreign-CAs in total imports of the compiling country, it needs to be stressed that many parent companies sell their products through their foreign affiliates for reasons of commercial strategy, which means that those affiliates have a high propensity to import. It would also be interesting to look at the contribution that foreign-CAs make to the host country's overall trade balance.

Intra-firm exports of goods by foreign-CAs in total exports of goods and intra-firm imports of goods by foreign-CAs in total imports of goods

576. These are indicators used to measure a particular category of trade by multinationals – trade between an affiliate and its other parent company and other foreign affiliates of the same group (intra-firm trade). These indicators were developed exclusively for total goods and it would also be possible to construct them by industrial sector and country of origin and destination. It would, on the other hand, be more difficult to construct them for services.

577. This category of trade is a sub-category of the total trade by foreign-CAs, but it is of particular interest in that it reveals the intensity of commercial links between affiliates and parent companies. When an affiliate has a commercial or distribution function, its parent

OECD HANDBOOK ON ECONOMIC GLOBALISATION INDICATORS – ISBN 92-64-10808-4 – © OECD 2005

company's exports to that affiliate could represent the bulk of this trade. If the affiliate is rather a producer of semi-finished goods (intermediate goods), the parent company probably imports them to a large extent in order to manufacture finished goods, possibly for re-export to other destinations. Methodological and conceptual aspects of intra-firm trade will be discussed in the second part of this chapter.

5.2.3. *Supplemental indicators*

5.2.3.1. *Extent of trade globalisation in the compiling country*

578. These indicators provide further measures of the extent of trade globalisation in the compiling country. They complement the corresponding reference indicators.

Propensity to export by industry: share of exports (X_{ij}) of a country i and industry j in the gross production (X_{ij}) of that country (X_{ij}/P_{ij})

579. For a compiling country, this is an important ratio for measuring the trade intensity of one of the industries, which is usually called the propensity to export. To calculate it, exports and production have to be measured using the same industrial classification such as ISIC Rev. 3 or NACE Rev. 1, unless production data are available in a product classification (SITC Rev. 3, HS or CPC). One difficulty that should be borne in mind in making international comparisons is the importance of sectors' secondary activities. There are several methods of estimating exports by industry, each of which treats secondary activities differently.

- If the totality of the exports of a product is assigned to the industry that is specialised in producing it, exports related to an industry's secondary activities are all assigned to a single industry.
- If the exports of a product are assigned to all the industries that produce it in proportion to their share of production, export data by industry reflect their primary and secondary activities.
- If exports by industry are estimated from industrial surveys, they will reflect the industry's primary and secondary activities. However, if the survey is one of exporters, the exporter may not be the producer, which makes it difficult to interpret the export/production ratio. In such surveys, the wholesale trade is a big exporter even though it does not produce any goods, or very few.

580. This *Handbook* recommends that exports by industry be estimated by the second approach. Unfortunately, such estimates are not available for many countries. Even in the case of countries that do compile data in this way, they are still difficult to interpret, since the weight of an industry's main activity (degree of specialisation) may vary widely from one country to the next. This is a difficulty however that is not specific to trade or production data. Another factor to consider when using this indicator is the vertical integration within industry groupings. For example, in country (A) the motor vehicle manufacturer sources a large proportion of its parts from other domestic motor vehicle parts manufacturers. All of this output is recorded in the same two-digit ISIC activity 34 and so P_{ij}, will record the output of all of these activities. The motor vehicle manufacturer in country (B) however produces all parts within the company, and so P_{ij}, will be lower in this case even if the manufacturers in country (A) and (B) produce the same quantity of identical cars.

581. A better indicator could be attained by removing from the denominator P_{ij}, any intra-industry transactions between domestic industries (see Section 5.4.3).

Penetration of imports (P_M) to meet domestic final demand (DF), intermediate demand (DI) and total domestic demand (DT).

582. These supplementary indicators are variants of the proposed reference indicator (3) shown in Box 5.1 above. To understand them properly, it is worth recalling an accounting principle of input-output tables. The total demand for a good in an economy is equal to the total supply of that good. Total domestic demand (DT) is the sum of intermediate consumption (DI) and domestic final demand (DF). Total supply for domestic consumers is the sum of domestic supply (gross production less exports) and external supply (imports).

583. Insofar as total domestic demand can be broken down into a component for intermediate consumption and a component for domestic final demand, imports can be intended for each of the two components. The reference indicator for import penetration is therefore biased since the denominator denotes only domestic final demand but the numerator includes all imports, some of which are used to produce goods for export. The supplementary indicators for import penetration shown below attempt to remedy this shortcoming. The total imports/total domestic demand ratio may be written as follows:

PM = M/DT = (MI + MF)/(DI + DF) where:

PM = import penetration (adjusted);

M = total imports;

DT = total domestic demand;

MI = imports for intermediate demand;

MF = imports for domestic final demand;

DI = intermediate demand;

DF = domestic final demand.

584. For a proper understanding of this indicator, two underlying indicators need to be developed:

PM = MI/DI and PMF = MF/DF where:

PMI = penetration of imports for intermediate demand ; and

PMF = penetration of imports for final demand.

585. The first indicator (PMI) measures the degree of international integration of the production process but also the degree of vertical integration within the domestic industry. A better indicator would be to measure DI net of domestic intra-industry transactions. It should be noted that the more detailed the classification of industries the lower the bias introduced by not correcting for intra-industry transactions. The second indicator (PMF) measures the share of final demand met from abroad (imports).

586. The global indicator is the weighted sum of these two components:

$$PM = PMI * \frac{DI}{DT} + PMF * \frac{DF}{DT}$$

587. This relation shows that a country's global indicator of import penetration depends on the degree of import penetration and the weight of each type of demand. Furthermore, each component depends on the degree of penetration at industry level and the weights of the industries. Cross-country differences thus reflect differences between the penetration ratios specific to an industry as well as differences in industrial structure. Industry level import penetrations would be useful to sort out these two effects but their computation

OECD HANDBOOK ON ECONOMIC GLOBALISATION INDICATORS – ISBN 92-64-10808-4 – © OECD 2005

requires several simplifying assumptions. This *Handbook* encourages countries to use the method proposed above to experiment with the estimation and analysis of industry level import penetration ratios.

Foreign penetration ratio

588. When foreign-CAs are present in a host country's economy, they may be regarded as the competitors of firms controlled by the residents of that country. The import penetration ratio which is proposed as a reference indicator could thus be widened. A foreign penetration ratio P_R could be defined which takes into account the share of foreign firms in local production plus total imports

$P_R = (S_F - X_F + M)/DF$ where

S_F = local sales of foreign-CAs.

X_F = exports of foreign-CAs.

M = total imports.

DF = final domestic demand.

589. If imports by foreign-CAs intended for their own production are available (M_{FP}), then the foreign penetration P'_R could be adjusted as follows:

Adjusted foreign penetration ratio: $P'_R = (S_F - X_F + M - M_{FP})/DF$

5.2.3.2. *Extent of trade globalisation related to parent companies in the compiling country*

590. These indicators show the role of parent companies in host countries' trade. It would be desirable that these indicators also be constructed by industrial sector and country of origin and destination but the reference indicators only relate to totals.

Parent companies' share of total exports and of total imports

591. In Chapter 3, two categories of parent company located in a compiling country were distinguished:

- Parent companies under the ultimate control of residents of the compiling country (*e.g.* General Motors in the United States, Toyota in Japan).
- Foreign-controlled parent companies (*e.g.* Chrysler in the United States).

592. Each of these two categories has CAs abroad. When measuring the share of exports by the parent companies of a country in the total exports of that country, it is important to distinguish the exports from each of the two categories of firm. For exports, two indicators could be constructed:

$X_{Parent,\,dc}/X$ and $X_{Parent,\,fc}/X$

where:

$X_{Parent,\,dc}$ = exports by parent companies under domestic ultimate control;

$X_{Parent,\,fc}$ = exports by parent companies under foreign ultimate control;

X = Total exports of the compiling country.

593. Equivalent ratios can be calculated for imports.

594. Parent company exports in a compiling country are distinguished from exports by other firms, the majority of which are SMEs. Because of their size, sector and especially the

degree of their internationalisation, the share of exports by parent companies is usually very large in a country's exports and imports.

Intra-firm exports of goods by parent companies in total exports of goods and intra-firm imports of goods by parent companies in total imports of goods

595. These indicators are used to assess the degree of international integration of compiling country firms as measured by trade flows. A higher share of parent companies' intra-firm exports (imports) in relation to total exports (imports) shows that the compiling country is more integrated with the rest of the world in terms of corporate relationships. These indicators were developed exclusively for total goods but it would also be possible to construct them for services and by industrial sector and country of origin and destination.

5.2.3.3. Extent of trade globalisation related to MNEs in the compiling country

596. These indicators are simply the addition of the foreign-CAs' and parent companies' corresponding indicators. They are a more global measure of the extent of trade globalisation due to MNEs in the compiling country. Where intra-firm trade is concerned, the data corresponding to foreign-CAs measure flows between the latter and their parent company group abroad, whereas the data for parent companies in the compiling country measure flows between the latter and their affiliates abroad.

5.2.3.4. Extent of international integration of production and distribution processes

597. The globalisation of production and distribution is one of the key characteristics of economic globalisation. It explains part of increasing trade at the world level. The degree of international integration can be measured by several trade-related indicators that are described below.

Import content of the production and exports of the compiling country

598. As pointed out earlier, a proportion of imports of goods is intended for use in production of exports. This supplemental indicator measures the importance of imports in the production process of exports. A higher import content reflects a higher integration of production with other trading countries. Section 5.3.1 provides details on how to compute the share of GDP related to exports. This indicator is in essence the corollary of reference indicator 4 shown above, since the sum of GDP generated to produce one-unit of export and imports used in producing one-unit of export is 1.

Share of re-exports in the GDP of the compiling country

599. One aspect of globalisation that affects trade is the internationalisation of the distribution of goods. Some countries have become important distribution centres for regional markets. This indicator tries to capture this phenomenon. Countries with higher share would tend to play a relatively more important role in the global distribution of goods. This indicator complements the analysis of the share of total exports in GDP, as it provides the portion related to distribution. This proportion needs to be taken into account as re-exports usually don't generate as much value added and employment as domestic exports.

Share of intermediate goods in the compiling country's merchandise exports and imports

600. One feature of the internationalisation of production is the multiple origins of the components of a particular product. These components are very often produced in different countries and imported in order to be used for the production of final goods. The source of these imports could be affiliates of parent companies or other non-affiliated firms. Box 5.4 discusses in more details the role of trade in intermediate trade within the international division of production processes.

601. The importance and extent of these imports are taken into account by measuring the import content of production and exports (see indicators proposed above). However, other indicators may also be useful for measuring the following:

- Share of exports and imports of intermediate goods in total exports and imports of a country.
- Imports of intermediate goods *a)* by parent companies located in the compiling country, *b)* by the affiliates under foreign control in the compiling country, and *c)* by other non-affiliated firms.
- Share of imports of intermediate goods in intra-firm imports.
- Share of imports of intermediate goods in intra-industry imports.
- Geographical diversification of intermediate goods imports.

Share of intra- and extra-regional exports and imports

602. For any given region, what we measure here is its intra- and extra-regional trade as a percentage of its total trade or its intra-regional trade as a percentage of its extra-regional trade (see measurement aspects in Box 5.6). The more a region's economies are integrated, the greater will be the share of intra-regional trade. Given the increasing number of regional free trade agreements, it is important to determine whether trade is becoming more intra-regional than it is international. If this is indeed the case, this could give rise to considerable debate and have an impact on policy issues.

603. All these indicators are useful to the comprehensive analysis of the degree of integration of the production processes. Not all of them are however presented in the list of reference indicators.

5.2.3.5. *Degree of geographic diversification (globalisation) of trade in the compiling country*

Herfindahl index of total exports and Herfindahl index of total imports

604. If trade intensity indicators, such as *X/GDP* are similar for two countries, it may be helpful for some comparative purposes to measure the geographical diversification of exports using the Herfindahl index of concentration. The most internationalised country will be the one which exports its goods to the largest number of countries which are very far away and which have no common borders.

605. We assume that X represents the total exports of compiling country A, which are destined for n different countries.

606. Herfindahl's index of geographical concentration for country A's exports is the sum of the squares of the market shares held in each country of destination i, *i.e.*

$$H = \sum_{i=1}^{n} \left[\frac{X_i}{\sum_{i=1}^{n} X_i} \right]^2$$

607. If each of the n countries of destination received the same export value, the Herfindahl index would be equal to:

$H = \frac{1}{n}$ (see also Chapter 2, Annex 2.5, Box 1).

608. Countries which receive very low export values influence the Herfindahl index very little and can if necessary be left out of the calculations. Herfindahl indexes can also be computed for imports.

5.2.4. *Experimental indicators*

5.2.4.1. *Trade balances based on capital ownership*

609. Trade balances based on capital ownership are experimental estimates that can be used to develop new globalisation indicators and to assess trade flows based on capital ownership rather than residency. Conventional trade flows measure the flow of goods and services across borders. Foreign direct investment represents another way to deliver products to other markets without crossing borders. Trade balances based on capital ownership try to take account of these "deliveries". Section 5.4.1 provides the conceptual framework for developing these trade balances and some of the results from the United Sates.

5.2.4.2. *New forms of trade relationships*

610. One of the key features of economic globalisation is the rapid development of telecommunications. This has favoured the emergence of new forms for relationships between buyers and sellers and between producers. These new forms of trade relationships can explain an increasing share of trade flows. In fact, the share of intra-firm trade between Canada and the United States diminished after the Free Trade Agreement between these two countries, in spite of increased economic integration. This suggests that other forms of trading arrangements – other than through corporate integration – are at work. The following presents some possible trade relationships that facilitate trade:

- International sub-contracting: firms contracting some aspects of product design, processing, etc. to other foreign firms.
- Distribution arrangements: distributors and producers forming alliances for the production and distribution of goods and services.
- Electronic commerce: the rapid evolution of Internet and electronic commerce has facilitated the international distribution of goods and services, opening trade flows to all economic agents of all sizes.

611. The first two forms of trading relationships are not necessarily new but they seem recently to have become an increasing source of trade. "Seem" is used because there is not much data to verify this assertion. There are no data measuring the first two phenomena.

OECD HANDBOOK ON ECONOMIC GLOBALISATION INDICATORS – ISBN 92-64-10808-4 – © OECD 2005

France has launched a qualitative survey in early 2003 to start obtaining information about the different types of relationship including international sub-contracting that firms can form to improve their performance. Electronic international commerce is measured by several countries. This *Handbook* encourages countries to develop these measures for future inclusion. This *Handbook* contributes to this endeavour by suggesting a definition and conceptual framework for the development of statistics on international sub-contracting (see Section 5.4.2).

5.2.4.3. *Intra-industry trade*

612. International trade is often characterised in terms of the principle of comparative advantage, based on relative cost or price differentials across countries. A country exports goods produced by it in which it enjoys comparative advantage, and imports other goods produced by industries that are at a disadvantage. Regardless of transport costs, for instance, international trade can be expected to take place between countries that are economically different (in terms of technological know-how, capital intensity or resource endowments), and its form should be the same in each industry, *i.e.* exports (where there is a competitive advantage) or imports (where there is a comparative disadvantage). The classic pattern is therefore "inter-industry" trade between countries that differ.

613. In practice, however, most international trade takes place between countries that are developed (and in many respects economically similar) and it often takes the form of "intra-industry" trade, *i.e.* simultaneous exports and imports within industries. It usually takes place between wealthy countries that have reached a similar level of development, are reasonably open to foreign producers, and where geographic proximity implies low transport costs.

614. Emerging in the late 1970s, the "new theory of international trade" laid emphasis on the imperfection of competition by incorporating many aspects of industrial economics such as economies of scale or product differentiation.[1] The new theory provided a simple explanation for the expansion observed in intra-industry trade, namely that, between similar countries, consumer demand for often differing ranges of similar (horizontally differentiated) goods produced with increasing returns will be met by *producer* specialisation.

615. In the mid-1980s, Helpman and Krugmann (1985)[2] succeeded in bringing the two schools of thought around the notion of integrated equilibrium. They associate monopolistic competition with intra-industry trade in similar goods between similar countries, whereas the principle of comparative advantage still holds for inter-industry trade between widely differing economies, *i.e.* those separated by a marked difference in the proportion of factors or levels of technology. Thus intra-industry trade is viewed as the corollary to economic integration: greater integration between similar and/or convergent countries is said to generate new gains in trade, while limiting the adjustment costs incurred when resources are moved between industries in a country. This new theory strongly influenced economic policy, one example being the *ex ante* studies on the impact of the Single Market in Europe.[3]

616. It would be desirable to estimate the proportion of trade accounted for by intra-industry trade as an indicator of the degree of economic integration between economies. However, attempts to measure intra-industry trade have been criticised for a variety of reasons (see Section 5.3.5. for further discussion). This *Handbook* encourages researchers to perfect these measures so that they can finally be used as globalisation indicators.

5.2.5. *Variables required and availability*

617. Box 5.2 lists the variables required to construct the proposed globalisation indicators related to trade, except for trade related to MNEs that are presented in Box 3.2 (Chapter 3). Except for the experimental indicators, the variables are readily available in all OECD countries. It should be noted however that the input-output tables are not as current as the other accounts in the SNA and are not published every year in most countries.

Box 5.2. Variables required to construct globalisation indicators related to trade*

Variables	Availability in the OECD countries	
	Available in most countries	Not or rarely available
GDP, final consumption expenditure accounts		
Total GDP	X	
Total exports	X	
Domestic exports	X	
Re-exports	X	
Total imports	X	
Input-output tables		
Use matrix	X	
Supply matrix	X	
Final demand matrix	X	
GDP, production accounts		
Gross output by industry	X	
Trade statistics by country of origin and destination		
Total exports	X	
Total imports	X	
Trade balances based on capital ownership		X
New forms of trade relationships		X
Intra-industry trade		X

* Variables related to trade by MNEs are shown in Box 3.2.

5.3. Conceptual and methodological considerations

5.3.1. *Computing input-output based indicators*

618. An important but less known aspect of globalisation is the link between a country's imports and production and exports. This link may be complex if a number of countries are producing parts of the same final goods and services.

619. One way of measuring the relationship is through the use of input-output tables. Input-output tables measure the interrelationships between the producers of goods and services (including imports) within an economy and the users of these same goods and services (including exports). In this context they can be used to estimate the contribution that imports make in the production of any good (or service) for export. For example, if a motor car manufacturer imports certain components (*e.g.* the chassis) the *direct import contribution* will be the ratio of the value of the chassis to the total value of the car. And if

OECD HANDBOOK ON ECONOMIC GLOBALISATION INDICATORS – ISBN 92-64-10808-4 – © OECD 2005

the car manufacturer purchases other components from domestic manufacturers, who in turn use imports in their production process, those imports must be included in the car's value. These indirect imports should be included in any statistic that attempts to measure the contribution of imports to the production of motor cars for export. The total direct and indirect imports are known as "embodied imports".

620. In an input-output framework the relationship between producers and consumers can be simply described as follows:

$$g = A*g + y$$

where:

g: is an $n*1$ vector of the output of *n* industries within an economy.

A: is an $n*n$ matrix describing the interrelationships between industries (I-A) is known as the Leontief matrix, where a_{ij} is the ratio of inputs from domestic industry *i* used in the output of industry j.

Y: is an $n*1$ vector of final demand for domestically produced goods and services, including domestic exports.

621. Assuming that no other imports (re-exports) are recorded, total imports embodied within exports can be shown as:

$$\text{Embodied imports} = m*(1 - A)^{-1}*e \quad (1)$$

where:

m: is a $1*n$ vector with components m_j (the ratio of intermediate imports purchased to output produced, in industry j)

e: is a $n*1$ vector of exports by industry.

622. Estimates of imports of goods embodied in exports of goods can be calculated by including only imported goods in "m", and setting all exports of services in *e* above to zero, assuming that goods industries produce goods only and services industries produce services only. By adapting the equation above to reflect Supply-Use table data sources this assumption can be relaxed. In this case Equation 1 above can be rewritten as $m*(1 - DB)^{-1}*Dx$, where x is a $n*1$ vector of exports by product, DB = A and Dx = e, B is an $n*n$ matrix where b_{ij} is the ratio of inputs of domestically produced product i used in the output of industry j. This approach can be applied to the equations below by replacing each occurrence of "A" and "e" with "DB" and "Dx".

623. And so the "import content of exports" (the share of imports used in production to make one unit of exports) is equal to:

$$m*(I - A)^{-1}* e/E \quad \text{where } E = \sum_{i-1}^{n} e_i \text{ (total exports).}$$

624. Similarly, the embodied imports in exports by industry *j* can be shown as:

$$\Sigma_i\, m_i*L_{ij} \quad \text{where: } L_{ij} \text{ is the ij}^{th} \text{ element of the Leontief inverse } (I - A)^{-1}.$$

625. In addition the share of imports used in the production process to produce exports is equal to:

$$m*(I - A)^{-1}*e/M \quad \text{where, } M = m*g \text{ (total imports).}$$

626. In the same way, one can estimate the total indirect and direct contribution of exports to value added by replacing the import vector m above with an equivalent vector that

shows the ratio of value added to output (v). So, the contribution of exports to value added is equal to:

Contribution of domestic exports to value added = $V*(I - A)^{-1}*e$, and

the value added content of domestic exports = $V*(I - A)^{-1}*e/E$, and

the share of value added embodied within domestic exports = $V*(I - A)^{-1}*e/V$, where V = total value added.

627. The formulas above demonstrate how to compute several relevant indicators that are not listed as indicators in Box 5.1. They are provided as potentially additional indicators to be included in analysing globalisation in countries' economies.

5.3.2. *Measuring trade involving MNEs: global and intra-firm trade*

628. Given their international orientation, MNEs are expected to account for a sizeable share of cross-border trade flows. Available data confirm that the shares of foreign-CAs in host-country exports and imports tend to be much larger than their shares in other measures of economic activity (such as host-country sales, value added, or employment).[4] Some of this trade may represent flows of intermediate inputs from parent companies to foreign manufacturing affiliates, which in turn may export part of their output either back to the investing country or to regional markets. Trade by multinational firms may also take the form of cross-border shipments to wholesale trade affiliates that are set up to market the products of their parent companies.

5.3.2.1. *Conceptual framework*

629. From the perspective of an individual compiling country, trade flows that involve multinational firms consist of 1) the exports and imports of foreign-CAs located in the compiling country, and 2) exports and imports associated with domestically located parent companies and their CAs abroad.[5] The trade flows of foreign-CAs include both intra-firm trade (*i.e.* trade with the CAs' foreign parent group and trade with unrelated firms. Trade flows associated with parent companies in the compiling economy and their CAs abroad include intra-firm trade between the parents and their CAs abroad, trade between the parent companies and other foreign firms (including both associates and unaffiliated firms), and trade between the CAs abroad and unaffiliated firms located in the compiling country.

5.3.2.2. *Trade by foreign-CAs*

630. Tables 5.1 and 5.2 present a breakdown of trade flows by foreign-CAs according to the affiliates' ownership ties with their foreign trading partners. For a given CA, the primary distinction is between trade with the CA's foreign parent group[6] and trade with other foreigners. For a compiling country, trade between foreign-CAs and their foreign parent groups constitutes intra-firm trade associated with foreign MNEs' activity in the country.

631. In the breakdown shown in Tables 5.1 and 5.2, a CA's trade with other foreigners includes trade with the foreign affiliates it may have, as well as trade with unaffiliated foreign enterprises. Any trade between the foreign-CA and its own affiliates abroad constitutes a portion of intra-firm trade associated with the compiling country's direct investment abroad.

Table 5.1. **Exports by foreign-CAs in the compiling country**

Total	To the foreign parent group	To other foreigners		
		Total	To foreign affiliates	To unaffiliated foreigners
(1)	(2)	(3)	(4)	(5)

Table 5.2. **Imports by foreign CAs in the compiling country**

Total	From the foreign parent group	From other foreigners		
		Total	From foreign affiliates	From unaffiliated foreign enterprises
(1)	(2)	(3)	(4)	(5)

5.3.2.3. *Trade associated with parent companies and their CAs abroad*

632. A breakdown of trade flows by parent companies according to their ownership ties with foreign trading partners is shown in Tables 5.3 and 5.4. For a given parent company, a major break is between trade with its CAs abroad and trade with other foreigners. Trade between the parent companies and their CAs abroad typically will constitute the major portion of intra-firm trade associated with parent companies and their CAs abroad. Trade with other foreigners includes trade with associates abroad, which is also regarded as intra-firm trade, as well as trade with unaffiliated foreigners. If a given parent company in the compiling country is itself foreign-controlled, trade with other foreigners also includes trade with its foreign parent group, which constitutes a portion of intra-firm trade for foreign CAs.

633. A compiling country's trade with its CAs abroad includes both intra-firm trade between domestically located parent companies and their CAs abroad (Tables 5.3 and 5.4, column 2) and arm's-length trade between unaffiliated firms in the compiling country and the CAs abroad (Tables 5.3 and 5.4, column 7). It should be noted that arm's-length trade with the CAs of a given parent company may include exports or imports by firms that are parents of other CAs abroad.

5.3.2.4. *Main limitations of data collection and their interpretation*

a) Potential duplication in recorded trade flows

634. In a compiling country's surveys of MNEs operations, a foreign-CA that has its own CAs abroad may be counted both as a foreign-CA (in a survey on inward investment) and as

Table 5.3. **Exports involving parent companies and their CAs abroad**

Total	Exports by parent companies in the compiling country					Exports by unaffiliated firms in the compiling country
	To their CAs abroad	To other foreigners				To affiliates controlled by compiling country parent companies abroad
		Total	To their foreign parent groups (if they are foreign-controlled)	To their associates abroad	To unaffiliated foreigners	
(1)	(2)	(3)	(4)	(5)	(6)	(7)

Table 5.4. **Imports involving parent companies and CAs abroad**

<table>
<tr><td rowspan="3">Total</td><td colspan="5">Imports by parent companies in the compiling country</td><td>Imports by unaffiliated firms in the compiling country</td></tr>
<tr><td rowspan="2">From their CAs abroad</td><td colspan="4">From other foreigners</td><td rowspan="2">From affiliates abroad controlled by compiling country parent companies</td></tr>
<tr><td>Total</td><td>From their foreign parent groups (if they are foreign-controlled)</td><td>From their associates abroad</td><td>From unaffiliated foreigners</td></tr>
<tr><td>(1)</td><td>(2)</td><td>(3)</td><td>(4)</td><td>(5)</td><td>(6)</td><td>(7)</td></tr>
</table>

a parent company of CAs abroad (in a separate survey on outward investment). There thus exists the potential for some duplication between data collected on the trade of foreign-CAs and data collected on the trade of parent companies.

635. The areas in which there could be potential duplication of intra-firm trade flows are shown in Tables 5.1, 5.2, 5.3 and 5.4. As a comparison of the tables reveals, data collected on trade between foreign-CAs and their affiliates abroad (Tables 5.1 and 5.2, column 4) could partly duplicate data on the intra-firm trade of parent companies in compiling countries (Tables 5.3 and 5.4, columns 2 and 5). Similarly, data on trade between parent companies and their foreign parent groups (Tables 5.3 and 5.4, column 4) will duplicate part of the data on trade between foreign-CAs and their foreign parent groups (Tables 5.1 and 5.2, column 2).

636. For arm's-length trade, part of the data on trade by foreign-CAs with unaffiliated foreigners (Tables 5.1 and 5.2, column 7) may duplicate a portion of the data on trade by parent companies with unaffiliated foreigners (Tables 5.3 and 5.4, column 6). In contrast to the data involving intra-firm transactions, the degree of duplication in this data between foreign-CAs and parent companies cannot be identified precisely based on the breakdowns in the tables.

637. Apart from any duplication that may result from a company in the compiling country being counted both as a foreign-CA and as a parent company, data collected on trade between CAs abroad and unaffiliated firms in the compiling country (Tables 5.3 and 5.4, column 7) may include trade with parent companies of other CAs (Tables 5.3 and 5.4, column 6), as well as trade with foreign-CAs (Tables 5.1 and 5.2, column 4). Thus, a broad measure of MNE trade constructed by summing the trade flows associated with parent companies and foreign-CAs could involve some duplication.

b) Intra-firm trade

638. It is useful to compare intra-firm trade (total and by sector) with the total trade of affiliates under foreign control and parent companies. At the same time, given the size of intra-firm trade, one has to be able to compare the weight of that trade in a country's overall trade and, if possible, by geographical area. Data on total trade have to be collected in the surveys of the activity of MNEs in order to ensure the necessary comparability between the two categories of data. Data must be collected in international classifications such as ISIC Rev 3.

5.3.2.5. *Transfer pricing*

639. "*Transfer prices*" are defined as the prices used for internal exchanges and transactions between parent companies and affiliates belong to the same group located, in principle, in different countries. But they may also apply to transactions between parent companies and affiliates located in the same country.[7] Valuations implicit in such prices are needed to comply with various legal requirements of the different countries in areas such as customs clearance, tax and financial reporting. However, how transfer pricing affects aggregate trade data and what compilers might do to take it into account is not totally clear.

640. The prices used for this valuation will not always be the same as market prices which, indeed, may not exist. Although customs, tax or other regulations may seek to impose an arm's length standard for intra-firm transfers, where products or services traded within a firm have unique attributes, market prices may not exist. Even when they do, it would not be easy for the authorities to monitor compliance with the arm's length standard. Parent companies who decide this valuation may decide the prices of goods and services supplied to their affiliates in the light of circumstances, most importantly as regards their impact on tax liabilities. For example, in countries where profits are highly taxed, transfer prices on imported inputs may be increased so that declared profits will be reduced, while in countries where taxes are lower, such transfer prices may be reduced so that the level of profits declared will be comparatively high.

641. Transactions requiring transfer prices include those involving goods, services and intangibles (essentially property rights and other items of technology trade). Given that such prices do not correspond systematically to market prices, as would be established for transactions between unrelated parties, their valuation will not normally be on the same basis as that of other international transactions.

642. Since the major practical issues raised by transfer pricing concern taxation, tax authorities have devoted considerable attention to the question of what principles should be applied to the determination of transfer prices. To best achieve an equitable distribution of taxation across countries in which a group operates and, at the same time, to minimise the risk of unrelieved double taxation, OECD member countries have chosen to treat each enterprise within a group as a separate entity and have adopted an "*arm's length principle*" for pricing transactions between these entities (see Annex 5.1). The arm's length principle, *i.e.* that pricing should be based on what would have occurred had the transacting entities been unrelated, would put the valuation of intra-firm trade flows on the same basis as that of other trade flows if it could always be applied accurately. However, there is often limited or no basis for such a valuation so in practice an element of arbitrariness in the valuation of intra-firm trade is unavoidable. Unfortunately, there is little that statistical compilers can do about transfer pricing. So users must interpret intra-firm trade data cautiously in light of these considerations.

5.3.2.6. *Recommendations for data collection*

643. Historically, detailed data on international trade flows have been available mainly for trade in goods, which is routinely reported in customs declarations. Data on trade in services, which generally must be collected in surveys, tend to be much less detailed. In addition, for intra-firm trade in services, companies may have particular difficulties in reporting the types of services involved. A variety of services may be performed at company headquarters on behalf of the entire MNE and the associated expenses allocated

worldwide, without a precise breakdown of the specific types of services provided to each CA. Because of these practical limitations, it is recommended that the initial data collection efforts for trade involving MNEs focus primarily on trade in goods.

644. For compiling countries, it is recommended that first priority be given to the collection of data on total exports and imports of goods by foreign-CAs. In conjunction with national data on trade in goods collected from customs declarations, these data can be used to determine the share of foreign-CAs in the country's total exports and imports of goods, one of the reference indicators listed in Section 5.2.2 of this chapter.

645. Data on exports and imports of goods by foreign-CAs can be collected through national surveys of the operations of foreign-CAs (which can also provide data for a number of the reference indicators discussed in Chapter 3). As an alternative to conducting separate surveys for foreign-CAs, it may be possible to identify foreign-CAs exports and imports through the inclusion of a foreign-control identifier either in national business registers or in the customs documents used to collect data on trade in goods.

646. In collecting these data, an effort should be made to identify the trade in goods between the foreign-CAs and their foreign parent groups.[8] The share of intra-firm trade in the compiling country's total exports and imports of goods – one of the reference indicators listed in Section 5.2.2 – reveals the degree to which cross-border flows of goods take the form of internal transactions within foreign MNEs. Another measure that can be constructed is the share of this intra-firm trade in the total exports and imports of goods by foreign-CAs; this measure reveals the extent to which these enterprises rely on their parent group abroad as a market for their exported output and as a source for their imported intermediate inputs, or for other products distributed to host countries. Other analytically useful measures can be constructed by taking the ratios of foreign-CA total or intra-firm exports and imports to their gross output or sales (two of the variables discussed in Chapter 3). In analyzing these measures, it would be useful to examine their variation by industry and by country of control.

647. For trade data collected through surveys of affiliate operations, it is desirable to present the data by primary industry of the CA. Particular priority should be given to providing breakdowns for trade by CA in manufacturing (which relates to the production of goods by CAs) *versus* trade by CAs in wholesale trade (which relates to distribution and marketing activities by CAs). Industry detail within manufacturing is also desirable for analysis. In some cases, it may be useful to compare data on CAs exports and imports by manufacturing industry with national totals on exports and imports of goods concorded by industry (on the basis of the industry that produces the goods); however, such comparisons should be made with caution. In particular, the ratio of exports or imports by foreign-CAs in a given manufacturing industry to the national total for exports or imports of goods produced by that industry should not be interpreted as a precise share. For one thing, some of the goods produced in a given industry may be exported or imported by CAs in industries outside of manufacturing (such as wholesale trade). In addition, for imports, the goods imported by CAs classified in a particular industry need not be goods produced by that industry.

648. It is also desirable to present data on the exports and imports of foreign-CAs by country of the controlling owner – information which is generally included in data collected through surveys of affiliate operations. For foreign-CAs, the preferred ownership concept is that of the ultimate controller. It should be made clear that the country of

ultimate control is not necessarily equivalent to the country of destination for CA exports or the country of origin for CA imports.

649. Geographic breakdowns of foreign-CAs exports by country of destination and imports by country of origin would be very useful for analysis; however, such detail may be difficult to collect in surveys of affiliate operations. Information of the on the geographic destination of affiliate exports and the geographic origin of affiliate imports might be more readily available from national customs data that are tagged to identify trade flows associated with foreign ownership.

650. Product-level data on the exports and imports by foreign-CAs are also analytically useful, and can easily be combined with comparable national data to compute foreign-CAs' shares by product group. Detailed product data may be difficult to collect in surveys of affiliate operations, but should be readily available from national customs data that are tagged to identify trade flows associated with intra-firm trade.

651. Another breakdown that would be informative but may be difficult to collect concerns the intended use of imports by foreign-CAs. In this breakdown, total and intra-firm imports by foreign CAs are distinguished according to whether they are intended to serve as intermediate inputs for further manufacture by the CAs, as capital goods added to the CA's plant and equipment, or as marketed goods to be resold by the CAs without further manufacture. Data on imports intended for further manufacture by the CAs are particularly useful for research concerned with the international fragmentation of production between different units of MNEs.

652. Turning to trade flows associated with the compiling country's MNEs, it is recommended that priority be given to the collection of data on total exports and imports of goods by parent companies located in the compiling country. In conjunction with national data on trade in goods collected from customs declarations, these data can be used to determine the share of parent companies in the country's total exports and imports of goods, one of the reference indicators listed in Section 5.2.2 of this chapter.

653. As with the data on trade by foreign-CAs, data on exports and imports of goods by parent companies can be collected either through specially designed surveys of the operations of parent companies and their CAs abroad or through the inclusion of a parent-company identifier in national business registers or customs documents. For trade data collected in surveys, it is desirable to present the data by primary industry of parent and by country of destination or origin.

654. Compiling countries that conduct surveys on the operations of parent companies and their CAs abroad are encouraged to present data on intra-firm trade in goods between parent companies and their CAs abroad. In conjunction with national data on trade in

Box 5.3. **Recommendations for measuring trade involving MNEs**

Priority should be given to the following measures:

i) For *inward investment*, total exports and imports of goods by foreign-CAs (column 1 of Tables 5.1 and 5.2) and intra-firm flows of goods between foreign-CAs and their foreign parent groups (column 2 of Tables 5.1 and 5.2).

ii) For *outward investment*, total exports and imports of goods by parent companies (column 1 of Tables 5.3 and 5.4).

goods collected from customs declarations, these data can be used to determine the share of this intra-firm trade in the country's total exports and imports of goods, a supplemental indicator listed in Section 5.2.3 of this chapter.

5.3.3. *Measuring trade in intermediate goods*

655. There are several ways of measuring the importance of the international division of production processes, and for identifying trade in intermediate products.

i) Business surveys are the most fertile source of information. Because they allow for the microeconomic pinpointing of flows, the precise identification of the destination and nature of products (same-state resale, further processing, etc.), and cross-referencing with databases on such variables as value added, profitability or innovation, they are an ideal research tool. Yet, owing to their cost and complexity, such surveys exist only for a limited number of countries (*e.g.* the United States, Japan and France), they are not regularly updated, and their methodologies are generally not compatible, making comparisons between countries difficult.

ii) Input-output tables offer a symmetrical solution. They involve working with broad industries (and grouping portions of firms rather than firms) and they show the extent to which industries use outside inputs. A portion of these relationships passes through international trade. The international division of the production process can be identified by the (intermediate) use of the goods traded. This method has the advantage of using reliable calculation principles and relatively well-stocked databases. However, the tables are updated only at intervals of several years, they are generally published with a considerable time lag, and the data are available only at fairly highly aggregated levels, both in sectoral and geographic terms. Also, for many countries, the use of input-output tables is subject to the limitation that is necessary to estimate imported intermediate inputs for a given industry indirectly by applying an economy-wide share of imports in the supply of a given good for each good used as an intermediate input in the industry.

656. Another approach is to take into account the final use of products. The United Nations Broad Economic Categories Classification makes it possible to group products from the Standard International Trade Classification (SITC) according to their nature (primary or processed product) or in terms of their final use (intermediate goods, capital goods or consumer goods).[9] However, in order to apply this method, additional information is needed. This last classification is defined in terms of products. It has the advantage of classifying each product both *by stage of production and by industry*. This is important, for example, when it comes to distinguishing the degree to which the apparent specialisation in final products is based on prior imports of intermediate goods from the same industry.

5.3.4. *Measuring intra-regional and extra-regional trade*

657. Regional free trade agreements and increasing regional economic integration have increased the importance of intra-regional trade flows. These can be measured in terms of: 1) the overall structure of and trends in intra-regional trade and 2) the nature of the products traded, whether goods or services. The first set can be used primarily with regard to manufacturing and non-manufactured goods rather than services. It is also still not possible to make a simple distinction between goods and services for intra-regional trade.

Box 5.4. Trade in intermediate goods within the international division of production processes

The internationalisation of production is a fundamental aspect of business strategies, and a key feature of economic globalisation. With their ties to their home country becoming increasingly tenuous, firms are supplying a global market by expanding their location choices. At the same time, the flow of foreign direct investment, strategic alliances and international subcontracting agreements allow for the increasingly refined specialisation of production units. The "international division of production processes" reflects the reorganisation of firms' value added chain on a regional and even world-wide basis. This is a specific form of the international division of labour, which is swiftly replacing older forms of internationalisation that were based on importing raw materials and exporting finished goods. It makes itself felt in the exchange of intermediate goods and thus has a direct influence on the volume and nature of international trade. International trade in intermediate goods implies an increasing degree of interlocking between countries' productive apparatus and poses some specific challenges.

The importance of economies of scale, which lead to ever smaller numbers of increasingly specialised production units, and the need to standardise processes upstream, while differentiating downstream in order to meet consumer demands for variety or quality, have combined to impose new ways of articulating products and production processes.

With technological progress and market globalisation, it is now possible to break up the production process of a given good into an increasing number of successive, upstream-downstream stages, and to increase in this way the number of intermediate goods that enter into the manufacturing process. Upstream goods (often highly standardised) are produced on a large scale by highly specialised plants (which may be located in different countries) and these are then combined or assembled in various ways, downstream, to create a broad range of widely differentiated varieties, closely adapted to specific markets.

Exports within an industry are often dependent in part on imports of goods produced by the same industry. Intra-industry trade measured at the less-detailed sector level thus comes in part from the international division of the production process. The "intra-firm trade" of multinational firms, which is a particular form of this division of labour, is thus associated by some economists with "intra-industry" trade. For example, they may point to differences in production and marketing costs between the parent corporation and its affiliates abroad:[1] a strategy of cost minimisation will lead a multinational firm to produce a single variety in a single country (through an affiliate), and sell it in other countries, while acting in symmetrical fashion with other varieties, thereby generating export and import flows within the same industry.[2]

The empirical link between these two theoretically distinct concepts – intra-firm and intra-industry – depends on the degree of detail in the classification nomenclature used. Take for example the case where a parent company sells components to an affiliate abroad for assembly, and then purchases the final product from that affiliate. The fact that a firm is focusing its efforts on R&D and on the manufacture of sophisticated components, while performing the (unskilled) labour-intensive work of assembling those components through an affiliate abroad (where labour costs are lower) certainly constitutes a form of intra-firm trade, but it should not necessarily be interpreted as "intra-industry" trade (which is based on substitutable products). It reflects in effect an international division of production processes within a multinational firm.[3] Note, finally, that this division of labour is not limited to exchanges within industries or firms, but can also take place between industries and firms.

Box 5.4. **Trade in intermediate goods within the international division of production processes** *(cont.)*

1. See Mainardi (1986).
2. Moreover, empirical studies have found a correlation between the growth of intra-firm trade and that of intra-"industry" trade: see for example Greenaway (1986).
3. See for example Catwell on the link between international trade and international production: Vertically integrated production necessarily creates intra-firm trade, but this is not the same thing as intra-industry trade. In any set of trade data, there is a problem with aggregating different categories, whenever the classificationselected is too broad, so that different products are grouped together within the same category of industries. For example, vertically integrated intra-firm trade is very important in the automotive sector, but the various categories of components used may differ greatly from one industry to the next. Under these conditions, the appearance of intra-industry trade may be no more than a statistical illusion. Despite this, Pomfret (1986) thinks that vertical specialisation, including intra-firm vertical integration, offers an important explanation (at least statistically) for intra-industry trade (Catwell 1994, page 314).

658. *Intra-regional* exports and imports relate to flows between each individual country in the region and all the others. *Extra-regional* trade (exports and imports) is equal to flows between all the countries in the region and the rest of the world, less intra-regional flows. The more countries become an integral part of a region, the more intra-regional trade will exceed extra-regional trade in importance. This could raise certain questions concerning trade policy, for example when countries belonging to a free-trade area cease trading or trade very little with countries that are not members. These indicators can measure to what extent the multiplication of free-trade agreements influences world trade. Countries belonging to a free-trade area could thus be likened to one country, allowing its market shares in world exports to be measured.

659. Measuring the intensity of intra- and extra-regional trade is not an easy task. Simple indicators, such as the intra-regional share of a region's trade or the ratio of intra-regional trade to world trade, can give misleading information, as shown by Anderson and Norheim (1993).[10] These authors advocate the use of intra-regional trade intensity indices which are however also subject to some methodological limitations. An alternative proposal has been made by Iapadre (2004).[11]

660. In the case of multinationals, an additional difficulty is that flows of manufacturing trade and flows of services are mixed together, since a firms' entire trade is assigned to its main activity. The United States is probably the only country that collects data on

Box 5.5. **Recommendations for measuring intra- and extra-regional trade**

In order to construct the proposed indicators in Box 5.7, countries which belong to a free trade region are invited to measure:

- Intra-regional trade of goods excluding it systematically from the global trade of these regions with the rest of the world (see Box 5.6). This implies the availability of data on the bilateral trade flows of each country with all the other countries of the same region.
- In the future, countries are invited to develop two categories of data:
  a) Intra and extra-regional trade flows of manufacturing products concerning multinational firms (parent companies and foreign affiliates) located inside each region.
  b) Global trade as well as intra- and extra-regional trade on services concerning multinational enterprises (see MSITS).

Box 5.6. **Measuring intra and extra regional trade**

The increase in the number of regional free-trade agreements is creating a new statistical need for trade indicators to take the regions concerned into account as a geographic whole. The two basic indicators to be constructed are intra-regional and extra-regional trade.

Intra-regional trade

Let it be assumed that a free trade area comprises *n* countries. The exports of the countries within that region is the sum of exports of each country to all the other countries in the region. Thus:

$$X_{Intra}^{N} = \sum_{i=1}^{n} \sum_{j=1}^{n-1} X_i^j \quad \text{where:}$$

X_{Intra}^{n} = the value of intra-regional exports of the *n* countries of the region;

X_i^j = the value of exports of country i of the region to the other countries *j* (with $i \neq j$) of the region.

The same formula can also be used for imports.

Extra-regional trade

Extra-regional trade for exports would be the total exports of each of the region's countries to all the world's countries minus intra-regional trade. Thus:

$$X_{Extra}^{n} = \sum_{i=1}^{n} X_i^{World} - X_{Intra}^{n} \quad \text{where :}$$

X_{Extra}^{n} = the value of extra regional exports of the n countries of the region;

X_i^{World} = the value of exports of each of the region's countries to all the world's countries.

With these basic indicators it is possible to construct two other relevant indicators: the ratio of a free trade area's intra-regional trade to world trade, and the market share of that area.

Ratio of regional trade to world trade

The ratio to be calculated is:

$$X_{Intra}^{n} / X_{world}$$

This ratio may increase more during the initial phase following the free trade area's creation and subsequently stabilise if intra-regional exports grow at the same rate as world exports.

Export market share of a region

The indicator of export market share must treat the free trade area as if it were a single country. Then the indicator would be:

$$100 \quad X_{Extra}^{n} / X_{world}$$

All of the above indicators can be calculated for the industrial sector as a whole (goods and services) and also for individual industries.

Box 5.7. Indicators of intra-regional trade

Indicators for free trade regions	Availability (OECD zone)		
	Available for all countries	Available for a few countries	Desirable but not available
a) Structure of trade			
Total intra-regional trade as a percentage of total extra-regional trade	X		
Intra-regional trade in goods as a percentage of extra-regional trade in goods	X		
Intra-regional trade in services as a percentage of extra-regional trade in services		X	
Region's share of goods export markets	X		
Share of intra-regional and extra-regional trade in global trade	X		
Total trade by multinationals as a percentage of total trade		X	
b) Nature of trade of a region			
Share of trade in intermediate goods		X	
Share of trade in finished products			X
Share of trade in intra-industry goods	X		
Share of trade in inter-industry goods	X		
Share of trade in high, medium and low-technology goods*	X		

* See Chapter 4.

multinationals' trade separately for goods and for services referring in the same firm. The same distinction is made for data on the sales of affiliates, irrespective of the industries to which they belong. In contrast, for the total trade of all firms, other distinctions can be drawn exclusively for manufactured goods, especially for intermediate and finished goods, customs data by product. This information can tell us, for example, whether intra-regional trade concerns finished rather than intermediate goods, in which case it would be useful to check whether extra-regional trade in intermediate goods is with affiliates belonging to countries in the area, or with unaffiliated firms.

661. Another distinction is that between intra-industry and inter-industry goods. A final distinction relates to the technology content of trade (high, medium, low). All these distinctions can tell us something about specialisation within the region or free trade area, as well as corporate organisation between the various countries of the area and the import dependency in each category of goods. Box 5.6 explains how to calculate the main variables and indicators of intra- and extra-regional trade while Box 5.7 summarises the various indicators proposed and their availability.

5.3.5. *Intra-industry trade*

662. Different types of trade are captured in measurements of intra-industry trade: *a)* "horizontal trade" in similar products with differentiated varieties (*e.g.* cars of a similar class and price range); *b)* trade in "vertically differentiated" products distinguished by quality and price (*e.g.* Italy exports high-quality clothing and imports lower-quality clothing). Horizontal intra-industry trade enables countries with similar factor endowments to benefit from economies of scale by specialising in "niche" products. Trade in vertically differentiated products may reflect different factor endowments, particular skills of the workforce or high fixed research and development costs. Vertical

 OECD HANDBOOK ON ECONOMIC GLOBALISATION INDICATORS – ISBN 92-64-10808-4 – © OECD 2005

specialisation, for example, to use cheap unskilled labour for assembly purposes or specialised personnel for research and development.

663. The most commonly used indicator of intra-industry trade is the Grubel-Lloyd index (see Box 5.8.). However, it has been shown that this index actually measures only the extent of trade overlap between two partner countries. Intra-industry trade turns out to be more important than what appears from the Grubel-Lloyd measure when it is recognised that all two-way trade within the same industry should be considered as intra-industry trade, regardless of the degree of overlap between exports and imports. Alternative indicators have been proposed by Abd-el-Rahman (1986)[12] and Vona (1991)[13] and extensively applied by Fontagné and Freudenberg (1997).[14]

664. Whatever indicator of intra-industry trade is selected, it is generally claimed that intra-industry trade is in part a statistical illusion. In fact, many empirical studies of intra-industry trade suffer from a geographic or sectoral aggregation bias:

- A geographic bias appears when different partners of a given country are pre-grouped for calculation purposes.[15]

Box 5.8. **The measurement of intra-industry trade**

Intra-industry trade flows are conventionally defined as the two-way exchange of goods within standard industrial classifications. The extent of intra-industry trade is commonly measured by Grubel-Lloyd indexes based on commodity group transactions. Thus, for any particular product class i, an index of the extent of intra-industry trade in the product class i between countries A and B is given by the following ratio:

$$IIT_{i.AB} = \left(\frac{(X_i + M_i) - |X_i - M_i|}{(X_i + M_i)} \right) \bullet 100 \qquad [1]$$

This index takes the minimum value of zero when there are no products in the same class that are both imported and exported, and the maximum value of 100 when all trade is intra-industry (in this case X_i is equal to M_i). Bilateral indices of intra-industry trade in the product class i between country A and all its trading partners are obtained as a weighted average of the bilateral indices [1] for each partner country B, using as weights the share of total trade of A accounted for by trade with B. Bilateral indices of intra-industry trade between country A and country B for total manufacturing are the weighted average of the indexes in [1] for all product classes i, with weights given by the share of total trade of i over total manufacturing trade:

$$IIT_{AB} - \sum_i \left(\frac{(X_i + M_i) - |X_i - M_i|}{(X_i + M_i)} \right) \bullet \left(\frac{(X_i + M_i)}{\sum_i (X_i + M_i)} \right) \bullet 100 \qquad [2]$$

A degree of caution must be used when comparing and interpreting intra-industry indices because their measurement crucially depends on the level of disaggregation chosen for the analysis. In the current context of assessing the importance of the division of the production process across countries, it should be recognised that, as well as measuring trade in intermediate goods at various stages of production, much intra-industry trade is trade in similar, but often highly differentiated, finished products.

Source: *OECD Economic Outlook 71*, June 2002, p. 160.

- The empirical detection of intra-industry trade is closely linked to the level of sectoral aggregation used for calculation: the more products that are in fact different (in terms of factor or technology content) are grouped together under the same heading (industry, branch), the greater is the risk of significant overlap between exports and imports, and hence the appearance of "intra-industry" trade relating to heterogeneous products.

665. On this point, there is no consensus among economists as to the appropriate sectoral level. While some economists (such as Balassa and Lloyd) recognise the problem of heterogeneous products within an industry, the problem cannot be resolved by disaggregating too far, because this will separate goods that may in fact be produced by the same industry. As others see it, the most detailed level possible must be used, because the sectoral level selected for calculation affects not only the measure of intra-industry trade (and its importance compared to inter-industry trade), but also its interpretation.

5.4. Guidelines for developing experimental trade indicators

5.4.1. Calculating trade balances based on capital ownership

666. Another measurement issue is preparing supplemental balance of payments accounts that better recognize the role of foreign affiliates as a means of delivering goods and services to international markets. In such accounts, "trade" is construed broadly to include not only cross-border exports and imports, but also deliveries through foreign affiliates. However, the latter are entered in the accounts, not at their full value, but in a way that reflects only the return to the capital ownership by the parent company. The trade balance is redefined to reflect both channels of delivery, thus capturing the effects on the compiling country of sales that originate both within and beyond its geographical borders.

667. The conventional measure of the trade balance reflects a country's performance in international markets in terms of the net value of goods and services transactions between firms and persons residing in that country and those residing abroad. Sales of goods and services by foreign affiliates of companies which have invested in other foreign persons, and sales by foreign affiliates in host countries to other persons in those countries, are not regarded as exports and imports and are therefore excluded from the trade balance.

668. In a framework based upon capital ownership, in contrast, sales by foreign affiliates are no longer disregarded, but are entered in the accounts in a way that reflects the return to the direct investor's ownership interest in the affiliate (which, in conventional balance of payments accounts, may be labelled "direct investment income"). Returns to investors in the compiling country generated by the sales of goods and services by their foreign affiliates are added to the conventional measure of cross-border exports, to yield a measure of the compiling country's total receipts arising from cross-border sales and sales by foreign affiliates. Similarly, returns accruing to the foreign owners of affiliates located in the compiling country are added to cross-border imports, to yield a comparable measure of the compiling country's total payments. Entering the effects of affiliate sales in this way recognizes these sales as a separate and distinct method of supplying foreign markets, while at the same time ensuring that only the portion of the sales that accrues to the benefit of the home country is included as revenue from that country's foreign sales. The grouping of these items recognizes that cross-border trade and sales through affiliates both are methods of active participation in international markets. In this regard, they lie in sharp contrast with other items in the current account, including the more passively

generated income on portfolio investment and the fundamentally different types of transactions recorded under current transfers.

669. To show the linkages between the returns generated by direct investors and the activities of affiliates that generate these returns, if the necessary data are available, details may be added showing the gross sales and expenses (as well as any profits accruing to local or third-country investors) that, when netted against one another, give rise to this return. (As a practical matter, it may be difficult to collect information on expenses directly, in which case expenses may be estimated residually, as the difference between the return to direct investors and the sales that generate the return.) Again depending on data availability, expenses could be further broken down to show major items of interest, such as compensation of employees, thus providing a more detailed picture of the activities generating and underlying the return to direct investors.

670. Having constructed these more comprehensive measures of receipts and payments resulting from international sales and purchases, a balance is calculated equal to the difference between them.

671. Accounts compiled on this basis have been presented periodically in the United States since the early 1990s. The basic structure of the accounts and key figures for the year 2000 are shown below in Table 5.5. In addition to the items discussed above, the table adds details on whether the cross-border trade is with unrelated parties or with affiliated parties and, for the latter, on whether the trade is with foreign parent companies or with foreign affiliates. In the table, trade with affiliated parties is defined as all trade with enterprises having a direct investment relationship. In addition, net receipts of direct investment income and the underlying sales and expenses are derived using data for all affiliates, rather than only those affiliates that are foreign-controlled. These procedures help to maintain consistency between these accounts and the standard accounts that define direct investment relationships using a 10% ownership criterion, as recommended by BPM5 and BD3.[16] They also help to avoid the inconsistency that would arise in the case of a minority-owned affiliate that is held indirectly, through a directly held controlled foreign affiliate; the direct investor's return from such an affiliate would be included in income from the controlled affiliate, but the minority-owned affiliate's sales and expenses would not be recorded because of the absence of foreign control.

672. Table 5.5 shows that, for the United States during 2000, the trade deficit calculated on the basis of capital ownership (line 37) was smaller than the deficit shown in the traditional accounts based on the location of production (line 36). This difference can be explained by the fact that receipts generated by US parent companies from sales by their affiliates abroad exceeded payments accruing to parent companies in other countries from sales by their affiliates in the United States.

673. Other methods of constructing supplemental accounts based on capital ownership have been suggested. For example, in the United States, a National Academy of Sciences (NAS)[17] study panel proposed accounts that differ from those described above in two major ways. First, rather than deducting from the affiliate's sales *all* costs and profits other than the return to direct investors, these accounts would deduct only the cost of purchased intermediate inputs, leaving an amount equal to the affiliate's value added in production. Because value added may include a major component of locally incurred costs, such as for compensation of employees, this method may result in too gross an indicator for purposes of gauging the effect of changes in affiliates' sales on the economy of the investor (home)

Table 5.5. **Ownership-based framework of the US current account, 2000**

Billions of dollars

1	**Exports of goods and services and income receipts**	**1 417.2**
2	**Receipts resulting from exports of goods and services or sales by foreign affiliates**	**1 213.9**
3	**Exports of goods and services, total**	**1 064.2**
4	To unaffiliated foreigners	736.5
5	To affiliated foreigners	327.7
6	To foreign affiliates of US companies	247.4
7	To foreign parent groups of US affiliates	80.3
8	**Net receipts by US companies of direct investment income resulting from sales by their foreign affiliates**	**149.7**
9	Non-bank affiliates	147.9
10	Sales by foreign affiliates	2 891.5
11	Less: Foreign affiliates' purchases of goods and services from the United States	247.4
12	Less: Costs and profits accruing to foreign persons	1 971.1
13	Compensation of employees of foreign affiliates	302.6
14	Other	1 668.5
15	Less: Sales by foreign affiliates to other foreign affiliates of the same parent	525.1
16	Bank affiliates[1]	1.8
17	**Other income receipts**	**203.3**
18	**Imports of goods and services and income payments**	**1 774.1**
19	**Payments resulting from imports of goods and services or sales by US affiliates**	**1 503.7**
20	**Imports of goods and services, total**	**1 442.9**
21	From unaffiliated foreigners	952.4
22	From affiliated foreigners	490.5
23	From foreign affiliates of US companies	195.4
24	From foreign parent groups of US affiliates	295.1
25	**Net payments to foreign parents of direct investment income resulting from sales by their US affiliates**	**60.8**
26	Non-bank affiliates	56.9
27	Sales by US affiliates	2 334.7
28	Less: US affiliates' purchases of goods and services from abroad	389.4
29	Less: Costs and profits accruing to US persons	1 888.4
30	Compensation of employees of US affiliates	329.7
31	Other	1 558.7
32	Less: Sales by US affiliates to other US affiliates of the same parent[2]	n.a.
33	Bank affiliates[1]	3.9
34	**Other income payments**	**270.4**
35	**Unilateral current transfers, net**	**–53.4**
	Memoranda:	
36	Balance on goods and services	–378.7
37	Balance on goods, services, and net receipts from sales by affiliates (line 2 minus line 19)	–289.8
38	Balance on current account	–410.3

1. Details on underlying sales and expenses are not available for bank affiliates.
2. Not available but, because affiliates are required to report on a consolidated basis, probably immaterial.

country. However, it may be more reflective than either the standard accounts or the accounts presented above of the way multinational firms view their worldwide operations. A second difference is that the NAS proposal redefines the boundary between "domestic" and "foreign" entities, in that firms are categorized as one or the other based on their ownership rather than their residency. In the case of foreign affiliates, for example, sales back to the home country are considered domestic-to-domestic transactions and are excluded, while sales in the country of location are regarded as international transactions that are to be included. By redefining this boundary, these accounts are not so much a satellite of the conventional accounts, but rather a different type of account, which may serve a different purpose.

674. Still another proposal was made by DeAnne Julius,[18] writing in 1990 for the Council on Foreign Relations. As with the NAS proposal, she suggested assigning nationality to firms based on ownership rather than residency, but she netted out *all* payments by affiliates to foreigners rather than only their expenses for intermediate inputs. Furthermore, she considered these payments as imports of the home country rather than as a deduction from affiliates' sales. While this approach represents a fundamental restructuring of the accounts, the fact that all of the affiliate's payments to foreigners – both those for factor services (labour and capital) and those for intermediate inputs – are recorded as trade results in balances identical to those derived under the accounts described above and presented in Table 5.5.

Box 5.9. **Recommendations on calculating trade balances based on capital ownership**

Countries that wish to do the foregoing calculations for their own case will need to collect data on:

- Local procurement of goods and services by foreign affiliates located in their country, from all countries save their own.
- Local procurement of goods and services by foreign affiliates located in their country.

5.4.2. Measuring international subcontracting

Main features

675. Globalisation has stiffened competition, thereby driving firms to produce better, faster and more cheaply. To do so, many firms have had to sharpen their focus and devote themselves exclusively to the activities that constitute the core of their business. A typical approach is to outsource other work through subcontracting.

676. A firm that subcontracts work abroad does so in order to devote its time and human resources to those areas where it has a competitive advantage over other firms. Subcontracting also allows a firm to take advantage of highly-targeted know-how that is only available outside the firm, and often beyond national frontiers. In the latter case we speak of international subcontracting. Increasingly, subcontracting firms have become specialised businesses with capabilities that are much in demand.

677. One effect of such specialisation in any given line of business is "multi-tier subcontracting". The buying firm (the "principal") engages a first-tier subcontractor, who in turn will arrange with a second-tier or even a third-tier subcontractor to do some portion of the work that falls beyond its own field of expertise.

678. The principal kinds of subcontracting are "*structuralsubcontracting*", where a firm's strategy leads it to call upon the capabilities of companies outside its own group and leads to a regular, ongoing relationship, and *occasional or ad hoc subcontracting* may occur where a firm engages another business on a temporary basis to supply goods or services that it would normally produce itself but cannot do so at the moment, within the deadlines imposed by the order it must fill.

679. An important distinction needs to be made between subcontracting and co-operative arrangements or partnerships. To appreciate this difference it is useful to distinguish two categories of subcontracting. The *first* involves relatively commonplace, "low-tech" goods

Box 5.10. **Subcontracting defined**

Subcontracting (broad meaning)

Subcontracting occurs when one firm, the prime manufacturer or contractor ("principal"), contracts with another firm, the subcontractor or "supplier", for a given production cycle, one or more aspects of product design, processing or manufacture, or construction or maintenance work.

The output is generally incorporated into the principal's final products. Subcontracting can also involve services, particularly studies, accounting, engineering, R&D, advertising, computer services or legal advice. Most of these services are of the kind that can be subcontracted abroad (international subcontracting).

The "supplying" firm must adhere strictly to the "principal's" technical or commercial specifications for the products or services in question.

and services, such as catering, cleaning, transportation, accounting services, intermediate inputs for various kinds of machinery, etc. The *second* category concerns goods and services that have a high technological content and are subject to constant innovation.

680. The relationship between the principal and the supplier will differ between the two categories. In the first category the principal, having a broader range of choice, can often exert heavy pressure on prices and deadlines and is able to replace subcontractors with relative ease.

681. On the other hand, suppliers of the second category are more closely involved in the design of the product or service, and they in effect assume the role of a partner. This type of subcontracting may be called a "*subcontracting partnership*".

682. A typical example of this type of subcontracting is the relationship that exists between automobile makers or aircraft manufacturers and their respective equipment suppliers (landing gear, instrument panels).

683. Both cases generally involve high-tech goods where the suppliers must do more than simply fulfil an order. They must also participate in designing products and monitoring technological trends, and may even impose certain innovations on their prime contractors. The latter are in fact much more dependent on their subcontractors than are first category principals. Nevertheless, such arrangements cannot generally be regarded as co-operation agreements.

684. In co-operation agreements, the partners often establish reciprocal financial ties (through cross-shareholding arrangements) and may undertake to share costs and risks or to pool their efforts to develop a new technology.

Main indicators

685. A central feature of subcontracting is that the same firm can engage subcontractors abroad, while simultaneously acting as a supplier under subcontract to other businesses. Indicators must take due account of this dual aspect.

686. A first category of indicators could cover subcontracting of the kind where the principals are domestic firms of a given country, while a second category could relate to subcontracts where the principals are foreign firms and the subcontractors are domestic firms of that country. Amongst a given country's domestic firms, a distinction needs to be made between resident-controlled enterprises and foreign-CAs in the same country. In

principle, transactions between affiliates, whether under resident or foreign control, should not be treated as subcontracting activity. These transactions are covered by the indicators of multinationals' activity and intra-firm trade in particular. From this point of view, international subcontracting should be regarded as an alternative to direct investment. Resident-controlled firms can be order givers or takers with non-affiliated firms abroad, while their foreign-CAs can be order givers or takers with independent firms abroad.

687. Another useful distinction concerns subcontracting for manufactured goods vs. services, and it applies equally to firms classified either as manufacturing or service businesses. The specific question is whether a firm that is primarily engaged in a manufacturing sector outsources a portion both of its manufacturing goods and of its services (the reverse situation is far less common). When it comes to subcontracting for services abroad, it is useful to note that this can be done not only with businesses but also with universities and other public or private institutions.

688. It is also interesting to determine whether such subcontracting is of a structural or *ad hoc* nature.

689. Other distinctions relate to the nature of the products and the characteristics of the firms involved. Thus, products may be intermediate or finished goods, while the firms involved may be large companies or SMEs. In fact, SMEs are often involved in "subcontracting partnership" arrangements.

690. French surveys have shown that the smaller an SME, the more likely it is to be involved in such arrangements. At the same time, SMEs are highly dependent on the least elaborate and most conventional form of subcontracting.

Figure 5.3. **International subcontracting typology of a compiling country**

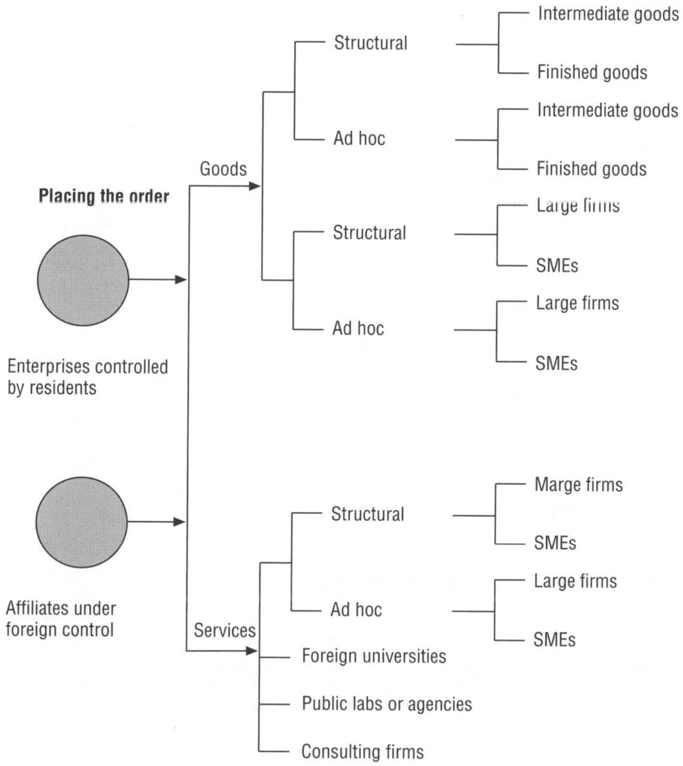

691. Figure 5.3 offers a typology of the different forms of international subcontracting.

692. By contrast, Box 5.11 which summarises the major indicators required, does not cover all the aspects and forms shown in Figure 5.3.

693. What is needed is to collect data by sector and by country of destination and origin for the two subcontracting categories discussed above, while distinguishing between domestic firms and foreign-controlled firms.

694. These indicators would appear to be very limited in their availability at both the domestic and international level. One of the major difficulties here is that many countries do not systematically collect the detailed domestic data needed for these indicators, while the underlying concepts need to be better harmonised.

Box 5.11. **Main indicators of international subcontracting**

Basic data and indicators	Availability		
	Available in most countries	Available in some countries	Desirable but not available
1. Firms placing the order are firms controlled by the residents of country A			
Manufacturing orders placed abroad by firms controlled by the residents of country A, by sector:			
– With non-affiliated firms			X
Service orders placed abroad by these firms, by sector:			
– With non-affiliated firms			X
– With other institutions (universities, public labs, etc.)			X
Manufacturing orders placed abroad by foreign-CAs of country A, by sector:			
– With non-affiliated firms.			X
Service orders placed abroad by foreign-CAs of country A, by sector:			
– With non-affiliated firms			X
– With other institutions (universities, public labs, etc.).			X
The same indicators, by country of destination			X
2. Firms placing the order are foreign firms approaching country A			
Manufacturing orders received from abroad by firms controlled by the residents of country A, by sector:			
– With non-affiliated firms			X
Service orders received from abroad by firms controlled by the residents of country A, by sector:			
– From non-affiliated firms			X
Manufacturing orders received from abroad by foreign-CAs of country A, by sector:			
– From non-affiliated firms			X
Service orders received from abroad by foreign-CAs of country A, by sector:			
– From non-affiliated firms			X
The same indicators, by country of origin			X
3. Ratios*			
Ratio of international subcontracting to domestic subcontracting			X
Ratio of orders placed abroad to total imports			X
Ratio of orders received from abroad to total exports			X

* These ratios can be calculated for all firms, and separately for domestic and foreign firms, as well as by sector and by country of destination or origin.

Notes

1. Traditional theories, based on perfect competition, eliminate firms from the analysis *de facto*, since single-product firms are considered to be identical, so that product, branch and firms become one and the same. See also P. Krugman (1990), *Rethinking International Trade*, MIT Press.
2. See Helpman E. and P. Krugmann (1985), *Market Structure and Foreign Trade*, MIT Press, Cambridge.
3. The implicit assumption in the *ex ante* work on the Single Market, extrapolating from past evidence, was that the development expected in intra-European trade would above all be intra branch, thereby containing adjustment costs while providing major gains in scope and efficiency (see for instance European Commission, 1990). For an *ex post* study of the impact of the Single Market on the nature of trade within the EU, see CEPII (1997).
4. Foreign-controlled affiliates account for substantially larger shares of exports and imports than of employment, turnover, or value added in most OECD member countries for which data are currently available; see OECD (2001), *Measuring Globalisation: The Role of Multinationals in OECD Economies*. For example, in the case of the United States, the shares of foreign-controlled affiliates in US exports and imports of goods are each more than three times as large as their shares in US GDP or employment.
5. Excluded from this taxonomy of trade involving multinational firms are trade flows between foreign parent companies and unaffiliated firms in the compiling country; such flows typically fall outside of the scope of data that can be collected in surveys of multinational-firm operations.
6. The concept of the foreign parent group goes together with those of "fellow subsidiaries" or "related enterprises" used in international definitions of direct investment capital; see Paragraph 40 of the *OECD Benchmark Definition of Foreign Direct Investment* (Third Edition, 1996) and Paragraph 368 of IMF's *Balance of Payments Manual* (Fifth Edition, 1993).
7. In the third chapter of this *Handbook*, it was recommended that intra-firm trade calculations should consider firms within a group, where the affiliates are under the direct or indirect majority control of the parent corporation. In certain specific cases, minority controlling interests might also be taken into account (see Chapter 3). The term "associated enterprises" used in the OECD *Transfer Pricing Guidelines* states that two enterprises are associated if one of the enterprises participates directly or indirectly in the management, control or capital of the other or if "the same people participate directly or indirectly in the management, control, or capital" of both enterprises.
8. It is probably easiest to collect such data through surveys of affiliate operations. If the affiliate trade data are collected from customs documents instead, a question could be included on the documents asking filing parties that are foreign-controlled to specify the amount of trade that is with foreign parent companies and other affiliated foreign firms.
9. See M. Freudenberg and F. Lemoine "Central and Eastern European Countries in the International Division of Labor in Europe", *CEPII Working Paper No. 99*, 5 April 1999 (available at *www.cepii.fr*).
10. Anderson, K. and H. Norheim (1993), "From Imperial to Regional Trade Preferences: Its Effect on Europe's Intra- and Extra-regional Trade", *Weltwirtschaftliches Archiv*, Vol. 129, pp. 78-102.
11. Iapadre, L. (2004), "Regional Integration Agreements and the Geography of World Trade: Measurement Problems and Empirical Evidence", United Nations University, Comparative Regional Integration Studies, UNU-CRIS e-working papers, w-2004/3.
12. Abd-el-Rahman, K. (1986), "Ré-examen de la définition de la mesure des échanges croisés de produits similaires entre les nations", in: *Revue Économique*, Vol. 37, No. 1, pp. 89-115.
13. Vona, S. (1991), "On the Measurement of Intra-industry Trade: Some Further Thoughts", in: *Weltwirtschaftliches Archiv*, Vol. 127, No. 4, pp. 687-700.
14. Fontagné, L. and M. Freudenberg (1997), "Intra-industry Trade: Methodological Issues Reconsidered", working paper No. 97-01, Centre d'Études Prospectives et d'Informations Internationales (CEPII).
15. As an example, assume that for a given industry, country A exports goods worth 100 to country B and imports goods of the same value from country C. If the two partners B and C are considered as a unit, there will obviously be an overlap between exports (to B) and imports (from C): this trade would be classified as intra-industry, *i.e.* it would be purely artificial. On the other hand, if each partner is treated separately, it will be seen that A is exporting to B and importing from C: in this case, the transactions would be classed as inter-industry trade with each partner. The latter configuration is perfectly compatible with conventional theories, once the concept of "the chain of comparative advantage" is introduced (Deardorff, 1979; Lassudrie-Duchêne and Mucchielli, 1979).

For example, an "intermediate country" would import a capital-intensive good from a country where capital is abundant, while exporting the same product to a country where capital is relatively scarce.

16. Where intra-firm trade is concerned, the treatment also is consistent with the Manual on Statistics of International Trade in Services, which defines "trade with related enterprises" as "trade with all enterprises" with which there is a direct investment relationship.

17. National Research Council (1992), Panel on Foreign Trade Statistics, "Behind the Numbers: US Trade in the World Economy", Anne Y. Kester (ed.), National Academy Press, Washington DC.

18. Julius DeAnne (1990), *Global Companies and Public Policy*, Council on Foreign Relations Press, New York.

ANNEX 5.A1

Arm's Length Principle

Box 5A1.1. **Arm's length principle**

When independent enterprises deal with each other, the conditions of their commercial and financial relations ordinarily are determined by market forces. When associated[1] enterprises conduct transactions among themselves, their commercial and financial relationships are not necessarily subject to the same market influences. This sometimes provides scope for manipulating profits which may have tax advantages, especially since there may be a genuine difficulty in accurately determining a market price in the absence of market forces or when adopting a particular commercial strategy. It must be remembered that the need to make adjustments in order to approximate arm's length dealing arises regardless of any contractual obligation that parties may have accepted to pay a certain price, and whether or not they are deliberately attempting to minimise their tax burden. Thus, a finding of transfer pricing problems is not the same thing as a finding of fraud or tax evasion, even if transfer pricing policies are sometimes used for such purposes.

Transfer prices affect both the amount of tax payable by the associated enterprises and the tax receipts of the host country when they do not reflect the play of market mechanisms and the arm's length principle. OECD member countries have agreed that, for taxation purposes, the profits of associated enterprises may be adjusted to ensure that the arm's length principle is respected.[2]

The arm's length principle is generally applied by comparing the conditions of the transaction between associated enterprises and those of a comparable transaction between comparable independent enterprises operating under comparable circumstances, thereby providing broad parity of tax treatment for MNEs and independent enterprises. The arm's length principle has also been found to work effectively in the vast majority of cases. Nevertheless, there are some significant cases in which the arm's length principle is difficult and complicated to apply, for example, in MNE groups dealing in the integrated production of highly specialised goods in unique intangibles, and/or in the provision of specialised services.

A practical difficulty in applying the arm's length principle is that associated enterprises may engage in transactions that independent enterprises would not undertake. Such transactions may not necessarily be motivated by tax avoidance but may occur because in transacting business with each other, members of an MNE group face different commercial circumstances than would independent enterprises. For example, an independent enterprise

Box 5A1.1. **Arm's length principle** *(cont.)*

may not be willing to sell an intangible (*e.g.* the right to exploit the fruits of all future research) for a fixed price if the profit potential of the intangible cannot be adequately estimated and there are other means of exploiting the intangible.

In order to establish the degree of actual comparability and then to make appropriate adjustments to establish arm's length conditions (or a range thereof), it is necessary to compare attributes of the transactions or enterprises that would affect conditions in arm's length dealings.

The methods used for detecting whether the arm's length principle is applied are described in *OECD Transfer Pricing Guidelines for Multinational Enterprises and Tax Administration* (OECD, 2001) where the following factors are identified for consideration:

The *specificcharacteristics* of the goods or services in question (for example, quality, reliability, form of transaction, type of asset or expected advantage, etc.).

Functional aspects (manufacturing, R&D, distribution, marketing, risk splitting, etc.).

Contractual provisions (distribution of responsibilities, risks and profits among parties, etc.).

Economic situation (markets involved, existence of substitute goods or services, purchasing power of consumers, etc.).

Business strategies (innovation, diversification, market penetration, etc.).

1. "Associated" as used here does not necessarily imply a majority controlling relationship as it does in the third chapter of this *Handbook*.
2. According to Article 9 of the OECD Model Tax Convention, "where conditions are made or imposed between two enterprises in their commercial or financial relations which differ from those which would be made between independent enterprises, then any profits which would, but for those conditions, have accrued to one of the enterprises but, by reason of those conditions, have not so accrued, may be included in the profits of that enterprise and taxed accordingly".

ISBN 92-64-10808-4
OECD Handbook on Economic Globalisation Indicators

Main Sources of Basic Data Concerning Globalisation Indicators

Main sources of basic data

1. The main sources of available data are presented in this chapter to help users select the source best suited to the types of indicators they wish to construct. Details on classification systems, countries and available variables are presented in the thematic chapters. Basic data are collected by the national statistical offices of member countries that are then compiled by international organisations such as the IMF, the WTO, UNCTAD, the World Bank, EUROSTAT or the OECD through use of questionnaires that request specific tabulations of the data.

Foreign direct investment

2. Data on direct investment refer to flows and stocks of each country's inward and outward investments corresponding to equity stakes of at least 10% in host country firms.[1] They are collected at international level by the IMF, OECD, and EUROSTAT. Data on the economic activity of multinational firms are collected regularly by the OECD (for the OECD countries) and by EUROSTAT and by UNCTAD.

IMF. The IMF has long been collecting data on: *a)* flows and stocks of direct investment for all countries in the world in connection with the balance of payments. It also gathers statistics on *b)* portfolio investments;[2] *c)* other investments; and *d)* financial derivatives, according to the standard balance of payments components.

OECD-EUROSTAT. FDI statistics are based on a joint survey and the database covers 30 OECD members (including 15 EU countries). The data provide detailed information on inward and outward FDI income and financial flows and FDI positions. They are presented according to *i)* partner country (geographical breakdown); and *ii)* economic sector (industry breakdown using the two-digit ISIC Revision 3). Moreover, the database is designed to cover in detail all the subcomponents of direct investment [FDI financial flows and positions: equity capital, reinvested earnings and other capital; FDI income: income on equity and income on debt (interest)]. Plans have been made to shift to a more detailed sectoral breakdown in the near future.

UNCTAD. The Division on Investment, Technology and Entreprise Development established a database on the inward and outward flows and stocks of foreign direct investment classified by type of investment, by industry and by region for more than 180 countries. It maintains also a database based on data from Thompson Financial that reports cross border mergers and acquisitions.

Economic activity of multinational firms

AFA: Activity of Foreign Affiliates. This database corresponds to the OECD Secretariat's annual surveys and at present covers 18 countries and 18 variables in manufacturing. These data based on the SITC Revision 3 classification concern majority-owned foreign affiliates (some countries also provide data on minority-owned affiliates), in contrast to investment flow statistics for the balance of payments. Some variables, like intra-firm trade or local procurement by foreign affiliates in host countries, are available only for a small number of countries.

This database covers both inward and outward investments, but we shall see in Chapter 3 that the number of countries having data on the activities of their offshore affiliates is more limited, as is the number of variables collected.

FATS: Foreign Affiliates Trade in Services. These data are collected jointly between OECD and EUROSTAT (Directorate B, Unit 5: International Trade in Services, Direct Investment, Balance of Payments, database New Cronos). The database contains statistics on the activity of multinationals of 19 OECD countries of which 12 from the European Union, for both inward and outward investments in services, and covers five variables (turnover or production, number of employees, value added, exports and imports). The breakdown by sector follows the ISIC Revision 3 classification or NACE Revision 1 and covers 38 industries, and the geographical breakdown comprises 120 partners.

EUROSTAT: New Cronos/Theme 4/SBS/FATS (Directorate D, Division 2: Structural Business Statistics). This database contains data on the economic activity of foreign affiliates in the EU Member States broken down by individual country of ownership. It covers manufacturing industry and services at a detailed level of disaggregation and contains information on ten variables.

UNCTAD: Database on FDI/TNC (Foreign Direct Investment/Operations of Transnational Corporations). This database contains data on the economic activity of majority-owned, as well as minority-owned foreign affiliates, applying where possible the principle of ultimate beneficiary ownership. The classification by industries is based on the ISIC Rev. 3. Data availability can vary across countries.

Trade

3. Trade data are collected in each country by a variety of public agencies, including customs authorities, banks, ministries of trade and industry, and national statistical services. At the international level, such data are centralised by the United Nations, OECD, WTO, IMF and EUROSTAT. Before supplying details on the contents of the databases of the main international organisations, it is useful to explain the main differences concerning the nature of the data available.

4. The categories of trade data include customs statistics (on manufactured and non-manufactured goods), balance of payments data on both goods and services (collected in most countries by central banks), national accounts data which combine customs and balance of payments statistics (compiled by national statistical services) and data on the trade of multinational firms (goods and services) which are collected in OECD and EUROSTAT surveys of the member countries.

 OECD HANDBOOK ON ECONOMIC GLOBALISATION INDICATORS – ISBN 92-64-10808-4 – © OECD 2005

5. Certain groupings of products or sectors can be used to construct specialised trade databases, such as those on high-tech products, intermediate goods and other product categories.

- United Nations (COMTRADE database)

  The United Nations' COMTRADE database encompasses all countries in the world and covers manufactured and non-manufactured goods. Data from the 30 OECD countries are collected by the OECD and subsequently forwarded to the UN. These data, which are also broken down by countries of origin and destination, correspond exclusively to customs data classified by product (using SITC Revisions 2 and 3 and, more recently, the Harmonised System).

- OECD (FTS, BILAT, SIST, AFA, FATS, HighTech databases)

  FTS: Foreign Trade Statistics. This is a product database covering the 30 OECD countries as reporting countries, plus three non-OECD countries (including China). The data are broken down according to the following classification systems: SITC Revisions 2 and 3, and the Harmonised System for recent statistics.

  OECD Tariffs and Trade database. The query and reporting system brings together trade data from the OECD's ITS database and corresponding tariffs for OECD member countries at the Harmonised System six-digit level. Tariff data (MFN 1996 and bound post-Uruguay round) have been elaborated using available sources and have been approved by OECD countries. The system also provides users with useful statistics on tariffs and analytical tools, including revealed comparative advantage measures and trade intensity indices.

  BILAT: Bilateral Trade. This database covers the 30 OECD countries as reporting countries and corresponds to a conversion of product data to industry data, through a conversion key from SITC Revision 3 to ISIC Revision 2 and soon Revision 3.

  SIST: Statistics on International Services Transactions. This contains data exclusively on trade in services compatible with the breakdown in the IMF's BPM5 and national accounts data. It covers 29 OECD reporting countries and the European Union. Data are collected jointly with EUROSTAT.

  AFA: Activity of Foreign Affiliates (OECD). This is the trade-related segment of the aforementioned database on foreign-controlled multinational manufacturers, arranged by sector and not by product. The data use ISIC Revision 3 and also include intra-firm trade for some countries.

  FATS: Foreign Affiliates Trade in Services (OECD-EUROSTAT). This contains data on trade in services by majority-controlled foreign affiliates, from the database presented above. The data differ from those of SIST insofar as they relate solely to majority-owned affiliates (and not to all firms, as is the case for balance of payments statistics) and are broken down according to ISIC Revision 3, which differs from the BPM5 (balance of payments) classification.

  High Tech: High Technology Trade (OECD-EUROSTAT). This database covers exports and imports of high-tech products (about 150 manufactured products) broken down by countries of origin (the 30 OECD countries) and destination and by geographic regions, using the SITC Revision 3 classification. It also contains unit values for this trade. Soon, it will also encompass trade by range of high-tech products and will include data using the Harmonised System.

- WTO (IDP: Integrated data base)

  This database contains information on WTO Members' tariffs and imports, linked at the level of tariff lines. On the trade side, the IDB contains imports by country of origin, in value and quantity, by tariff line. On the tariff side, it contains MFN (Most Favoured Nation) current bound duties and MFN current applied duties. For some countries, information covering preferential duties is also included. Product descriptions at the tariff line level are also part of the database. Access is restricted to WTO Members only.

- EUROSTAT (COMEXT database)

  This is a database containing monthly trade data reported to Eurostat by each of the 15 Member States in the European Union (exports and imports), with 250 partner countries as well as information concerning the mode of transport. The products are classified according to the Combined Nomenclature (more than 10 000 codes) on the tariff nomenclature in case of extra-community imports (more than 20 000 codes). Information is further analysed to produce price and volume indices. Also seasonally adjusted figures will be disseminated during 2002.

Globalisation of technology

6. Databases relating directly to the globalisation of technology are developed at the international level essentially by the OECD, and in part by EUROSTAT.

- OECD databases

  Research and Development. The R&D data collected in conjunction with globalisation surveys deal with R&D performed in the countries by foreign affiliates (expenditures and researchers) and R&D performed by offshore affiliates of domestic firms. Data on foreign financing of all domestic enterprises are collected during regular surveys and are available in the MSTI and R&D databases.

  Internationalisation of patents. These indicators can be constructed from data that is contained in, or that is being incorporated into, the OECD database on patents. This database is compiled from data forwarded by national patent offices (European Patent Office, US Patents and Trademarks Office, Japanese Patent Office). When it is completed, the OECD patent database can be used to compute indicators such as: the number of patents issued to OECD country inventors, by technological category or by industry, patents issued jointly to inventors from more than one country and citation counts. Some of these indicators, along with counts of "families of patents" (a "family" being defined as a set of patents issued in different countries to cover a single invention) are in the process of being published by the OECD (see: *OECD Science, Technology and Industry Scoreboard, 2003 edition*; and *Main Science and Technology Indicators2002-3*).

  Technology balance of payments. The OECD Secretariat's annual survey of technology receipts and payments fulfils a significant portion of the need for the indicators. Even so, and despite their importance, data on transactions between parent companies and affiliates are available for only a limited number of countries.

  Co-operation agreements and transnational alliances. The basic data are collected by private sources which in many cases favour certain categories of agreements and alliances, which explains the multiplicity of sources and the diversity of their contents.

- EUROSTAT databases

EUROSTAT's New Cronos database contains information on certain categories of R&D, including data by region, but it does not distinguish the R&D activity of multinational firms. The data on trade in high-tech products contained in the New Cronos database are the same as the OECD's data. With regard to patents, the New Cronos database contains information on EPO patent applications by region and technological classes (IPC). Negotiations underway with the OECD should ultimately give EUROSTAT free access to the OECD databases.

Notes

1. It should be made clear, however, that not all countries (and not all those in the OECD) apply the 10% ownership criterion to define instances of foreign direct investment.
2. [See IMF comment to provide further description of other types of direct investment or be amended to refer to the relevant paragraph in Ch. 2]

   a) Flows and stocks of direct investment. See also: *Balance of Payments Statistics Yearbook*, which publishes portfolio investment data from numerous countries, broken down into: *i)* assets and liabilities; *ii)* instruments (equity investments and debt instruments), the latter being further broken down into bonds and other debt instruments, and money market instruments; *iii)* sectors (other monetary authorities, government, banks and other sectors).

   b) Direct investments are broken down into: *i)* equity capital, *ii)* reinvested earnings and *iii)* other capital (see also Chapter 2).

   c) Other investments: This is a residual item encompassing all transactions involving financial assets and liabilities not included in items corresponding to direct investment, portfolio investments or reserve assets. They include commercial credit, loans, currency and deposits and other assets and liabilities.

   d) Reserve assets: This category includes monetary gold, SDRs, reserve positions in the IMF, holdings of foreign exchange and other claims.

   See also *Co-ordinated Portfolio Investment Survey Guide,* which can be found on the IMF Web site, at: *www.imf.org/external/np/sta/pi/cpisgd.htm.*

   See also *Co-ordinated Portfolio Investment Survey Guide* (IMF, May 1996).

Acronyms Used in this Handbook

ANBERD	Analytical Business Enterprise Research and Development
APEC	Asia-Pacific Economic Cooperation
BERD	Business enterprise R&D expenditure
BoP	Balance of payments
CEPII	*Centre d'études prospectives et d'informations internationales*
COPC	Current operating performance concept
CPC Vers. 1	Central Product Classification, version 1.0
EBOPS	Extended balance of payments services
EC	European Commission
Eurostat	Statistical Office of the European Communities
FATS	Foreign Affiliates Trade Statistics In the present Manual "FATS" statistics refers to statistics pertaining in the service activities of foreign affiliates as opposed to all the activities of foreign affiliates as is the case in other publications, especially those of Eurostat.
FCS	Fully Consolidated System
FDI	Foreign direct investment
Foreign CAs	Foreign-controlled affiliates
FTE	Full-time equivalent
GATS	General Agreement on Trade in Services
GATT	General Agreement on Tariffs and Trade
GDP	Gross domestic product
GEP	Global external position
GFCF	Gross fixed capital formation
GNERD	Gross national expenditure on R&D
HS	Harmonised System
ICFA	Industrial Classification of Foreign Affiliates
IIP	International investment position
IMF	International Monetary Fund
IMF BoP Derivatives	IMF Financial Derivatives
IMF BoP Guide	IMF Balance of Payments Compilation Guide 1995
IMF BPM5	IMF Balance of Payments Manual, 5th edition
ISIC Rev. 3	International Standard Industrial Classification, Rev. 3
M	Imports
M and A	Mergers and acquisitions
MNEs	Multinational enterprises
MSITS	Manual on Statistics on International Trade in Services
n.e.c.	Not elsewhere classified

NACE Rev. 1	General Industrial Classification of Economic Activities
NAFTA	North America Free Trade Agreement
NAICS	North American Industry Classification System
NPI	Non-profit institute
OECD	Organisation for Economic Co-operation and Development
R&D	Research and development
SITC Rev. 3	Standard International Trade Classification
SMEs	Small and medium-sized enterprises
SNA 1993	System of National Accounts
SPEs	Special purpose entities
TBP	Technological balance of payments
TRIMS	Trade related investment measures
TRIPS	Trade related aspects of intellectual property rights
UBO	Ultimate beneficiary owner
UN	United Nations
UNCTAD	United Nations Conference on Trade and Development
WTO	World Trade Organization
X	Exports

Glossary

Activity of multinational enterprises

In principle quantitative or qualitative information directly concerning multinational firms could be classified under activity of multinational enterprises. However, within the framework of this *Handbook*, data on the activity of multinationals covers all economic and industrial data which are not associated with FDI, portfolio or other financial transactions. At the present time, the data collected by the OECD within the framework of the surveys on the economic activity of multinationals include 18 variables, notably gross output, turnover, value added, number of people in employment, employee compensation, gross operating surplus, gross fixed capital formation, R&D expenditures, number of researchers, total exports and imports, intra-firm exports and imports, and technological payments and receipts.

Affiliate under control abroad

An affiliate under control abroad is an enterprise controlled directly or indirectly by a parent company which is controlled by residents of the investor country.

Affiliate under foreign control

In a compiling country, an affiliate under foreign control is an enterprise controlled by another enterprise located abroad which is its parent company.

Affiliated financial intermediaries

The clarifications of the IMF Committee on Balance of Payments Statistics promulgated in May 2002 indicate that for the purposes of balance of payments data, financial intermediaries are defined as being: *i)* other depository institutions (banks, other than the central bank); *ii)* other financial intermediaries, except insurance companies and pension funds; and *iii)* financial auxiliaries. The definition would therefore include Special Purpose Enterprises (SPEs) – principally engaged in financial intermediation for a group of related enterprises – and enterprises such as security dealers, whose function is the provision of services auxiliary to financial intermediation for a group of related enterprises. Transactions between affiliated financial intermediaries (that is, financial intermediaries that are in a direct investment relationship) should be *excluded* from the direct investment data, except for transactions in the form of equity capital or permanent debt. Transactions between *i)* direct investment enterprises that are not financial intermediaries, and *ii)* affiliated financial intermediaries (including SPEs primarily engaged in financial intermediation for a group of related enterprises), should be *included* in the direct investment data.

All-inclusive concept

The application of this concept is one of the two main approaches to measuring earnings. The concept is explained in the *International Accounting Standard No. 8, "Unusual and Prior Period Items and Changes in Accounting Policy"*. When earnings are measured on the basis of this concept, income is considered to be the amount remaining after allowing for all items (including write-offs and capital gains and losses), causing any increase or decrease in the shareholders' or investors' interests during the accounting period, other than dividends and any other transactions between the enterprise and its shareholders or investors (see also the entry for ***Current operating performance concept.)***

Asset/liability principle

The Financial Account of the balance of payments records an economy's transactions in external financial assets and liabilities. The transactions are classified by 1) functional type of investment (*direct investment*, *portfolio investment*, *other investment*, and *reserve assets*); 2) assets and liabilities or, in the case of direct investment, direction of investment; 3) type of instrument; and, in some cases, 4) domestic sector and 5) original contractual maturity. This distinction between external assets and liabilities is of primary importance for the functional types of investment other than direct investment. Transactions should be recorded on a straight asset/liability basis. Even when a net basis is used for recording the Financial Account of the balance of payments, transactions in financial assets should be shown separately from transactions in financial liabilities (see also the entry for the ***Directional principle***).

Balance of payments

Statistical system through which economic transactions occurring during specific time periods between an economy and the rest of the world can be summarised in a systematic way. The fifth edition of the IMF *Balance of Payments Manual(BPM5)* provides conceptual guidelines for compiling balance of payments statistics according to international standards.

Bilateral sources

Involve the use of direct investment statistics that are compiled by other countries, or by international organisations.

Bonds and money market instruments

Include bonds, debentures, commercial paper, promissory notes, certificates of deposit, and other tradable non-equity securities, other than financial derivatives.

Book value

Is the value at which an equity or other capital asset or liability is recorded in the balance sheet of an entity and can reflect a number of valuation methods:

- Historical cost.
- Replacement cost.
- An interim adjusted price that is not the current market price.

- Fair market value.
- Current market price.

Control (of an enterprise)

The notion of control for an enterprise implies the ability to appoint a majority on board of directors to run the enterprise, guide its activities and determine its strategy. This ability is exercised by a single direct investor or a group of associated shareholders acting in concert and controlling the majority (+50%) of ordinary shares or voting power. The control of an enterprise may be direct or indirect, immediate or ultimate.

Current operating performance concept (COPC)

The application of this concept is one of the two main approaches to measuring earnings. The concept is explained in the International Accounting Standard No. 8, "Unusual and Prior Period Items and Changes in Accounting Policy". When earnings are measured on the basis of this concept, such earnings consist of income from normal enterprise operations before non-recurring items (such as write-offs) and capital gains and losses are accounted for (see also the entry for the ***All-Inclusive concept***).

Debtor/creditor principle

There are two principles that may serve as the basis for geographic allocation of direct investment financial flows: the debtor/creditor principle and the transactor principle. The debtor/creditor principle allocates transactions resulting from changes in the financial claims of the compiling economy to the country or residence of the non-resident debtor, and transactions resulting in changes in the financial liabilities of the compiling economy to the country of residence of the non-resident creditor, even if the amounts are paid to or received from a different country (see also the entry for the ***Transactor principle***.)

Direct investment (foreign direct investment)

Is defined as international investment by a resident entity in one economy (direct investor) with the objective of obtaining a lasting interest in an enterprise resident in a direct investment enterprise. The "lasting interest" implies the existence of a long-term relationship between the direct investor and the enterprise and a significant degree of influence by the direct investor on the management of the direct investment enterprise. Direct investment involves both the initial transaction between the two entities and all subsequent transactions between them and among affiliated enterprises, both incorporated and unincorporated.

Direct investment enterprise

Is an incorporated enterprise in which a foreign investor owns 10% or more of the ordinary shares or voting power or an unincorporated enterprise in which a foreign investor has equivalent ownership. Ownership of 10% of the ordinary shares or voting stock is the criterion for determining the existence of a direct investment relationship. An "effective voice in the management", as evidenced by an ownership of at least 10%, implies that the direct investor is able to influence, or participate in, the management of an enterprise; absolute control by the foreign investor is not required.

Direct investment enterprises comprise:

- subsidiaries (an enterprise in which a non-resident investor owns more than 50%);
- associates (an enterprise in which a non-resident investor owns between 10% and 50%) and;
- branches (unincorporated enterprises wholly or jointly owned by a non-resident investor);

that are either directly or indirectly owned by the direct investor.

When the 10% ownership requirement for establishing a direct investment link with an enterprise is met, certain other enterprises that are related to the first enterprise are also regarded as direct investment enterprises. Hence the definition of direct investment enterprise extends to the branches and subsidiaries of subsidiaries of the direct investor (so-called "indirectly owned direct investment enterprises"). The OECD *Benchmark Definition of Foreign Investment,* and the IMF *Balance of Payments Textbook* and *Balance of Payments Compilation Guide* describe the scope of enterprises, both directly and indirectly owned, that should be included in the definition. The OECD's specification of this group of enterprises is referred to as the "Fully Consolidated System".

Direct investment financial flows

Are transactions between a direct investor in one economy and a direct investment enterprise in another economy, and among affiliated direct investment enterprises that are in a direct investment relationship, other than those that are resident in the same economy.

Direct investment income

Comprises income on equity and income on debt accruing to a direct investor resident in one economy from the ownership of direct investment capital in an enterprise in another economy (See also the separate entries for these two elements).

Direct investment position data

Are stock data showing an economy's direct investment assets and liabilities at a given point in time.

Direct investment relationship

A direct investment relationship is created when an enterprise resident in one economy owns 10% or more of the ordinary shares or voting power for an incorporated enterprise, or the equivalent for an unincorporated enterprise, that is resident in another economy. Direct investment enterprises that are considered to be in a direct investment relationship with a direct investor are also considered to be in direct investment relationships with each other.

Direct investor

Is an individual, an incorporated or unincorporated public or private enterprise, a government, a group of related enterprises (incorporated or unincorporated) or individuals, that has a direct investment enterprise (that is, a subsidiary, associate or branch) operating in an economy other than the economy or economies of residence of the foreign direct investor or investors.

Directional principle

Unlike other financial investments, direct investment is not recorded in the balance of payments on a strict asset/liability basis. Direct investments are recorded on a directional basis (that is, as resident direct investment abroad, or non-resident direct investment in the reporting economy). Capital invested by the direct investment enterprise in its direct investor (reverse investment) is regarded as an offset to capital invested in the direct investment enterprise by a direct investor and its related enterprises. That is, such capital is regarded as disinvestment by the direct investor rather than as an asset of the direct investment enterprise, except when the equity participations are at least 10% in both directions and two direct investment relationships are therefore established (see also the entry for ***Reverse investment***.)

Dividends

Are the distribution of earnings allocated to shares and other forms of participation in the equity of incorporated private enterprises, co-operatives, and public corporations. These can be recorded on the date they are payable, on the date they are paid, or at some other point in time and can be recorded either gross or net of withholding taxes.

Economic territory

"Economic territory of a country consists of the geographic territory administered by a government; with this territory, persons, goods and capital circulate freely" (BPM5 §59).

Enterprise

The ***enterprise*** (as defined by Council Regulation EEC No. 696/93 of 15 March 1993) is "the smallest combination of legal units that is an organisational unit producing goods or services, which benefits from a certain degree of autonomy in decision-making, especially for the allocation of its current resources. An enterprise carries out one or more activities at one or more locations. An enterprise may be a sole legal unit. This definition is more precise than the one provided by SNA 1993, where an **enterprise** is defined as "an institutional unit engaged in production. An enterprise may be a corporation (a quasi-corporate enterprise being treated as if it were a corporation in the System), a non-profit institution, or an unincorporated enterprise" (SNA 1993, §5.1). When referring to statistical units, an enterprise is an institutional unit that regroups one or more establishments under its control.

Enterprise group

The ***enterprise group*** (according to Council Regulation EEC No. 696/93) is an "association of enterprises bound together by legal and/or financial links. A group of enterprises can have more than one decision-making centre, especially for policy on production, sales and profits. It may centralise certain aspects of financial management and taxation." Its activities may be in the industrial, service or banking sectors, and sometimes concurrently in two or all three (conglomerates). It may be located within a country (in which case it is a domestic group) or, as is more commonly the case, in several countries (multinational group).

There are two types of enterprise group to be considered associated with outward investments:

a) The first is an association of enterprises or establishments directly or indirectly majority-controlled by a parent. All the enterprises and their parent are located in the same country and represent one enterprise with consolidated accounts.

b) The second is a group comprising parents and indirectly controlled by affiliates located in different countries or MNE.

Equity capital

Comprises: *i)* equity in branches; *ii)* all shares in subsidiaries and associates (except non-participating preference [preferred] shares, which are treated as debt securities and included under direct investment, other capital); and *iii)* other capital contributions, including non-cash acquisitions of equity (such as through the provision of capital equipment).

Establishment

The ***establishment,*** as defined in the System of National Accounts (SNA 1993), is an enterprise, or part of an enterprise, that is situated in a single location and has the most homogeneous production, or whose principal productive activity accounts for most of the value added. In the European System of Accounts, this entity is also called a "local kind-of-activity unit". The establishment theoretically has no legal autonomy, but this is not necessarily true as there are many single establishment firms that have legal autonomy while its accounts contain all information relating to such factors as employment, gross value of production and intermediate consumption, apart from overheads, which are reported in the enterprise's accounts.

Financial intermediaries

For the purposes of balance of payments data, financial intermediaries are defined as being: *i)* other depository institutions (banks, other than the central bank); *ii)* other financial intermediaries, except insurance companies and pension funds; and *iii)* financial auxiliaries. The definition would therefore include Special Purpose Enterprises (SPEs) primarily engaged in financial intermediation for a group of related enterprises, and enterprises such as security dealers, whose function is the provision of services auxiliary to financial intermediation for a group of related enterprises.

Foreign direct investment

(See entry for ***Direct investment***.)

Foreign parent group

A foreign parent group consists of 1) the foreign parent; 2) any foreign person, proceeding up the foreign parent's ownership chain, that owns more than 50% of the person below it, up to and including the ultimate controller and 3) any foreign person, proceeding down the ownership chain(s) of each of these members, that is owned more than 50% by the person above it.

Immediate host/investing country

Geographic analysis of direct investment transactions is complicated by holding companies; that is, when the ultimate parent enterprise's investment in a foreign country is held through another subsidiary in a third country. Because the principle of classification used in balance of payments regional statistics is based on the change of ownership, direct investment flows should be compiled only in respect of the immediate host/investing country. The same rule applies for the international investment position statement; liabilities should be classified by the country of residence of the owner of the claim, and assets should be classified by the country of the liability holder. However, it is suggested that the stock of net assets of direct investment could also be compiled in respect of the ultimate host or controlling country, as supplementary information.

Income on debt (interest)

Consists of interest payable on inter-company debt to/from direct investors from/to associated enterprises abroad. It covers interest on the borrowing and lending of funds (including debt securities and suppliers' credits) between direct investors and direct investment enterprises.

Income on equity

Comprises *i)* dividends and distributed branch profits; and *ii)* reinvested earnings and undistributed branch profits (See also the entries for ***Dividends*** and for ***Reinvested earnings and undistributed branch profits***).

Indirectly owned direct investment enterprises

In principle, foreign direct investment statistics cover all enterprises in which direct investors have, directly or indirectly, a direct investment interest. The OECD's *Benchmark Definition of Foreign Direct Investment* and the IMF's *Balance of Payments Textbook* and *Balance of Payments Compilation Guide* describe the scope of enterprises, both directly and indirectly owned, that should be included in the definition. The OECD's specification of this group of enterprises is referred to as the "Fully Consolidated System" (FCS). Once a group of related enterprises has been defined, the FDI transactions data should include: *i)* the relevant share of the reinvested earnings of the indirectly-owned enterprises; and *ii)* all equity and other capital transactions made directly between resident enterprises of the group and non-resident enterprises of the same group, without consideration of the percentage of equity directly held by these enterprises in each other. Similarly, the position data should include *i)* the relevant share of the reinvested earnings of the indirectly-owned enterprises; and *ii)* all equity capital and inter-company debt positions held directly with all indirectly owned direct investment enterprises, without consideration of the percentage of equity directly held by these enterprises in each other.

Influence

An investor exercises an influence on the management of an enterprise if he owns directly at least 10% of the ordinary shares or voting power of this enterprise without controlling it directly or indirectly.

International investment position

Is the balance sheet of the stock of external financial assets and liabilities of an economy. The concepts and guidelines for compiling international investment position data are set out in the fifth edition of the IMF *Balance of Payments Manual*.

International subcontracting (international outsourcing)

International subcontracting occurs when one firm, the prime manufacturer or contractor ("principal"), contracts with another firm, the subcontractor or "supplier", for a given production cycle, one or more aspects of production design, processing or manufacture, or construction or maintenance work. The output is generally incorporated into the principal's final products. Subcontracting can also involve services, particularly studies, accounting, engineering, R&D, advertising, computer services or legal advice.

International Transactions Reporting System (ITRS)

An ITRS measures individual balance of payments cash transactions passing through the domestic banks and may also measure *i)* individual cash transactions passing through the foreign bank accounts of enterprises, *ii)* non-cash transactions and *iii)* stock positions. Statistics are compiled from forms submitted by domestic banks to the compilers and may also be compiled from forms submitted by enterprises to the compiler.

Intra-firm trade

Intra-firm trade consist of trade between parent companies of a compiling country with their affiliates abroad and trade of affiliates under foreign control in this compiling country with their foreign parent group.

Intra-industry trade

Different types of trade are captured in measurements of intra-industry trade:

a) Trade in similar products ("horizontal trade") with differentiated varieties (*e.g.* cars of a similar class and price range).

b) Trade in "vertically differentiated" products distinguished by quality and price (*e.g.* exports of high-quality clothing and imports of lower-quality clothing).

Inward

Refers to direct investment in the reporting economy for the purposes of the present document.

Listed voting stocks

Are equity/shares that give voting rights to the holder and are listed on an official stock exchange.

Market price

Is the amount of money that willing buyers would pay to acquire a financial asset from a willing seller. The use of market price for valuation of assets and liabilities is one of the key principles of balance of payments compilation.

Nomenclature générale des activités économiques dans les Communautés européennes (NACE)

Refers to the industrial classification as defined in Revision 1 which is used by EUROSTAT.

Non-voting stocks

Equity/shares that do not give voting rights to the holder. The category includes participating preference shares (See also the entry for ***Voting stocks***).

Offshore enterprises

In balance of payments statistics, the residency of so called "offshore enterprises" is attributed to the economies in which they are located without regard to the special treatment they may receive by the local authorities, such as exemptions from taxes, tariffs, or duties. Off-shore enterprises can be engaged in the assembly of components manufactured elsewhere, in the processing of re-exported goods, and in trade and financial operations, and can be located in special zones (*e.g.* special trade zones, free-trade zones, or tax-havens).

Other capital

Covers the borrowing or lending of funds between *i)* direct investors resident in one economy and their subsidiaries, branches, and associates resident in other economies, and *ii)* enterprises within a group of related direct investment enterprises that are resident in different economies. The instruments covered include loans, debt securities, suppliers' (trade) credits, financial leases, and non-participating preference [preferred] shares (which are treated as debt securities).

Outward

Refers to direct investment abroad, for the purpose of the present document.

Ownership

The notion of ownership is different from those of control, since the first corresponds to a majority or to a minority financial ownership of an enterprise. A majority direct ownership (+50%) of ordinary shares or voting power from a single investor should also imply the control of this enterprise by this investor while a minority ownership could imply an indirect control of this enterprise (through another enterprise). In other words, the notion of ownership is not sufficient to indicate if an enterprise is or not under influence or control.

Parent company

a) Inward investment

The parent company of an affiliate under foreign control in a compiling country is the first foreign investor outside the borders of this country, exercising direct or indirect control over the foreign affiliate. If the first foreign investor is also under foreign control, the parent company could be a company other than the ultimate control company at the head of the group.

a) Outward investment

From the point of view of a compiling country, the parent company of its affiliates abroad controlled by residents of this country is the consolidated enterprise (enterprise group) comprising the domestic firms which the preceding firm controls directly or indirectly in the compiling country.

Perpetual inventory method

Refers to the process of deriving data on stocks (position data) from transaction data. Under this method, for which a stock estimate for some base point in time is required, the compiler may calculate the value of a stock at the end of a period as being equal to the value of the stock at the beginning of the period, plus the impact of transactions and non-transaction changes in the value of the stock during the period.

Quasi-corporations

Enterprises that produce goods and services in an economy other than their own, but do not establish separate legal corporations in the host country. Quasi-corporations that are in a direct investment relationship with the parent enterprise are deemed to exist if:

- Production is maintained for one year or more.
- A separate set of accounts is maintained for the local activities.
- Income tax is paid in the host country.

Quasi-corporations are often involved in construction or the operation of mobile equipment in another economy. The fifth edition of the IMF *Balance of Payments Manual* (*BPM5*) recommends that quasi-corporations be included in the direct investment data.

Reinvested earnings and undistributed branch profits

Comprise, in proportion to equity held, direct investors' shares of *i)* earnings that foreign subsidiaries and associated enterprises do not distribute as dividends ***(reinvested earnings***), and *ii)* earnings that branches and other unincorporated enterprises do not remit to direct investors ***(undistributed branch profits).***

Reinvested earnings of indirectly owned direct investment enterprises

Are treated as follows under the Fully Consolidated System. Assuming that: *a)* Company A in Country 1 owns 51% of Company B in Country 2, which in turn owns 51% of Company C in Country 3, and *b)* the reinvested earnings of Company B is 500 and the reinvested earnings of Company C is 100, the income of Company A from reinvested earnings is 281, that is:

51% of the reinvested earnings of Company B: .51x500 = 255

51% of 51% of the reinvested earnings of Company C: .51(.51x100) = 26

(Table 4 of Annex I of the OECD *Benchmark Definitionof Foreign Direct Investment* gives a more detailed example.)

Residence

The concept of residence is not based on nationality or legal criteria, although it may be similar to concepts of residence used for exchange control, tax and other purposes in many countries. The concept of residence is based on a sectoral transactor's centre of economic interest (...). It is necessary to recognize the economic territory of a country as the relevant geographical area to which the concept of residence is applied. An institutional unit is a resident unit when it has a centre of economic interest in the economic territory of a country (BPM5, §58).

Reverse investment

Occurs when a direct investment enterprise acquires a financial claim on its direct investor(s). Because direct investment is recorded on a directional basis, capital invested by the direct investment enterprise in its direct investor (reverse investment) is regarded as an offset to capital invested in the direct investment enterprises by a direct investor and its related enterprises, except in instances when the equity participations are at least 10% in both directions.

Such reverse investment transactions are recorded based on the direction of the direct investment relationship:

1) When the claims are not sufficient to establish a second, separate direct investment relationship, the reverse investment transactions should be recorded according to the directional principle of the direct investment relationship as follows:

- As *direct investment in the reporting economy, claims on direct investors* in the data for the economy in which the direct investment enterprise is resident.
- As *direct investment abroad, liabilities to affiliated enterprises* in the data for the economy in which the direct investor is resident.

2) When the equity participations are at least 10% in both directions, two direct investment relationships are established. In these circumstances, equity and other capital transactions between enterprises are recorded as direct investment claims and liabilities in both directions, as follows:

- As *direct investment abroad* for transactions on assets.
- As direct investment in the reporting economy for transactions on liabilities.

Special Purpose Entities (SPEs)

Are 1) generally organised or established in economies other than those in which the parent companies are resident, and 2) engaged primarily in international transactions but have few or no local operations. SPEs are defined either by their structure (*e.g.* financing subsidiary, holding company, base company, regional headquarters), or their purpose (*e.g.* sale and regional administration, management of foreign exchange risk, facilitation of financing of investment). SPEs should be treated as direct investment enterprises if they meet the 10% criterion. SPEs are an integral part of direct investment networks as are, for the most part, SPE transactions with other members of the group.

For SPEs that have the primary function of serving as financial intermediaries:

- All transactions, except those with affiliated banks and affiliated financial intermediaries, should be recorded in the direct investment data.
- Transactions with affiliated banks and affiliated financial intermediaries should be excluded from the direct investment data, except transactions in equity capital and permanent debt.

Statistical units

The statistical units correspond to the following three levels of production: *a)* the establishment; *b)* the enterprise; and *c)* the enterprise group.

Technological balance of payments

Technological balance of payments corresponds to cross-border technological receipts minus technological payments.

Technological payments and receipts

Technological payments and receipts correspond to four types of transactions between countries:

1. Technology transfers (patents, unpatented inventions, licences linked to patents, know-how).
2. Transfers of design (sales, licences, franchises), trademarks and patterns.
3. Provision of technical services (technical and engineering studies, and technical assistance).
4. Provision of industrial R&D.

Time of recording

The time of recording for transactions and, hence, for holdings, is governed by the principle of accrual accounting. For financial claims and liabilities, changes of ownership are considered to have taken place at (or be proxied by) the time that the parties to the transactions record them in their books or accounts. If no precise date can be fixed, the reporter may use the date on which the creditor received payment or the date on which some other financial claim was satisfied. For direct investment income data, dividends should be recorded as the date they are payable and income on debt (interest) as it is accrued.

Transactor principle

There are two principles that may serve as the basis for geographic allocation of financial flows: the debtor/creditor principle and the transactor principle. The transactor principle allocates transactions resulting from changes in the financial claims and liabilities of the compiling economy to the country of residence of the non-resident party to the transaction (the transactor), even if this is not the country of residence of the direct investment enterprise or direct investor (See also the entry for the ***debtor/creditor principle***).

Transfer pricing

Transfer prices are defined as the prices used for internal exchanges and transactions between parent companies and affiliates belonging to the same group, located in principle in different countries. But they may also apply to transactions between parent companies and affiliates located in the same country. Valuations implicit in such prices are needed to comply with various legal requirements of the different countries in areas such as customs clearance, tax and financial reporting.

Ultimate beneficial owner

The notion of ultimate beneficial owner corresponds more to the concept of "ownership" than to the "control" concept. When a parent company abroad is not owned more than 50% by another natural or legal person, the foreign parent and the ultimate beneficial owners are the same. In the framework of this handbook, the term "ultimate beneficial" is replaced by the term "ultimate controlled" or "ultimate control unit". In reality, there could be several ultimate beneficiaries, but only one ultimate control unit.

Ultimate control enterprise (ultimate control unit)

An investor (company or individual) is considered to be the ultimate control investor if it is at the head of a chain of companies and directly or indirectly controls all the enterprises in the chain without itself being controlled by another investor.

Ultimate host/investing country

Geographic analysis of direct investment transactions is complicated by holding companies; that is, when the ultimate parent enterprise's investment in a foreign country is held through another subsidiary in a third country. The compilation of foreign direct investment statistics on income and financial flows based on the ultimate source of such flows would require a basis for the recording of transactions other than the change-of-ownership principle that is recommended in the fifth edition of the IMF *Balance of Payments Manual*. Therefore, direct investment flows should be compiled only in respect of the immediate host/investing country. The regional allocation of the international investment position statement should also be compiled on the basis of the immediate host or investing country. However, it is suggested that the stock of direct investment net assets could also be compiled in respect of the ultimate host or controlling country, as supplementary information (See also the entry for the ***Immediate host/investing country***).

United Nations International Standard Industrial Classification for all Economic Activities (ISIC)

Refers to the industrial classification as defined in the third version of ISIC.

Unlisted voting stocks

Are equity/shares that give voting rights to the holder, but are not listed on an official stock exchange.

Valuation of stocks (position data)

The fifth edition of the IMF *Balance of Payments Manual (BPM5)* and the OECD *Benchmark Definition of Foreign Direct Investment* recommend using market price as the basis for valuation. However, it is recognised that, in practice, book values from the balance sheets of direct investment enterprises (or investors) are often used to determine the value of the stock of direct investment (See also the entry for ***Book value***).

Voting stocks

Equity/shares that give voting rights to the holder. These can either be "listed voting stocks" (that is, equity/shares that are listed on an official stock exchange), or "unlisted voting stock" (that is, equity/shares that are not listed on an official stock exchange (See also the entry for ***Non-voting stocks***).

OECD PUBLICATIONS, 2, rue André-Pascal, 75775 PARIS CEDEX 16
PRINTED IN FRANCE
(92 2005 06 1 P) ISBN 92-64-10808-4 – No. 53765 2005